CHINA'S NEW
RED GUARDS

CHINA'S NEW RED GUARDS

THE RETURN OF RADICALISM AND THE REBIRTH OF MAO ZEDONG

JUDE BLANCHETTE

OXFORD
UNIVERSITY PRESS

OXFORD
UNIVERSITY PRESS

Oxford University Press is a department of the University of Oxford. It furthers the University's objective of excellence in research, scholarship, and education by publishing worldwide. Oxford is a registered trade mark of Oxford University Press in the UK and certain other countries.

Published in the United States of America by Oxford University Press
198 Madison Avenue, New York, NY 10016, United States of America.

First issued as an Oxford University Press paperback 2022

Library of Congress Cataloging-in-Publication Data
Names: Blanchette, Jude, author.
Title: China's new Red Guards : the return of radicalism and the rebirth of Mao Zedong / Jude Blanchette.
Description: New York : Oxford University Press, [2019]
Identifiers: LCCN 2019002681 | ISBN 9780190605841 (hardcover) |
ISBN 9780197577554 (Paperback) | ISBN 9780197577615 (Digital-Online)
Subjects: LCSH: China—Politics and government—2002– |
Authoritarianism—China. | Nationalism—China. |
Mao, Zedong, 1893–1976—Influence.
Classification: LCC DS779.46 .B625 2019 | DDC 951.06/12—dc23
LC record available at https://lccn.loc.gov/2019002681

1 3 5 7 9 8 6 4 2

Printed by Integrated Books International, United States of America

*Journalist Oriana Fallaci: "Will Chairman Mao's portrait above Tiananmen
Gate be kept there?"*
Deng Xiaoping: "It will, forever."

(Oriana Fallaci, "Deng: Cleaning Up Mao's 'Feudal Mistakes,'"
Washington Post, August 31, 1980)

CONTENTS

—————◆—————

ACKNOWLEDGMENTS

Like many first-time authors, I'm now much more hesitant to critique any other fellow-book writer, for I understand just how difficult it is to put together 60,000 words of coherent and persuasive text, let alone to write an actually great work. This book, which I hope passes the persuasive bar, would have been worse were it not for the significant help, guidance, and intervention of a large number of people.

My first debt of thanks goes to the inestimable Susan Shirk, who not only gave me support and the confidence to think I could tell this story, but also helped connect me to her agent. And it was Jill Marsal, of the Marsal Lyon Literary Agency, who patiently and skillfully guided me through the proposal process. While working for Susan at UC San Diego, I had the distinct good fortune of having an office directly across from Barry Naughton, whom I consider one of the wisest observers of China's great economic and political transformations. Barry was unfailing in his willingness to discuss this project in its early phases, and later, provided some much-needed corrections as I managed to completely mangle the politics surrounding Deng's 1992 Southern Tour. Evan Osnos gave me a quick, but necessary, pep talk on why neo-Maoism was a worthy topic, and Jim McGregor gave me a much-needed kick-in-the-butt that remains greatly appreciated. David McBride and

Emily Mackenzie at Oxford University Press were immensely patient and supportive throughout the project.

Of course, this project wouldn't have come to fruition without the conversations I had with the individuals mentioned in these pages. My own political outlook is much different from theirs, but they treated me with respect and honesty, and I hope I have repaid this kindness by accurately and sympathetically telling their story. Many of them must go unnamed, owing to the political sensitivities of neo-Maoism, and many of them would not agree to being lumped in with the neo-Maoists. Those I can publicly thank include Guo Songmin, Sun Jingxian, Sima Pingbang, Wang Xiaodong, Song Qiang, Liu Yang, Yang Fan, Zhang Hongliang, Cui Zhiyuan, and Li Kaicheng.

Other individuals who, in their own way, contributed greatly to this project include: Karl Gerth, Zhang Jian, Dai Qing, Wu Si, Mao Yushi, Anthony Garnaut, Brendan Mulvaney, Mark Wong, Fang Fang, Yuan Haiying, Ma Junjie, Hong Zhenkuai, Zhang Qingfang, Zhao Sile, Yang Kuisong, Greg Newburn, Dorothy Solinger, Thomas P. Bernstein, Joe Kelley, Rodney Faraon, Guang Lei, Richard McGregor, David Hoffman, Chun Han Wong, and Andrew Polk.

I'd like to also thank those individuals who provided excellent feedback on earlier drafts of the manuscript, including Kaiser Kuo, Julia Lovell, Chris Buckley, Peter Braden, Matt Willis, Ryan Manuel, Joseph Torigian, Andrew Chubb, Alec Ash, Tristan Evans, and Ric Stockfis.

I'd like to thank my parents, Joe and Peg, who have been my greatest champions and teachers. Thanks to my brother, Josh, who shares my passion for *Star Wars* and craft beer, and understands why it's absurd that the mayor in *Jaws* remains the mayor in *Jaws 2*. Thanks to Shackleton, our black Labrador, who kept me company on many long days of writing. Finally, to Katie, the love of my life, my best friend, and my intellectual confidante. She read and improved nearly every word of the manuscript, and I dedicate the book to her.

CHINA'S NEW
RED GUARDS

Introduction

China should maintain vigilance against the Right but primarily against the "Left."

—Deng Xiaoping, 1992[1]

ON APRIL 22, 2018, on a desolate stretch of highway outside of North Korea's capital city, a bus carrying Chinese tourists plunged off a bridge, killing thirty-six, including four North Koreans.

In a rare move, North Korean state media publicly acknowledged the traffic accident, with news reports showing the country's leader Kim Jong-un consoling the injured in a Pyongyang hospital.[2] According to South Korean media, four North Korean officials were executed and three members of the military were demoted as the result of an internal investigation into the causes of the accident.[3]

The Twitter account of China's state-run TV station initially reported the accident, but the post was quickly deleted. A brief report on China's flagship nighttime news program showed footage of the upturned bus shrouded by pouring rain. Yet for the next week, the identities of the passengers remained a mystery.

This was unusual. Normally, when Chinese citizens are killed abroad, the Communist Party of China (CCP) goes to great lengths to publicize their deaths, perhaps to highlight how dangerous the outside world can be when compared to China, or to reinforce the paternal concern the party has for its own. But this time the authorities remained silent.

Did this mean a high-ranking Chinese official was among the deceased? Was there a connection to the recent tensions between North Korea and the United States? Was the bus crash staged?

Online, rumors spread with abandon. Some said Mao Zedong's grandson was among the victims. Others claimed the driver of the bus was drunk or that he'd overloaded the vehicle with too many people and too much luggage.

When the list of the deceased was finally released more than a week later, the truth turned out more interesting than the rumors.

The individuals who died in North Korea that day were descendants of Chinese soldiers who'd fought in the Korean War sixty-five years earlier. They were traveling with a Chinese company called Spark Travel, a boutique tourist agency that took its name from a folk saying made popular by Mao Zedong, "A single spark can start a prairie fire." The company specialized in red tourism—visits to memorial sites and landmarks with significance to the CCP's revolutionary history, which had become a booming industry in China, estimated to bring in more than $44 billion in 2017.[4] Since its founding in 2015, Spark Travel led trips retracing the CCP's famed Long March, to the former party strongholds in Yan'an and Jinggangshan ("cradle of the Chinese revolution"), and on international trips to Karl Marx's birthplace in Germany and to Lenin's hometown in Russia.

For the fateful trip in April 2018, the company's website promised participants the chance to "visit the beautiful mountains of Korea, and feel the tensions at the 38th parallel," a reference to the boundary between North and South Korea more commonly known as the "Demilitarized Zone," or DMZ for short.[5] For just under $1,000, tourists could spend seven days touring North Korea's capital Pyongyang and venturing out into its countryside to visit Sanggamryŏng, the site of the legendary Korean War battle, later popularized in the 1956 Chinese film *Battle on Shangganling Mountain*. They would also visit the grave of Mao Zedong's son, Mao Anying, who died in the war. More importantly, Anying was killed by an American napalm bomb on November 25, 1950, making him not only a martyr to North Korea and China but one who had died at the hands of the United States, China's on-again, off-again foe.

Among the deceased was the head of Spark Travel, Diao Weiming. He was forty-five at the time of the accident and the father of a seven-month-old child. A flood of eulogies for Diao appeared on left-leaning websites in China. Guo Songmin, a former air force pilot who traveled to Moscow with Diao in 2017 to commemorate the one hundredth anniversary of the October Revolution, wrote that Diao's work on behalf of red tourism made him "immortal."[6] Peking University's Kong Qingdong, who once called Hong Kong residents "dogs of imperialism," believed that Diao should be awarded a "Sino-DPRK Friendship Medal."[7] People's Liberation Army (PLA) General Wang Lihua, a prominent hardline military commentator, wrote that Diao's efforts "inspired the great rejuvenation of the Chinese nation," borrowing from a slogan revived by China's current leader, Xi Jinping.[8]

He was born in 1967 at the height of the Great Proletarian Cultural Revolution, Mao Zedong's last great effort to purge the party of his political and ideological enemies, which engulfed the country in chaos for the better part of a decade and left more than one million dead.[9] Diao later worked for one of Shanghai's local tax bureaus before relocating to the southern city of Shenzhen, the epicenter of China's export juggernaut, to join a relative's company. He quickly grew dissatisfied with his boss, but more importantly, with the treatment of local migrant workers who were overworked and underpaid in sometimes appalling working conditions. Diao left the city in frustration and returned to Shanghai, where he began a spiritual journey of sorts.

As he worked odd jobs, he began reflecting on the economic and social costs of China's current economic model and the fate of the country's socialist legacy. After Mao's death in 1976, the country had undertaken a series of painful reforms to modernize its political and economic system with a goal of creating a more sustainable path to independence and prosperity. Agricultural workers were given more autonomy over their fields, urban workers were freed to pursue employment in new occupations and in different parts of the country, and foreign investment, technology, and expertise were (cautiously) welcomed into the domestic market.

The ensuing benefits were real, but the costs were high.

Even for those eager to leave behind the anarchy of the Mao era, the changes unleashed by these reforms were wrenching and provoked a series of uncomfortable questions. Deng Xiaoping had said, "Let some people get rich first," but how could a nominally socialist government allow such flagrant income inequality in the face of crushing poverty? How could China's leaders permit the wholesale destruction of the natural environment in the name of economic growth? Would an actual, existing socialist system permit the layoffs of an estimated 60 million workers from state-owned and collective sector enterprises, as the Chinese government had done between 1993 and 2006?[10]

Diao's search for answers brought him to a popular left-leaning and nationalist website called 乌有之乡, which translates as the "Land of Utopia" but is more widely known in English as "Utopia." The organization was formed in 2003 as a pan-leftist website and bookstore by intellectuals and activists who, like Diao Weiming, were angered by what they saw as the Communist Party's increasing capitalist drift, and the concomitant exploitation of the country's workers, peasants, and other marginalized groups.

The previous year, the CCP's charter had been amended to permit private entrepreneurs to join the party. Although many cadres publicly supported the move (one provincial official described it as "a creative usage and development of Marxist theory [that] is strongly theoretical, scientific, creative, and practical"[11]), it was highly controversial with more orthodox party members. In 2001, China joined the World Trade Organization (WTO) after nearly a decade of negotiations and key concessions on further liberalizing large sectors of its command-and-control economy. Han Deqiang, one of Utopia's founders, argued that accession would lead to the decimation of Chinese firms by their foreign competitors. "China will lose its independent industrial system and gradually become a production and processing base for multinational companies," he warned.[12]

The group was just one of many such websites that arose during the early 2000s out of the burgeoning space for intellectual discussion and political activism that cyberspace afforded. "With the Internet, we didn't need to go through the elite to speak our minds," one prominent intellectual affiliated with Utopia told me. "The Internet is the new 'big character poster,'" he added, referring to the tradition of drafting spontaneous political statements that had been a core feature of expression during the Cultural Revolution.[13]

Although it began as a relatively ecumenical gathering spot for a variety of leftist critics of China's market reforms, by the mid-2000s, Utopia evolved to become more dogmatic—and overtly political—in its activities. It began organizing student groups on Chinese universities, publishing open letters and petitions addressed to the Chinese government, and directly criticizing the CCP's most senior leaders, even going so far as to publicly call for the sacking of then-Premier Wen Jiabao for "grave errors and crimes."[14]

By the time Diao discovered Utopia in 2010, the explosion of information technology enabled the growth of a nationwide network of disenfranchised intellectuals, anti-GMO activists, environmentalists, disaffected migrant workers, nationalists, wealthy entrepreneurs, university students, and current and former high-ranking members of the CCP and PLA who rejected the triumphalism of Western liberal democratic capitalism, were skeptical of US-dominated globalization, and advocated egalitarian socialism under the leadership of a nationalist CCP. They found intellectual homes on websites like the Red Song Society, New Workers, Left Bank, Maoflag, China Workers Net, Protagonist, and Utopia. These websites cross-posted articles, co-sponsored events, and created a vibrant community, both online and off.

Collectively, they were dubbed "neo-Maoists," owing to their vocal support for modern China's founding father, Mao Zedong, as well as to distinguish them from other flavors of leftist thought in China, such as the New Left and the older generation of Maoists who came to power during the Cultural Revolution.[15] Like many such political labels, this appellation was coined by opponents who sought to discredit the movement by painting it as slavishly following Mao, or as group of naive and hopeless nostalgics pining for a return to a distant past.

There is some truth in this. As Utopia co-founder Han Deqiang declared in 2009, "Without the cult of personality for Mao Zedong, our Communist Party might have remained a sheet of loose sand and would have remained groping in the darkness. To destroy Mao's cult of personality is to destroy the spirit of the Communist Party."[16]

As their comfort navigating the online world indicated, however, neo-Maoists weren't advocating that China go back in time to the 1960s anymore than conservative-leaning Tea Party activists in America sought to actually wind back the clock to the eighteenth century and the age of George Washington. Rather, they believed that Mao Zedong offered a strategic vision and practical guidance that could help China resolve many of the "contradictions" that had emerged over the course of four decades of economic reforms, as well as to help the country navigate the challenges of the twenty-first century.

Yet there was genuine nostalgia for the Mao era, which remained a constant presence throughout the past four decades of Reform and Opening and was especially strong in areas that withstood the full brunt of reforms to the planned economy. In the north, SOE-heavy industrial cities faced the sudden shock of tens of millions of layoffs beginning in the mid-1990s. The aftershocks of smashing the "iron rice bowl" of guaranteed employment and social benefits are still felt today. In southern China, the post-WTO rise of the export economy, fueled by cheap and abundant labor, provided new opportunities for millions of migrants, but also injustice and oppression at the hands of unscrupulous employers and compliant local governments. In both north and south China, memories of the Mao era (real and imagined) powered a sense of grievance and opposition. "People without ability are all nostalgic about Mao's time," one textile mill worker told sociologist Ching Kwan Lee.[17]

Yet neo-Maoists also wrapped themselves in the mantle of Mao because they believed it provided a tactical advantage and a degree of protection from a regime that's highly intolerant of civic and grassroots activism. As one of the original members of the CCP and the founding father of the PRC in 1949, Mao holds an unrivaled position in party history and national lore. By dressing their political activities in Maoist symbolism, the neo-Maoists believed they could occupy the ideological high ground, thus raising the cost to the party for any overt repression. "How can you attack someone holding high the banner of Mao?" one grassroots activist told me.[18] Mao's image and words had been an important "weapon of the weak" since the onset of the reforms in the late 1970s, and it remains common at labor protests to see Mao's image prominently displayed. The "banner of Mao" wasn't quite the infallible amulet many neo-Maoists believed it to be (as this book explores in later chapters), but it did leave them far less exposed to state coercion than might otherwise have been the case.

The visibility of neo-Maoist groups like Utopia grew along with—or perhaps because of—their increasingly defiant and radical posture. While this made it easier to attract new members and readers, it also brought with it the attention of the authorities, and throughout the 2000s, neo-Maoist websites and the Chinese government seemed engaged in a drawn-out game of whack-a-mole. Websites would be closed only to reopen again days or weeks later. Utopia was closed repeatedly, only to reopen again, seemingly without consequence. Yet each censoring of a neo-Maoist website only seemed to confirm their original supposition that the party had abandoned true socialism. On February 22, 2008, three prominent neo-Maoist websites—Chinese Workers' Network, the Communist Party Network, and the Workers' and Peasants' Forum—were simultaneously closed on legal technicalities. Utopia's response was defiant. "In a country that claims to be socialist, in a country that claims that the working class is the leading class, in a country ruled by a self-proclaimed Communist Party, the authorities actually want to block websites and forums that insist on Marxism-Leninism and Maoism," the group thundered on its website. "When things get to this point, our leftist friends . . . should think hard."[19]

Evocative language like this appealed to many citizens who'd grown tired of the staid and formalistic utterings of the party's propaganda authorities. This included Diao Weiming, who began attending Utopia lectures on topics ranging from socialist ideology to revisionist accounts of the Mao Zedong era, as well as regularly reading the dozens of articles the group posted on its website each week. In Utopia, he found a community that shared his concerns with the direction of China's economic reform agenda, his frustration over the treatment of peasants and workers in an increasingly capitalistic system, and his view that the Communist Party was culpable in leading the country away from its legacy of socialism and egalitarianism.

In 2011, Diao traveled to Beijing to meet Utopia co-founder Fan Jinggang, who also ran the organization's day-to-day operations. Diao wanted to work for the group full-time, but he would first need to undergo "investigation and training" before he was approved for permanent employment.[20] According to one journalist who posed as a prospective Utopia employee in 2012, the training program was a "new Whampoa Military Academy," a reference to the famous military training ground created by Sun Yat-sen's KMT in 1924.[21] Applicants were typically between the ages of eighteen and twenty-five and were required to possess the minimum of a high school diploma, a healthy and strong physique, and a commitment to serve the motherland. In total, the training lasted sixty days, split into three sections: military-style drilling, lectures by well-known leftist and nationalist intellectuals, and a period of work-study in Nanjie Village, once called the "Last Maoist Village in China" by *The Atlantic* magazine.[22] Diao completed the training and joined Utopia in late 2011.

His work on North Korea began almost immediately. He led multiple trips to the country to celebrate its cooperation with China in their "victory" over the United States in the "War to Resist U.S. Aggression and Aid Korea," as the group still referred to the Korean War. In an announcement on its website, Utopia described one such trip to commemorate the "smashing of 30 years of influence by Western intellectuals that has led to the masses both supporting the US while also fearing it."[23]

A journalist for the liberal-leaning *Southern Weekend* published a biting exposé of Utopia's North Korea trips after posing as a sympathetic tourist.[24] He painted a picture of naïve "fellow travelers" who bumbled their way, seemingly unaware, through a highly controlled and choreographed Potemkin outing to the world's most repressive regime. ("You fellow comrades have made an extraordinary contribution to the North Korean economy," a North Korean official told the group after they'd purchased propaganda bric-a-brac at a Pyongyang souvenir store.) Many of the neo-Maoists didn't hide their unabashed support for the Kim family regime. One participant who traveled to North Korea with Diao and Spark Travel in 2017 said of the trip, "I personally saw the great achievements of the Korean people under the wise leadership of the three generations of Kim Il-sung, Kim Jong-il and Kim Jong-un. The truly socialist North Korea has such courage!"[25]

One day after North Korea tested a nuclear device in February 2013, Utopia released a seventeen-hundred-word letter congratulating Kim Jong-un, adding that the test "proves that the Workers' Party and comrade Kim possess the capability and resolution to lead the socialist country to prosperity."[26] In April 2014, Utopia hosted a banquet in Beijing for North Korean diplomats, which was an extremely rare instance of Chinese citizens having direct contact with North Korean officials outside of officially sponsored events. According to one report of the dinner, the highlight of the evening was a group rendition of "The Internationale" and "The East Is Red," China's de facto national anthem during the Cultural Revolution.[27]

The issue of North Korea had long been a sensitive topic for Beijing, owing to its reluctant embrace of the unpredictable pariah regime on the one hand, but viewing it as a buffer state between China and South Korea, a US ally, on the other. Even worse, by the time of Diao's death in the spring of 2018, war on the Korean Peninsula was a distinct possibility. In a series of Twitter posts and press conferences, US president Donald Trump declared he would respond to North Korea's threats against US territory with "fire and fury like the world has never seen." Kim Jong-un, in turn, made his own provocations toward the US territory of Guam in the Pacific Ocean. The CCP, meanwhile, was trying to navigate the volatility of Donald Trump and the unpredictability of Kim Jong-un, and it wanted to do so without the disruption of online nationalism, which was often a precursor to accusations that the party had failed to protect China's national interests. In addition, the outpouring of support for Diao Weiming and the other Utopia supporters who died with him in North Korea brought unwanted attention to China's long-term and increasingly strained fraternity with North Korea. And this, in turn, was making it harder for Beijing to pursue a possible strategic realignment away from the Communist dictatorship.

On May 19, in the lead-up to this historic summit between Trump and Kim, the CCP blocked Utopia's popular WeChat account with its estimated 130,000 followers, and soon after, its main website was shuttered as well, the sixth time this had occurred since its founding in 2003. Some speculated that the move was intended to pre-empt accusations of treason by the group if China made significant concessions to the United States in the course of its negotiations with the DPRK.[28]

Yet within days, Utopia's website was back up and running.

Compared to the ruthlessness the CPP normally imposes on errant organizations, intellectuals, and activists, this wasn't even a slap on the wrist. Grassroots lawyer Chen Guangcheng served a four-year prison sentence followed by years of unofficial house arrest after bringing a class-action lawsuit against a local-level family planning office in 2005. Writer and future Nobel Peace Prize winner Liu Xiaobo was arrested in late 2008 on charges of "state subversion" for his work organizing the "Charter 08" manifesto calling on the party to enact serious political reforms. After nearly a decade in prison, Liu died of cancer in 2017. Following his rise to power in late 2012, CCP general secretary Xi Jinping intensified the crackdown on civil society and intellectual discourse, arguably the most severe since the crushing of student demonstrations in Tiananmen Square in 1989. More than one hundred lawyers have been detained, dozens of influential magazines and websites were permanently closed, and countless academics and intellectuals have been punished for politically incorrect remarks.

Given Utopia's long history of political contention and its direct involvement in some of the country's most sensitive political issues, relations with North Korea being just one, why did the Communist Party appear to treat neo-Maoists with such relative leniency?

This book attempts to answer this question. I argue that neo-Maoism is a genuine political movement, one born out of widespread discontent with China's political and economic trajectory, nurtured by access to information technology like the Internet and the mobile phone, and sustained through deep connections with a small, but influential, group of political elites. These include individuals like Zhang Quanjing, the head of the Organization Department in the 1990s and now the deputy head of the Central Committee's "Party Building Directorate"; Hu Muying, the "princeling" daughter of Mao Zedong's former secretary, Hu Qiaomu, Wang Lihua, a hawkish propagandist in the People's Liberation Army, and Mei Xinyu of the Ministry of Commerce.

I also argue that neo-Maoism's longevity is surprising only because we've fundamentally misunderstood the nature of China's development following Mao Zedong's death in 1976.[29] In our collective imagination, the 1980s and 1990s—the Deng Xiaoping era—saw the relentless dismantling of the command economy and the forthright abandonment of the Maoist ideological infrastructure that underpinned it. Deng was lionized in the West for his decisive leadership in dragging China out of the chaos of the Cultural Revolution and into the modern (i.e., Western) world. This great transformation earned him a place as *Time* magazine's "Man of the Year" twice (in 1978 and 1985). He even received the same honor from William F. Buckley's virulently anti-Communist *National Review* magazine in 1985. If the epoch had a slogan, it was one reputedly uttered by Deng: "It doesn't matter whether a cat is black or white, as long as it catches mice." In place of Marxism and Leninism, class struggle, and the utopian dream of communism, CCP leaders appeared to embrace capitalism and the ethos of "to get rich is glorious." Even the Soviets saw China hurtling toward Western capitalism, warning that Deng's China was "reviving anti-socialistic forms of property," and according to one high-ranking Russian diplomat, "[The Chinese] have advanced the motto 'let's get rich' and everyone has escaped into trading. . . . In ten years, the capitalists and kulaks [rich peasants] will multiply."[30]

The brutal crackdown on student protests in Tiananmen Square in 1989 momentarily dislodged our Whiggish hopes for China, laying bare as it did the CCP's willingness to deploy violence when threatened. But we were comforted yet again by Deng's 1992 Southern Tour (discussed in chapter 1) and his renewed promise of market reforms. And clearly, as the dissolution of the Soviet Union in 1991 seemed to prove, China *had* to reform, for if it didn't, its political system would collapse under its own ideological deficiencies and political rigidities: "The system has exhausted itself. It has run out of ideas and energy, and especially in the provinces you get the sense that it's pretty much irrelevant," a Western ambassador told a Beijing-based journalist in 1991.[31]

Others argued that trade and commerce would force change. After a 1998 trip to China, columnist Max Frankel observed, "People who were required by the Emperor Mao a generation ago to hide their individuality in blue uniforms now sport sneakers, jeans and T-shirts heralding Michael Jordan and Colonel Sanders." The result, concluded Frankel, was that "Communism has expired. Commerce has exploded."[32] While campaigning for the US presidency in 2000, George W. Bush proclaimed, "Trade freely with China, and time is on our side."[33] Journalist Nicholas Kristof declared in 2004: "Communism is fading, in part because of Western engagement with China—trade, investment, Avon ladies, M.B.A.s, Michael Jordan and *Vogue* magazines have triumphed over Marx."[34]

If capitalism didn't kill off Marxism, the Internet surely would. In 1999, when China had a mere 2.1 million Internet users, Andy Kennedy of the *Washington Post* predicted that "the party's future looks even shakier as technological developments, such as the Internet, gradually erode its command over the flow of information."[35] Even as late as 2009, columnist Roger Cohen wrote, "Technology has taken the 'total' out of totalitarian. The Stalinist or Maoist dark night of the soul has been consigned to history by wired societies."[36]

With hindsight, it's cheap and easy to ridicule such predictions as naïve or ignorant. Certainly, there was enough "end of history" triumphalism going around after the collapse of the Soviet Union that the majority of journalists, academics, and intellectuals believed a "new world order" was imminent—and, crucially, permanent. Old ideologies such as communism, Marxism, protectionism, and nationalism would—in one of the most overwrought clichés of the era—be consigned to the dustbin of history. Technology was believed to be a universal acid that would corrode tools of state control over free thought and expression. Increased access to information about the crimes of the Mao era would irrevocably deplete any remaining pockets of nostalgia for the Great Helmsman. According to this line of thinking, the Communist Party was already completely pragmatic, its only ideology being economic development. "These are thinking people. You're not dealing with ideologues," said the late Singaporean leader Lee Kuan Yew of the Chinese leadership in a 2006 interview.[37]

Of course, much in this narrative is true. China in 1989, to say nothing of 2019, was far removed from the China of 1976, the year Mao Zedong died. But there was clearly an overabundance of romanticism as we watched China emerge from the bonfire of the Cultural Revolution. Perhaps more importantly, outside of a core group of academics, there was a distinct inability to listen to the complex intellectual debates raging inside China. As the nationalist writer Wang Xiaodong told me, "Westerners made the mistake of only talking to the intellectuals they liked or those intellectuals who thought [China] was doomed."[38] Had we paid attention to the multitude of voices arguing for different and often competing paths to modernity, we might have better calibrated our expectations. Instead, we imposed our own understanding of where China *should* go, such that we missed the signs pointing to a much messier, more complex, and far more interesting journey.

Thus, I hope to show in the pages that follow that despite the façade of strict party control and a "depoliticization" of the Chinese population, the past four decades of "Reform and Opening" have been replete with intense ideological and political struggles, with debates that raged during the first few decades of the post-Mao era still fueling social, political, and ideological divisions today. These debates were often obscured by a highly active system of censorship and repression, but they were there nonetheless, and they speak to deep divisions running through Chinese society, despite the outward appearance of political stability. Rather than a "unspoken social contract," wherein the Chinese people have agreed to avoid politics in return for economic growth and stability delivered by the CCP, we see that China has politics, too, with neo-Maoism being but one of the many intellectual currents rippling through the country in reaction to the political choices party leaders are making on behalf of the Chinese people.

As the epigraph to this chapter indicates, among the many ideological fault lines that have run through the past four decades after Mao's death, the political divisions on the left have longest vexed party leaders. A discussion of the shifting meanings of the term "left" throughout the history of the People's Republic of China has warranted entire books,[39] but in the contemporary context—that is to say, after 1992—the left's advocacy of Mao-inspired socialism (again, broadly and often imprecisely defined) has come to represent a deeply subversive ideology as Beijing focuses on growth-at-all-costs to the exclusion of social equity, the environment, and the rights of workers and peasants. Some on the so-called New Left have called Beijing's vision "developmentalism" in an attempt to remind the Chinese public that the economic reform agenda is just as much an "ism" as was socialism or Marxism. But the more biting criticism has been to point out that a nominally socialist government overseen by a nominally communist party had all but abandoned any pretense to pursuing the socialist vision that had animated the country since its founding. As political scientist Feng Chen points out, "as long as 'socialism' remains symbolically important for the Party's political legitimacy, the CCP has to bear the burden of justifying its current practices in socialist terms, which will therefore involve a protracted ideological battle with the leftists over what is authentic socialism and who represents it."[40]

This is not new, of course, and is not unique to China. As Mark Mazower writes in his brilliant study of the twentieth century:

> The decline [of the Communist Party of the Soviet Union] was most visible in Poland. In the official Kubiak Report, which it commissioned in September 1981 to reflect upon the causes and origins of the Solidarity crisis, its author—on the liberal wing of the Party—noted that the origins of social conflict lay not only in the political opposition but more basically, "when the gap between the declared aims of socialism and the results achieved widened." Solidarity proved that the workers of Gdańsk took socialism seriously—they criticized the perks of Party bosses and showed no signs of interest in capitalism or the market; it was precisely because the Party was no longer a convincing guide to socialism that the assault it faced was so devastating.[41]

And so it is in China, where the party, long the student of Soviet decline, feels exposed on its left flank, and the most effective way to impugn Beijing still remains to point out the distance between its socialist aspirations and the realities of authoritarian state capitalism. The story of neo-Maoism is, then, also a story about the struggle over national identity, with a central question being who speaks for authentic socialism and Marxism, and who the true political inheritors of Mao's legacy are. As a result, and in contradistinction to the recent debates over the "reinvigoration of ideology" under Xi Jinping,[42] this book argues that ideology has always played a central role in China's domestic discourse, including—indeed especially—Deng Xiaoping's deeply ideological commitment to political stability and economic growth that was "Reform and Opening."

This book also hopes to shed additional light on China's political system, specifically the intimate connection between abstract ideological debates and cold, hard political maneuvering and policy formulation. Looking back at the great political swings in China since Mao's death, we see a recurrent pattern whereby seemingly abstruse ideological discussions on topics like alienation, the nature of truth, or the definition of socialism are in fact groundwork for meatier policy debates that begin with references and reinterpretations of the existing theoretical canon. As scholar Tu Wei-ming explains, "Even if we choose to believe that the power struggle in China is more a political game than an ideological debate it is worth noting that the widely accepted way to exercise power in this political game is through ideological discourse."[43]

Operating as they do in this nexus of ideology and politics, one key question explored in this book is why does the party allow the neo-Maoists to exist at all? One thesis holds that Beijing remains unable to strike against a political movement that so closely identifies with Mao Zedong and the founding principles of the nation. This is certainly what some neo-Maoists believe:

> "What many people don't know is that the current government isn't afraid of the right wing, as even if it becomes more vocal, it has little support among the masses. In the worst case, it will form a handful of shameless and bloated interest groups. With the left it's different. While they lack finances, they hold high the banner of Mao Zedong while advocating the mobilization of the people."[44]

Yet this doesn't explain why Beijing has repeatedly shuttered neo-Maoist websites and organizations, nor the current campaign of repression against Marxist student groups for their involvement in labor disputes in southern China, a topic explored toward the end of this book. Clearly, when the party feels threatened, it acts.

A more convincing hypothesis is that the neo-Maoists serve a useful "radical flank" for more moderate leftists within the party-state.[45] The core of the neo-Maoist platform (such as a coherent platform exists) calls for strengthening party control and increasing the state's involvement in the economy, goals that clearly align with many elements within the political system. With neo-Maoist demands staking out the extreme boundary on any given policy issue, the demands of centrist (yet sympathetic) actors appear more reasonable by comparison.[46] More recently, neo-Maoists have proven their utility to the party leadership by slotting into the role of attack dogs for Xi Jinping's many campaigns to purify China's ideological sphere, including against "historical nihilism" and "universal values."[47] Critics of Xi have been hounded into silence by a torrent of online abuse at the hands of neo-Maoist netizens, allowing party authorities to appear hands-off in the process.

But this doesn't mean that the party and the neo-Maoists have found a permanent truce, and without institutionalized avenues for popular participation in policymaking, groups like Utopia will always feel tempted to move to the extreme in order to make their voices heard. This is a pattern we've seen play out again and again in issues ranging from labor rights to the treatment of ethnic minorities. Cornell University scholar Eli Friedman has called China "undeniably the epicenter of global labor unrest," owing to the denial of basic rights and legal procedures for the tens of millions of Chinese workers who power the country's export machine.[48] As one 2006 article reposted on the Utopia website put it starkly, "Why do workers take to the streets to defend their legitimate rights and interests? This is because they have been treated unfairly and have nowhere to speak."[49] There are many more such struggles in China, limited only by the party's iron grasp of information flows and its willingness to utilize coercion.

Mao Zedong and the history of the Mao era also permeate the discussion that follows, an unavoidable feature for a book on neo-Maoism. But Mao matters for reasons I initially failed to comprehend, the most important being that despite the remarkable transformation China has undergone since his death, the CCP has always viewed its legitimacy as being inextricably tied to Mao. Even during the heady days of the Deng Xiaoping era, when it was commonly assumed that China had "de-Maoified," the party was always careful to police the boundaries of Mao's legacy, which it ultimately saw as its own legacy. New spaces for historical investigation of the Mao era opened up, but there were always red lines that couldn't be crossed, most especially anything that could be perceived as challenging the party's legitimacy. Thus, Mao remains essential, yet contested and controversial, even within the party. (To take but one example: the fifth and final volume of Mao Zedong's *Selected Works*, which was published in 1977 under the editorship of Hua Guofeng, ends in 1957, the year before the catastrophic Great Leap Forward that led to tens of millions of deaths. This leaves nearly twenty years of Mao's rule completely absent from the official body of his speeches and writings.)

Of course, China's rulers are not alone in their struggle to control and manipulate historical narrative, which stretches across political systems.[50] "History everywhere is political," observed historian Eric

Foner.[51] Modern capitalist democracies such as the United States, Australia, Japan, and Germany still wrestle with the ghosts of the past, and contemporary political debates are often smuggled into the public square through discussions of nominally historical events. In Japan, argues writer Ian Buruma, "Whenever you hear a right-winger say, 'It's all a left-wing myth, we're not as guilty as people are saying,' what he's really saying is, 'We want to revise the Constitution and postwar order imposed by the United States.'"[52] Similarly in the United States, heated public debates about the removal of statues commemorating Confederate soldiers stand in for discussions about contemporary racism and police brutality. American conservative James Robbins laments, "Those who take pride in America emphasize stories that reflect the best about our country and inspire hope for the future. Progressives seek to demean and demolish, elevating the victims of the past as an indictment of the present. They wield history as a weapon on behalf of the aggrieved, never gratified by the progress made."[53] This is precisely what a neo-Maoist would say about the Mao era.

In Russia, Vladimir Putin has overseen a pronounced rehabilitation of Joseph Stalin, with the notorious twentieth-century tyrant now viewed as Russia's greatest historical figure by half the country.[54] Rather than embrace Stalin outright, Putin has been relatively muted on the deceased dictator, instead allowing pro-Stalinist intellectuals to promote revisionist accounts of the Soviet past that overlap with, if not reinforce, Putin's own conception of power and authority. As in China, individuals and organizations that seek to commemorate or remember the darker chapters of the Stalin era are silenced, or worse.

Like all countries, struggles over collective memory and historical truth have a particular salience owning to their impact on a country's political trajectory. But with China, this trajectory will have a significant impact on the entire world. A free press, a vibrant publishing industry, an independent academia, and a free and open Internet that can facilitate honest discussions about a nation's darker chapters are all absent, and under its current leader, the space for objective historical analysis is closing at a rapid pace. "Germany has reckoned with its Nazi past, America still talks about its history of slavery, why can't we Chinese talk about our own history?" says Li Zhensheng, a former newspaper photographer now barred in mainland China from showing pictures taken during the Cultural Revolution.[55] Writing in 1990, the dissident physicist Fang Lizhi argued, "Once each decade, the true face of history is thoroughly erased from the memory of Chinese society," a policy achieved through a "coerced forgetfulness," so that "any detail of history that is not in the interests of the Chinese Communists cannot be expressed in any speech, book, document, or other medium."[56]

As I write this introduction in early 2019, the US and China stand on the precipice of a "new Cold War," and like the Cold War with the Soviet Union, we're coming to see the divisions running, not only on economic and military lines, but along ideological ones as well. One of the key transformations over the past five years was *not* that China became bigger and stronger—that's been occurring for some time now—but rather, it was the unabashed pride China's leader Xi Jinping holds for the sickle and hammer and the role of the party in all aspects of China's political, economic, and social life. As he declared at the Nineteenth Party Congress in 2017, "Party, government, military, civilian and academic; east, west, south, north, center, the Party leads everything."[57] It's thus imperative that we better understand how the party sees itself and how it sees the world. This, in turn, depends on a more complete understanding of the domestic forces that exert influence on the CCP—be they economic, political, or ideological.

One of these forces, indeed a very important one, is the neo-Maoist movement.

I

Prologue—The Death of Mao Zedong

What [Mao] left to posterity is a complicated yet rich legacy, a fruit hard to consume, but impossible to discard. . . . His shade lingers in all corners of contemporary Chinese society.

—Qian Liqun, literary historian, Peking University[1]

AT 4 P.M. ON SEPTEMBER 9, 1976, public loudspeakers across China crackled to life with the most important announcement in the history of the People's Republic:

> Comrade Mao Zedong, the esteemed and beloved great leader of our Party, our army, and the people of all nationalities of our country, the great teacher of the international proletariat and the oppressed nations and the oppressed people . . . passed away at 00:10 hours, September 9, 1976, in Beijing because of the worsening of his illness.[2]

A spokesman for the PRC Foreign Ministry claimed Mao's death "plunged the 800 million people across the country into profound grief and deep mourning."[3]

In reality, reactions varied.

Li Zhengsheng, a staff photographer for the *Heilongjiang Daily*, knew his editor would want photos of a nation in mourning, but after visiting factories, villages, and military facilities, he was unable to find a single mourning peasant.[4]

Dai Kaiyuan, a factory worker in Sichuan Province, remembered a sixty-year-old man telling him, "Mao Zedong should have died earlier!"[5]

The writer Yu Hua recalled, "Everyone loved Chairman Mao, of course, so when his name was finally announced, everyone burst into tears. I started crying, too, but one person crying is a sad sight; more than a thousand people crying together, the sound echoing, turns into a funny spectacle, so I began to laugh. My body shook with my effort to control my laughter while I bent over the chair in front of me."[6]

For others, Mao's death was a catastrophe.

Shen Yingwei, an elementary school student in 1976, recalled hearing of an elderly blind women who began to smash her head against the ground upon hearing of Mao's death.[7] Shen's father, who had returned home for a mandatory mourning ceremony, told his son, "[Mao's] entire life he thought of nothing else but the people, and everything he did was for others. We will never forget him."[8]

The Chinese staff at the Agence France-Presse "broke down" upon hearing of Mao's death: "Slumped in their chairs, they sobbed loudly, their heads buried in their hands."[9]

Regardless of how one reacted to the news of Mao's death, everyone knew that China would never be the same. By the end of his twenty-seven years as the ruler of the People's Republic, he had achieved near godlike status. "Every sentence of Chairman Mao's works is a truth; one single sentence of his surpasses ten thousand of ours," declared his one-time heir, Lin Biao.[10] In 1969, nearly 90 percent of China's population is said to have worn a Chairman Mao badge.[11] His "little red book"—formally known as the "Quotations from Chairman Mao Zedong"—was printed nine hundred million times and his image reproduced more than two billion times during his reign.[12]

With Mao's disappearance, the Chinese people confronted not only a spiritual, political, and cultural vacuum but also an existential question: Where did China go from here? And more immediately, who would lead them there?

The decisions the party leadership would make to address these questions in the coming months and years would have enormous repercussions for China and for the world. As they navigated the uncertain terrain of the "post-Mao" era, however, Mao Zedong remained a constant reference point, with his legacy serving as both a burden and a ballast.

A skilled political infighter, Mao survived decades of intraparty leadership struggles, and by the time of his death, questions of policy, promotions, and purges were simple: just ask Mao Zhuxi (Chairman Mao). His opinions were often erratic and radical, but his outsize charisma and unquestioned authority made him the undisputed arbiter on questions of national importance. As his former interpreter later wrote, "For the first twenty-seven years of the People's Republic, Mao was China. Now that the anchor line had been cut, no one could say with certainty in what direction the country might drift. Anything was possible, even civil war."[13]

The possibility of civil war was real. Just hours after Mao's death was announced, the nation's military was placed on its highest level of alert for only the fifth time since the country's founding in 1949.[14] Believing Mao's death might be the pretext for a counterrevolutionary coup, thousands of militia cordoned off a one-square-mile section near the center of Beijing. A member of Mao's medical team, who had served him loyally and without incident for decades, became convinced that he was about to be purged.[15] Sidney Rittenberg, an American who spent decades in China working alongside the CCP's top leadership, recalled that in the days following Mao's death, "the newspapers began to bristle with a strange, unstated energy."[16]

Confusion over "what next?" enshrouded Beijing. Even with virtually all the CCP's Central Committee members in Beijing for Mao's funeral, by early October there had still been no formal meeting to decide the path ahead. Foreign diplomats were unsure if the National Day holiday on October 1 would proceed after witnessing "some workmen . . . putting up decorations and lights for National Day, while other workers were taking them down and still others putting them up again," according to one contemporaneous report.[17] Even the fate of Mao's corpse remained unclear after it disappeared from public view on September 17.

Whoever took command of the party had the unenviable (and near-impossible) task of trying to replace the supposedly irreplaceable Chairman Mao. Having purged one potential successor after another,

Mao had also made it seemingly impossible for anyone to build up the required power and prestige to run the system in his absence.

On paper, the succession issue appeared to be resolved in favor of Hua Guofeng. Hua had been a relatively obscure provincial official until he was elevated to the Politburo in 1973, and in the wake of State Council Premier Zhou Enlai's death in early 1976, he was promoted again to become the acting premier. Absent any formalized succession procedure, Hua's claim to the throne stemmed from a note scribbled by the dying Mao and addressed to Hua: "With you in charge, I'm at ease."

But a note, even by the hand of Mao Zedong, wasn't going to be enough.

Hua faced fierce competition from Jiang Qing, Mao's wife, and her three lieutenants, Yao Wenyuan, Zhang Chunqiao, and Wang Hongwen. Mao had dubbed them the "Gang of Four" in 1974, and the name stuck. For much of the preceding decade, the Gang of Four was a potent political force from its base at the Central Cultural Revolution Group, which possessed extraordinary power over domestic affairs. From its founding in May 1966 until it was finally disbanded at the Ninth Party Congress in 1969, the group maintained de facto oversight over all Cultural Revolution–related actions and policies. Jiang Qing was also a remarkable personality. She managed to survive decades of extreme uncertainty that accompanied her unique position as Mao's wife and possible heir. As she once told an assembly of high school students, "We do not fear chaos. Chaos and order are inseparable."[18]

But like Hua Guofeng, Jiang Qing's authority stemmed directly from Mao's tacit (and only occasionally explicit) support. With his passing, she was on her own. Long March veteran General Xu Shiyou warned Beijing: "If you don't arrest [Jiang Qing], I'll march north."[19]

He didn't have to.

Less than one month after her husband's death, Jiang Qing and her three accomplices were arrested on their way to a Politburo meeting. "Before Chairman Mao's bones are even cold you are already doing this," she scolded her captors. "What is this but a counterrevolutionary coup?"[20]

A Nanjing resident told one foreign diplomat, "The day we learned Jiang Qing had been arrested, not a bottle of alcohol was left in the city."[21]

But euphoria quickly turned to anger as the official media implicated the Gang of Four for all the chaos and destruction of the preceding decade. Lurid tales of excess soon emerged: private screenings of pornography, shipments of fresh lobster for extravagant meals, and Jiang Qing's penchant for foreign fashion.[22] One Shanghai newspaper called them "cunning and treacherous swindlers of sham Marxism," and if that wasn't enough, "maggots who disguised themselves as Leftists and climbed to higher positions."[23] "She is a very, very evil woman," Deng Xiaoping later remarked. Largely thanks to her, Deng had been stripped of his leadership positions in 1975, and he clearly held a grudge. "She is so evil," he continued, in a streak of barely concealed misogyny, "that any evil thing you say about her isn't evil enough, and if you ask me to judge her with the grades as we do in China, I answer that this is impossible, there are no grades for Jiang Qing, that Jiang Qing is a thousand times a thousand below zero."[24]

With the Gang of Four cast as counterrevolutionary villains, Mao Zedong was spared blame for the persecutions of the "anti-Rightist campaign," the mass starvation connected with the Great Leap Forward, and the chaos of the Cultural Revolution. Far from casting off the dead dictator's legacy, all sides in the brewing leadership struggled to cast themselves as his true inheritor. After all, the system still lurched along on the machinery he had constructed, and it was—and still remains—impossible to separate the legitimacy of the CCP from the legacy of Mao.

When the National Day celebration did finally go ahead, Hua Guofeng used the occasion to draw the mantle of Mao's memory publicly around him and (he hoped) the authority that came with it. As he stood with the members of the Politburo atop the Gate of Heavenly Peace, the same vantage point from which Mao had declared the founding of the PRC twenty-seven years earlier, he made clear that the leader's absence would be confined to the corporeal. "Chairman Mao," he declared, "will always live in our hearts."

Newspapers across the country took up the message, as calls went out for an "upsurge" in the study of Mao's written works as the "best concrete action to carry out Chairman Mao's behests."[25] On October 8, it was announced that Mao's remains would be displayed in a soon-to-be constructed mausoleum in the center of Tiananmen Square, a clear violation of Mao's stated desire to be cremated. "We should all be burnt after we die, turned into ashes and used for fertilizer," he had said in 1956.[26] But just as Stalin had decided to embalm Lenin's corpse and place it on public display in Moscow's Red Square, in China the needs of the regime outweighed the wishes of the dead.

This rush to embrace Mao's symbolic legacy, and anxiety about what might otherwise follow, was not confined to the capital. In his native Hunan Province, a party directive instructed the population to begin studying the official announcement of Mao's death, Hua Guofeng's funeral eulogy, and a newspaper editorial on the topic of Mao's legacy. Concerned about political instability, they mandated the people learn to sing "The Three Main Rules of Discipline and Eight Points for Attention," which spoke of the "iron discipline" the Red Army showed for Mao. "Sing it aloud, unite very closely around the Party center, and strengthen the Party's centralized leadership," demanded the authorities.[27] To show that even in death Mao was beyond reproach, officials in Nanjing city executed a thirty-one-year-old man for "his criticisms . . . aimed directly at our great leader Chairman Mao."[28]

With the Gang of Four now gone ("smashed" in the more evocative term of party propagandists) and the memory of Chairman Mao temporarily holding the system together, Hua Guofeng set about attempting to rebrand himself as the symbolic heir to Mao. On the anniversary of Mao's birthday in December 1976, he released a newly edited version of Mao's 1956 speech "On the Ten Great Relationships" and announced that he would be the editor of the fifth volume of *The Selected Works of Mao Zedong*, to be published in 1977. He also edited himself in to the national imagery: in propaganda posters, he was depicted eager and attentive at Mao's side, or as a stand-in for Mao with the same dress and hairstyle.

Hua's basic dilemma, and one that all subsequent leaders of the CCP would be forced to confront, was how to both preserve the legend of Mao (which, after all, was the only reason Hua was in power) while simultaneously reimagining it to provide the needed ideological leeway to rebuild the nation's economy after decades of misrule.

But Hua was no slavish follower of Mao's politics, and while later party propaganda minimized his role in those early years following Mao's death, recent scholarship has highlighted his pivotal role in kick-starting the economic reforms and helping to steer the country toward a more rational type of economic development.[29] And while the economic and political trajectory of China under the leadership of Hua is an interesting counter-factual, his time in power was relatively brief, owing to the political maneuverings of an four-foot, eleven-inch cadre from Sichuan Province named Deng Xiaoping.

Born in 1904, Deng had joined an overseas branch of the CCP in 1924 while living in France and dedicated his life to building and defending the party. He fought alongside Mao in the Red Army, and survived both the Long March and years working in the inner core of the party leadership in Yan'an, where purges were a regular occurrence. Soviet leader Khrushchev later wrote, "Mao regarded him as the most up-and-coming member of the leadership."[30] Indeed, while serving as vice premier in the early 1950s, at Mao's personal request Deng reviewed all government documents heading for the party center. While Mao clearly found Deng supremely capable, he also found him insufficiently ideological, accusing him of "paying no attention to the color of the cat as long as it catches mice," a charge with which Deng would no doubt have agreed. Perhaps worst of all, Deng did "not read books, and is ignorant about Marxism-Leninism."[31]

Deng had fallen out of favor with Mao on three separate occasions, but his final banishment from power ended in the summer of 1977, whereupon he and Hua Guofeng fell into an uneasy alliance that lasted until 1979, when Deng emerged as the de facto leader of the party. By 1981, Hua was completely sidelined.

With power, however, Deng and his allies were confronting a series of stark dilemmas: what was the right path forward for China's economy? No one at the time was arguing that China should become a capitalist system—that notion was then, as it is now (officially at least), a heretical suggestion. While everyone agreed that whatever happened, it had to be called socialism, it was far from clear what that would actually mean. Rather, the buzzword of the late 1970s was "modernization," which was politically neutral and ideologically safe—and also devoid of any specific policy proscriptions. Deciding what set of policies could actually deliver economic modernization was the hard part.

One of the ways the party sought answers was by visiting the outside world. In 1978 alone, twenty-one official delegations visited fifty-one countries, and the news from groups returning from Hong Kong, Japan, and Western Europe did not reflect well on the state of Chinese socialism.[32] "We thought capitalist countries were backward and decadent," remarked one official, adding, "When we left our country and took a look, we realized things were completely different."[33] Deng Xiaoping later put the matter more bluntly: "we must acknowledge that we are backward, that many of our ways of doing things are inappropriate, and that we must change."[34]

According to the official CCP history still told in the twenty-first century, the question of "which way forward" was decisively settled at the Third Plenum of the Eleventh Party Congress, held in Beijing on December 18–22, 1978. The meeting, now a core component of the CCP's post-Mao mythology, is often referred to as the "historical turning point" for modern China—the moment when China boldly and decisively blazed a path toward economic liberalization and integration with the outside world. It was at this meeting, the legend holds, that Deng Xiaoping's bold vision for "reform and opening" was first unveiled.

In fact, it was at the monthlong Work Conference just prior to the plenum that many of the immediate issues over economic policy were discussed and settled.[35] At the plenum itself, there was little discussion of reform (the word only appears twice in the official communiqué, while "market" was completely absent), and there were few new resolutions or policies. This point notwithstanding, the signs of change were clear. At the plenum's conclusion, Hua Guofeng announced that "large-scale, turbulent class struggles of a mass character have, in the main, come to an end." Also significant was the return to power of Chen Yun, the once-powerful economic planner who had been hounded out of Beijing during the Cultural Revolution. Now back in Beijing, Chen's rehabilitation was a powerful sign that pragmatic economic policy had returned.

But perhaps the most important outcome of the Third Plenum was the clear enhancement of Deng Xiaoping's power. Despite the fact that

Hua Guofeng presided over the meeting, Deng was the star, and from this point onward, he would be calling the shots.

At the "Theory Conference," convened the following month in Beijing, participants would spend weeks probing a new set of questions that the Work Conference and Third Plenum exposed on issues ranging from how to rehabilitate cadres accused of political crimes during the Mao era, and perhaps most important of all, how to summarize the historical achievements of Mao Zedong himself.

Hu Yaobang set the tone for the first half of the meeting in his opening remarks. The years since Mao Zedong's death had shaken the CCP to its core, he said. The defeat of the Gang of Four—"fake" Marxists and Maoists is how he described them—had been the party's "great achievement." But, he warned, there were still those in the leadership who possessed "mistaken viewpoints" that had to be addressed. What was needed, according to Hu, was for everyone to come together and reflect on the lessons of the past two, the past ten, and the past thirty years. What lessons had the party learned since assuming power in 1949? What had it learned from the chaos of the Cultural Revolution? What did the battles against the Gang of Four teach them? For Hu, it was clear: the party must emancipate its thinking, seek truth from facts, and avoid dogmatism. In short, the CCP must discard the ruling pathology of the Mao years and transform itself into a modern and more pragmatic governing apparatus.

That Hu Yaobang came out swinging was no accident, for he and his allies had already gauged the mood of the participants before the start of the conference. At Hu's insistence, a government think tank had distributed a questionnaire to research departments throughout the government and party in advance of the conference asking, among other questions, "What theoretical forbidden zones are there left for us to smash?"[36] The collected answers gave Hu and his allies confidence that there was a sufficient level of frustration with the status quo to warrant the aggressive tone.

One "forbidden zone," however, was meant to be left untouched. An article distributed to conference participants, written by CCP historian Liao Gelong, made the official position on Mao Zedong clear: "Our Party was led by Comrade Mao Zedong and thus our Party's victories and defeats cannot be separated from Comrade Mao Zedong. If we squarely face historical truths, this conclusion is inescapable."[37]

A similar tactic had been taken at the Third Plenum, when it was decided that a complete reckoning on the darker episodes of the recent past would be delayed until an "appropriate moment."[38] In other words, they understood that no consensus was likely to be reached so soon after Mao's death. Yet with all the historical and ideological baggage that had accumulated, participants at the Theory Conference understood that some sort of accounting with the past was unavoidable, so long was the shadow that it cast. As one participant pointed out, "After experiencing the Cultural Revolution, have we moved forward or backward? Tackling this problem is of the utmost importance for theoreticians, the Party and our country, and we should not leave this question to later generations to sort out."[39]

There was also the question of the political rehabilitation of those who had committed political "crimes" during the Mao era and spent the ensuing years enduring the consequences. Under the Maoist system, a "rightist" label would not only limit access to employment, food, or other necessities but would stigmatize one's entire family as well. During the Cultural Revolution, the designation would prove dangerous, even deadly.

One related consequence of the continuous political campaigns and their attendant purges had been to gut the government of qualified personnel. Hu Yaobang, perhaps more than any other high-ranking official, believed rehabilitation was not just expedient as a means of getting qualified scientists, academics, and government officials back to work but also as a way of signaling to the Chinese people that a new chapter had begun. Now that his patron Deng Xiaoping was a rising star, Hu moved aggressively to clear the names of those persecuted during the Mao era, arguing that China could not modernize without skilled party and government officials, tens of thousands of whom had been marginalized or worse over the previous two decades. There were also political calculations in play, for Hu knew that in doing so, he would engender a great amount of goodwill with those brought back into the system.

For many at the Theory Conference, these halfway measures were inadequate, and the only way to deal with the legacy of the Cultural

Revolution was to wholeheartedly denounce it, rehabilitate those who had been persecuted under it, and crush any remaining sympathy for the politics that animated it. The influential Marxist literary theorist Zhou Yang went even further, asking conference participants, "Was the Cultural Revolution the product of conspirators and some ambitious individuals such as Lin Biao and the 'Gang of Four,' or was it a problem with our theoretical line? Is there a problem with the theory of the continuous revolution under the dictatorship of the proletariat?"[40]

Some conference participants felt emboldened to attack yet another once-unthinkable target: Chairman Mao Zedong. This development was in many ways unavoidable, for there was no way to separate Mao from his revolutionary creations. Indeed, Mao himself had made this link explicit, once telling the Gang of Four that he had done two great things in his life: driving the KMT and the Japanese from mainland China and launching the Cultural Revolution.[41] Wang Ruoshui had earlier tested the waters in a session of party theoreticians in 1978, positing that the lesson of the Cultural Revolution was to avoid the "cult of personality," a reference to the godlike devotion Mao had attained.[42]

Most understood that diagnosing Mao's mistakes had to be done carefully. Li Xiulin proposed what would become the standard means of criticizing Mao. "The thought of Comrade Mao Zedong (including his words and actions) includes mistakes, while Mao Zedong Thought—just like Marxism and Leninism—is in itself a complete and correct system."[43] Thus, he argued, there was a difference between "thought" with a small "t" and big "T." The former represented the personal opinions and actions of Mao the man and, like the opinions of even the greatest leader, these were subject to occasional errors or logical deviations and thus were fair game for approved and "scientific" criticism—but the latter was sacred.

Others went further in their critiques, arguing that Mao's actions betrayed even his own core political ideals, including his vision of a "New Democracy" for China. The deputy head of the Propaganda Department went so far as to claim that Mao's push for socialism had been a "premature birth."[44]

By the Spring Festival holiday in mid-February, almost every aspect of the Mao era, including Mao Zedong himself, had come up for discussion. For those who believed China's future lay in economic integration with the outside world, particularly the United States, the seeming break with the Maoist past was a welcome and necessary development. For the tens of thousands of party and government officials hoping to have their political crimes annulled, the news coming from the Theory Conference was exhilarating. And for countless members of Chinese society, to hear that Deng Xiaoping was firmly in power and that the new ideology was pragmatism, not revolution, must have come as a welcome relief.

For the first half of the conference, Deng Xiaoping was on his historic trip to the United States, perhaps best remembered in the West for the images of Deng attending a rodeo in his ten-gallon hat. He was receiving regular updates from Beijing, however, and the news reaching him was not encouraging. Hu Qiaomu, Mao Zedong's former secretary, provided Deng with frequent and increasingly unsettling briefings. Hu was incensed by radical sentiment at the conference and warned Deng of a growing "anti-party" movement he felt was even greater than what had been seen during the 1956 "Hundred Flowers" campaign, when Mao Zedong briefly encouraged intellectuals to speak openly, only to be horrified by the depths of their frustration with the party.[45]

Hu's fear was not as far-fetched as it seemed: reports of resistance to a perceived "rightist coup" orchestrated by Hu Yaobang and Deng Xiaoping had trickled in from across China, and there was general unease among the military and other party organs that a "de-Maoification" was underway in Beijing.[46] At the end of the Third Plenum the previous December, Hu Qiaomu had described three winds blowing in China: an "anti-Communist wind," an "anti-socialist wind," and an "anti-Marxist-Leninist-Maoist wind."[47] As he warned his fellow party members, "The situation at present is very similar to the first half of 1957 when the anti-rightist campaign began. Don't force Chairman Hua [Guofeng] to launch another anti-rightist campaign."[48]

It wasn't just events in the Theory Conference that alarmed party conservatives. Several months earlier, Beijing citizens had begun to spontaneously draft "big character posters" calling for political and economic reform on a stretch of road in western Beijing. This new Democracy Wall, as it came to be known, was a forum for critiquing the excesses of the Mao era, and not surprisingly, it was initially supported by Deng Xiaoping, who saw it as a way to indirectly attack Hua

Guofeng. "What is the harm of a little opposition?," Deng said to party theoretician Yu Guangyuan in December 1978.[49] He told the chairman of the Japanese Socialist Party, "It's perfectly normal for people to put up posters. It's a sign of the stability of our country."[50]

The Western media quickly dubbed this the "Beijing Spring," and only the most cynical of observers could have doubted that the process of dethroning Mao was underway.[51] "The new thinking, the great democratic and human rights to which we aspire, which we seek, have today raised their heads in the great land of China," read one of the first posters, drafted by a group of writers who referred to themselves as "The Democratic Forum."[52] In January 1979, a poster called for Mao's body to be removed from the center of Tiananmen Square, calling it "feudal idolatry" and arguing that China needed to "thoroughly root out spiritual superstition, as well as the worship of idols."[53] Stories emerged of Chinese citizens who, when speaking of the crimes of the Gang of Four, would hold up five fingers and say, "Yes, yes, four!"[54]

While Deng professed to believe in "a little opposition," what he really meant was that he supported a little opposition so long as it was aimed at his political opponents. As his hold on power strengthened in the wake of the Third Plenum, the utility of these public displays of opposition diminished, and when they expanded into calls for political reform and criticism of Deng himself, his tolerance for discontent came to an end.

At just the moment party members were exploring the legacy of the Mao era at the Theory Conference, a former Red Guard and electrician at the Beijing Zoo named Wei Jingsheng posted a criticism of Deng's recent war with Vietnam in which he referred to him as a "fascist dictator."[55] In another poster, Wei called for the "Fifth modernization—Democracy," and in an article for the March edition of the magazine *Exploration*, he asked, "Do We Want Democracy or a New Dictatorship?" This was too much for Deng, for as permissive as the new atmosphere appeared, it was predicated on the unchallenged rule of the party, and when Deng believed a red line had been crossed, he was decisive in his use of state coercion, an instinct that was to play out repeatedly in the 1980s and culminating in the events of June 4, 1989. The coming crackdown against the Democracy Wall was signaled in the official media after it began to refer to activists as "anarchists" threatening social and economic stability.[56] On March 29, 1979, Wei Jingsheng was arrested and, after a sham trial, sentenced to fifteen years in prison for providing secret information on the Sino-Vietnamese war to a Reuters journalist.[57] Wei's arrest sent a chill through the Democracy Wall movement, and soon the wall itself was closed down. By year's end, there would be almost one thousand criminal cases stemming from a charge of "counter-revolution."[58] Less than a year after it had begun, the Beijing Spring was over.

Just before his arrest, Wei Jingsheng was asked by a foreign journalist why did he not believe party leaders would bring democracy to China. "Because," he responded, "they have been Communists all their lives."[59]

As he clamped down on dissent in the streets of Beijing, Deng turned his attention to a much larger problem: What to do about Mao?

From within moments of the chairman's death, when the decision was made to preserve his corpse rather than abide by his wishes for cremation, party leaders understood the importance of Mao's legacy to their own political survival. Now they had to figure out how to steer the country toward a new course of economic modernization while still claiming they remained loyal to Mao's vision.

Perhaps more than any other party official, Deng understood how precarious this balance was, having been in Moscow in 1956 when Soviet leader Nikita Khrushchev made his explosive "secret speech" denouncing the crimes of Stalin and his cult of personality. Deng had witnessed firsthand the shock, jubilation, confusion, and sense of betrayal that Khrushchev's revelations had unleashed, and now he was in a similar position. But whereas the Soviet Union had the luxury of having Lenin in the absence of Stalin, the CCP had only one founding father.

After returning to Beijing from the United States in the spring of 1979, Deng was convinced that a line had to be drawn under the growing criticisms of Mao Zedong, and he entrusted Hu Qiaomu with the responsibility of drafting a speech to be given at the end of the Theory Conference. Hu had earlier told his confidant Deng Liqun that he'd seen conference participants negate five fundamental principles: socialism, the dictatorship of the proletariat, the leadership of the party, Marxism-Leninism, and Mao Zedong.[60] If these were now opposed by the party, "then there's no reason for the CCP and the PRC to exist."[61]

The speech would become one of the most important of the post-Mao era. Entitled "Uphold the Four Cardinal Principles," it was delivered to conference participants on March 30, just four days before the close of the meeting.

As he stood before the hundreds of conference participants, Deng condemned the "doubts about socialism, the dictatorship of the proletariat, the Party's leadership, and Marxism-Leninism and Mao Zedong Thought" that had spread to "a small section of people," no doubt a reference to the Democracy Wall activists and many of those gathered before him. To avoid "small or big disturbances," Deng told the assembled audience that no matter what direction the country was to take, all must adhere to what he called the "four cardinal principles":

1. We must keep to the socialist road.
2. We must uphold the dictatorship of the proletariat.
3. We must uphold the leadership of the Communist Party.
4. We must uphold Marxism-Leninism and Mao Zedong Thought.

The speech next turned to those cadres overly zealous in their criticisms of Mao Zedong:

> Comrade Mao, like any other man, had his defects and made errors. But how can these errors in his illustrious life be put on a par with his immortal contributions to the people? In analyzing his defects and errors, we certainly should recognize his personal responsibility, but what is more important is to analyze their complicated historical background. That is the only just and scientific—that is, Marxist— way to assess history and historical figures. Anyone who departs from Marxism on so serious a question will be censured by the Party and the masses. Isn't that natural?[62]

In other words, anyone who does not "scientifically" criticize Mao would be punished, with the qualities of "scientific" evaluation to be determined by the party. The imprecision of these boundaries was, of course, precisely the point. From then on, any discussion of Mao

Zedong's demerits would have to proceed with great caution and only with official sanction.

The speech had a chilling effect. By setting out this new red line on Mao and on the four cardinal principles, Deng provided immediate succor to hardliners weary of the increasingly "anti-party" discourse in the halls of the Theory Conference and on the streets of Beijing. The dissident writer Liu Binyan would later refer to these as the "four sticks," for the frequency with which they were invoked to stifle dissent and debate.

Even with these new boundaries now in place, Deng and the rest of the leadership believed an official statement on Mao was needed. They had promised a verdict on Mao at the "appropriate time," and now that Deng was in charge, that time had arrived. Even then, it would take two years before the official view of Mao would emerge.

Once again, he called upon Hu Qiaomu, the CCP's "first pen," to draft the "Resolution on Certain Questions in the History of Our Party Since the Founding of the PRC." This was, and remains, the party's official evaluation of Mao Zedong and the history of the party since the founding of the PRC in 1949. Decades later, it still defines what is permitted in school textbooks, what academic research on Mao can be undertaken, and how Mao can be depicted in the media. While Deng hoped the document would settle the "Mao question" once and for all, thus freeing the CCP and the Chinese people to pursue economic modernization unencumbered by nagging historical questions, the resolution only served to institutionalize a new set of historical-political tensions. Throughout the 1980s, the resolution was used as both spear and shield by those looking to either cast off or protect Mao's legacy. For the neo-Maoist movement that would emerge decades later, the resolution remains the original sin of the Deng era—the point at which the CCP first sold out modern China's creator.

Work on the resolution began in March 1980 by Hu Qiaomu and his assistant Deng Liqun. The struggle for the two men in drafting the resolution was, in the words of one party historian, "how to correct the mistakes of Mao's later years while in all respects protecting his prestige."[63]

Deng delivered a preview of the upcoming resolution in an interview with Italian journalist Oriana Fallaci near the end of August. "It isn't only his portrait which remains in Tiananmen Square," he explained. "It is the memory of a man who guided us to victory and built a country. Which is far from being little . . . Do write this: We shall not do to Mao Zedong what Khrushchev did to Stalin at the 20th Soviet Communist Party Congress."[64]

In many ways, Deng Xiaoping's comments on the drafting process are more enlightening than the resolution itself. As drafts of the document were passed to Deng, he became more impatient with the overly negative portrayal of Mao, finding "the tone of the [third] draft as a whole is too depressing."[65] By the fourth draft, Deng was seeing some progress but still not enough praise: "If we don't mention Mao Zedong Thought and don't make an appropriate evaluation of Comrade Mao's merits and demerits, the old workers will not feel satisfied, nor will the poor and lower-middle peasants of the period of land reform, nor the many cadres who have close ties with them."

By mid-1981, Deng was handed the ninth and final draft. He expressed satisfaction that it would "sum up experience, unify thinking, and unite all our comrades as one in looking to the future."[66]

Not surprisingly, the resolution opens with a lengthy paean to the glories of Mao Zedong, Mao Zedong Thought, and the CCP's efforts in crushing feudalism, fascism, capitalism, and imperialism in China in order to establish the People's Republic of China. It takes note of the "Basic Completion of the Socialist Transformation" in a mere seven years, the progress in areas ranging from science to education, the PRC's contribution to world peace, and the great advancements in the living standards of the Chinese people.

It is when the reader arrives at Section 19 that it becomes clear this is a unique document. While it accuses Mao's one-time heir Lin Biao and the Gang of Four of "counter-revolutionary crimes," it concludes that "chief responsibility for the grave 'Left' error of the 'cultural revolution,' an error comprehensive in magnitude and protracted in duration, does indeed lie with Comrade Mao Zedong." It accuses Mao of becoming "arrogant" at the time his "prestige reached a peak," and, in a stinging rebuke, claims that Mao "gradually divorced himself from practice and from the masses, acted more and more arbitrarily and subjectively, and increasingly put himself above the Central Committee of the Party." But returning to Deng's admonition that Mao remain a celebrated figure, the resolution concluded: "If we judge his activities as a whole, his contributions to the Chinese revolution far outweigh his mistakes. His merits are primary and his errors secondary."

It's worth noting that the conventional wisdom which claims the document contains an "official" verdict that Mao was "70 percent right and 30 percent wrong" is erroneous. There is no such formulation in the 1981 "Resolution," nor is there any "official" 70 percent/30 percent evaluation in any other party document or speech. Mao himself used the 70/30 formulation (known in Chinese as the *san-qi kai*), commenting, "When it comes to the Cultural Revolution, my overall opinion is that it was basically correct, and only partially unsatisfactory. What we need to do now is research the unsatisfactory portion. 70/30 split—70% positive and 30% mistaken. This opinion will not necessarily be uniform."[67] He'd also used it to evaluate Stalin, writing, "you should at least give him a 70-30 evaluation, 70 for his achievements and 30 for his mistakes. This may not be entirely accurate, for his mistakes may be only 20 or even 10, or perhaps somewhat more than 30."[68] The 70/30 evaluation was used by one participant at the 1979 Theory Conference, but only in reference to the period between 1956 and 1966, and not to Mao himself. Deng also referenced it in his interview with Oriana Fallaci in 1980, saying, "[Mao] said that my mistakes were only 30 percent, my merits 70 percent, and he resurrected me [brought Deng back into the government] with 30/70."[69]

Some of the confusion seems to have come from a 1977 speech Deng gave entitled "The 'Two Whatevers' Do Not Accord to Marxism," in which he said, "[Mao] said that if one's work was rated as consisting 70 percent of achievements and 30 percent of mistakes, that would be quite all right, and that he himself would be very happy and satisfied if future generations could give him this '70-30' rating after his death."[70] Yet Deng isn't saying whether or not he agrees with this formulation, merely adding, "This is an important theoretical question, a question of whether or not we are adhering to historical materialism."

Regardless, the fact that Mao's legacy was being discussed at all was a testament to how much had changed since his death in 1976. The Gang of Four had been tried and convicted, Hua Guofeng had been sidelined, and power firmly grasped by Deng. "When China entered the 1980s," wrote the former party theoretician Ruan Ming, "a faint glow of light seemed to dawn, and it was possible to believe in a fundamental change in the political system."[71]

This optimism was not unfounded. The changes taking place in China were remarkable, but the story was incomplete. At the same time the narrative of "reform and opening" was beginning to take hold, the seeds for another were being planted.

Hints of a counternarrative were already visible in the continuing centrality of the deceased Mao Zedong over the country's political and ideological life and in the near-universal consensus among the party leadership that his legacy must be preserved if the CCP was to survive. Deng's intolerance for the Democracy Wall and the political guardrails he created with his "four cardinal principles" also spoke to continuities with the past.

The forces shaping this alternative narrative would take many different forms and be given many names: conservatives, statists, nationalists, Leninists, Communists, neo-authoritarians, reactionaries, and later, neo-Maoists. They were to disagree—often fiercely—over issues of ideology, politics, history, theory, and tactics. But on one key point they would always agree: China's road ahead would be long and torturous; but no matter what, they must advance under the banner of Mao Zedong.

2

Hard Truths

There are no Marxist quotations for what we are doing now.

—Party theorist Su Shaozhi, 1984[1]

ON PAPER AT LEAST, Deng Xiaoping's 1992 trip to the south of China was unremarkable.

Like many of the eighty-seven-year-old leader's previous tours, the agenda included visits to factories, meetings with government officials, and the occasional chat with local residents. But there were clues that this outing was different. The previous winter, the Shenzhen Party committee received word that Deng would come south for a brief family vacation. Local officials were told to keep the visit quiet and that no journalists would be accompanying Deng.[2] Even CCP general secretary Jiang Zemin was unaware of Deng's impending travels.[3] Just after New Year's Day in 1992, another telegram arrived: "Comrade Xiaoping will come south to rest. Please begin preparations to greet him and for his safety."[4] Deng finally departed Beijing in an unmarked train on January 17, accompanied by nearly twenty family members.

The pretense of vacation was dropped immediately: Deng's trip was an effort to solidify China's "post-Deng" trajectory, an era that was fast approaching. In 1989, he'd retired from the Central Military Commission, his final remaining formal title. And without a firm consensus in the top party leadership about the pace and direction of the economic reform agenda, he feared his great project of economic modernization might die along with him.

For more than two years, the reforms had been under sustained assault by a powerful coalition of conservative officials and ideologues. With Deng's assent, they had been empowered after the student protests in the spring of 1989, which culminated in the early hours of June 4 with PLA tanks and soldiers opening fire on the demonstrators, killing hundreds, possibly thousands. Their standing strengthened as the Soviet Union entered a terminal crisis.[5] From Poland to Hungary, Bulgaria to Czechoslovakia, the "Revolutions of 1989" foretold the demise of global Communism. In November, the Berlin Wall separating East and West Germany was torn down. On Christmas day, the Romanian dictator Nicolae Ceausescu and his wife, Elena, were executed by firing squad after an impromptu trial.

The leaders of the Communist Party of China saw the writing on the wall. "The problem now is not whether the banner of the Soviet Union will fall," Deng told his fellow party elders in the fall of 1989, "but whether the banner of China will fall."[6] There was unanimity among senior leaders, Deng included, that the only way to avoid the Soviet Union's fate was to ensure the iron grip of the Communist Party. There would be no *glasnost* (i.e., openness and transparency in government), and with the purge of the reformist party leader Zhao Ziyang on June 24, there would be no Chinese Gorbachev either.[7]

But on the question of *perestroika* (literally meaning "restructuring")—at least as it related to economic reform—the leadership was divided. More precisely, it was locked in fierce discussion about the scope and pace with which any such reform should proceed.

"Why do the people support us?" Deng asked in March 1990. "Because over the last ten years our economy has been developing and developing visibly."[8] To grow the economy, he argued, China needed to stick to the path of reform and opening. It could ill afford backsliding into isolation, to revert to rigid central planning, or to wall itself off from foreign capital and investment. But reforms could only exist within an environment of political stability, for Deng firmly believed, "The most important thing is that there should be no unrest in China and that we should continue to carry on genuine reform and to open wider to the outside. Without those policies, China would have no future."[9]

Economic modernization amid political stability. That was Deng's formula for China.

But whereas Deng saw in the rapid disintegration of the Soviet Union an argument for doubling down on reform, many of his colleagues saw it the other way around. Chen Yun, a onetime ally of Deng's in the early days of reform and opening, warned of "a dangerous tendency in enlivening the economy to shake off state planning. This is a grave tendency. It will certainly create chaos, affect the entire national economy, and lead to social turmoil."[10] Deng Liqun, who, like Chen, gradually shifted from Deng's ally to opponent as China's reforms weakened the party's grip on the economy and ideology, warned of international hostile forces that would bring regime change to China. "Some people estimate that since they have succeeded in Eastern Europe and are succeeding in the Soviet Union, the Western monopoly capitalist class headed by the United States will probably put the emphasis of 'peaceful evolution' on China, which refuses to give up the socialist system," he said in an internal speech.[11] Gong Xuezeng, a professor at the Central Party School, concluded the experience of the Soviet Union "proves that if the Communist Party abandons Marxism as its guiding ideology, abandons the leadership of the Communist Party, and abandons the socialist road, not only will it be unable to solve its national problems; on the contrary, this will lead to a national crisis, national division, and ultimately all national ethnic groups will suffer."[12]

The argument for retrenchment (temporarily) won the day. In the fall of 1989, the party released a "Thirty-Nine Point" economic program, which was a significant blow to the economic reform agenda. According to the plan, "Our present economic difficulties are conspicuously evident in worsening inflation, overall imbalances, irrational economic structure, and chaotic economic procedures. These difficulties did not just emerge suddenly in the last year or two; they are a concentrated reflection of deep-rooted problems that have accumulated over many years."[13] The resulting austerity program slammed the brakes on bank lending, fixed investment, wage increases, and price rises.

The official press was flooded with calls to halt, or at least slow, the market reforms. Chen Yun's son, Chen Yuan, co-authored an article in the *China Youth Daily* attacking "romantic capitalist ideas" that had infiltrated China.[14] The newly installed CCP secretary Jiang Zemin used his October 1 National Day speech in 1989 to clarify that there were only two types of reform, one based on the "four cardinal principles" and one based on "bourgeois liberalization."[15] Politburo member Li Tieying warned of "hostile forces both within and outside the country . . . using the economic, scientific, technological advantages of the international monopoly capitalist class . . . [to] advocate and propagate the ideological tide of bourgeois liberalization and to negate leadership by the Communist Party."[16] As one Hong Kong report described the situation that December 1991: "The conservative faction has seized upon the 'four cardinal principles' and 'anti-bourgeois liberalization' proposed by Deng Xiaoping and fiercely attacked, almost totally occupying the ideological front."[17]

Despite his reformist credentials, Deng took these arguments seriously. Since the beginning of the reforms in the late 1970s, he'd balanced two (often competing) goals: modernizing China's economy on the one hand and maintaining the unchallenged supremacy of the Communist Party on the other. "Without political stability and unity," Deng said in 1987, "it would be impossible for us to go on with construction, let alone to carry out the reform and pursue the open policy—none of those efforts could succeed."[18] When torn between the two, Deng always sided with party supremacy. Yet when party hardliners pushed too hard against the reforms—thus threatening to derail them—Deng used his considerable authority to re-right the agenda so long as he believed the political situation was in check.

This story played out again and again throughout the 1980s. To simplify, two groups vied for control of economic policymaking: reformists, led by State Council premier Zhao Ziyang and CCP general secretary Hu Yaobang, and "conservatives," a loose coalition of powerful senior-level officials, entrenched bureaucrats, aging revolutionaries, and die-hard Marxists.[19] This latter group, while never as tightly knit and coherent as outside analysts painted them to be, did coalesce around support for heavy industry, a strong state-sector, and a wariness of deficits and foreign investment.[20] In other words, they wanted to "conserve" core elements of the planned economy.

Two important figures in this regard were Chen Yun and Deng Liqun.

Chen was a cautious central planner, a craft he'd first learned during the two years he spent in Moscow in the mid-1930s.[21] Upon returning to China in 1937, he was tasked with establishing supply routes between the Soviet Union and the newly established party stronghold in Yan'an, Shaanxi Province. Chen, then thirty years old, was promoted to lead the Organization Department, the party's human resources organ. With only 30,000 CCP members when he took charge in late 1937, its membership ballooned to one million by the time he formally left the position in 1945.[22] This growth was accompanied by an extensive effort to conduct background checks to ensure there were no KMT spies or sympathizers within the party's ranks, as well as the creation of a voluminous filing system covering every cadre's background and conduct. While Mao Zedong had no interest in such detailed affairs, Chen Yun thrived in them. In 1943, while still nominally running the Organization Department, he was promoted to be the deputy head of the Finance and Economic Office.[23]

After the CCP's final victory over Chiang Kai-shek in 1949, Chen played a pivotal role in drafting the PRC's first Five-Year Plan. By the mid-1950s, however, Mao was impatient with the slow progress of the country's socialist transformation, and he chided circumspect bureaucrats like Chen for "tottering along like a woman with bound feet [and] complaining all the time. . . ."[24] Beginning in 1957, this rift widened as Mao pushed for a "Great Leap Forward" to boost industrial output with the goal of "catching up" with the United Kingdom within fifteen years. Chen's preference for doing things "carefully and prudently" (in his own words) was the opposite of the millenarian Mao, and as China descended into the Cultural Revolution in 1966, Chen's economic prudence was a political liability.[25] The head of China's intelligence services, Kang Sheng, criticized Chen for "only talking about the economy and ignoring politics. The only economic policy he talks about, as far as I can see, is the capitalist merchant economy."[26]

Soon thereafter, Chen, along with other senior leaders including Deng Xiaoping, was exiled from Beijing for the duration of the Cultural Revolution. Upon his return to politics at the Third Plenum in 1978, he was an active early participant in shaping economic policy, arguably playing a leading role through the end of 1980.[27] Yet as the reforms progressed, Chen's conservative temperament was increasingly at odds with the more aggressive reformers, including Deng's protégés Zhao Ziyang and Hu Yaobang. "Ours is a socialist system," Chen Yun declared in a 1982 speech. "Industry must mainly practice planned economy, and agriculture is no exception."[28] Even as his power and health waned throughout the 1980s, Chen's influence could be strongly felt on ideology and policy.

Like Chen, Deng Liqun had been a loyal party man for more than fifty years, having joined the CCP in 1936 at the age of twenty-one.[29] After studying at Peking University, he set out for Yan'an in 1938, where he became the editor of *Red Flag*, the party's premier ideological journal. While in Yan'an, Deng wrote a self-critical "big character poster" entitled "To Fire the Arrow at Myself" (把箭射向自己), which came to the attention of Mao Zedong through his secretary, Chen Boda.[30]

Like Mao, Deng was from Hunan Province, and also like Mao, he was born into relative prosperity. To have abandoned wealth and education for the cause of revolution is an indication of Deng's commitment, a point conceded by even his most ardent intellectual opponents. The liberal historian Yang Jisheng said Deng's political convictions "reflected his real beliefs; he wasn't seeking personal material gain."[31] As Deng himself later reflected, "The greatest happiness for a party member is to earn the trust of the party, his comrades, and the people."[32]

For most of his career, he served as a theoretician and propagandist. As President Liu Shaoqi's political secretary, he was at the heart of the decision-making process, that is, until Liu (and consequently Deng himself) was purged during the Cultural Revolution. Rehabilitated in 1975, he was called on by Deng Xiaoping to serve on the State Council, and in 1978 he was promoted to serve as vice-president of the Chinese Academy of Social Sciences. Deng Xiaoping recognized the formidable nature of "Little Deng," as he was known, calling him "a piece of steel," and "stubborn like a Hunan mule."[33] He was later promoted to run the Propaganda Department between 1982 and 1985 before Deng Xiaoping ordered him removed for his over-zealous attacks on party members he deemed insufficiently orthodox. In 1987, he was formally sidelined from power, but his influence as a leftist gadfly would remain. In his memoir, Zhao Ziyang described him as "the most powerful writer among those who oppose Deng Xiaoping's reforms."[34]

Pushback from conservatives like Chen Yun and Deng Liqun began almost immediately after China's first moves away from the planned economy. In July 1979, Deng spoke of the "fair number of people" who opposed "the Party's current political and ideological line," and who "yearn for the past, because the present policies do not yield much advantage to them."[35] In this, both Deng Xiaoping and Mao Zedong, two men with vastly different temperaments and political outlooks, shared a common critique of the vast party-state bureaucracy as a fundamentally "conservative" institution that needed to be "rectified."

Deng's jab at "yearning for the past" was perhaps unfair, but it was true that for many in the party hierarchy the reforms were indeed a zero-sum proposition. "The combination of a 2,000-year-old tradition of despotism and the inheritance of Stalinist institutions in China had produced a bureaucracy mainly concerned with itself," observed Hong Kong political scientist Ding Xueliang.[36] For nearly thirty years party cadres and government bureaucrats enjoyed immense power in dictating the lives and fate of the Chinese people, and now, these vestiges of control were dissipating at a remarkable pace. Relaxing party control over agriculture, industry, and enterprise necessarily entailed a re-distribution of power and resources away from government and party officials and toward ordinary members of society and the burgeoning private sector.

In many cases, systems that had existed for decades were upended in a matter of months, even days. In a rapidly changing China, village shops—not the local government office or the production brigade headquarters—were the center of social activity. Status symbols previously available only to cadres were now increasingly within reach of regular peasants. State media celebrated one village in northeast China for the simple fact that every male peasant owned a Western suit and tie.[37] Purchasing power, it seemed, was supplanting political power.[38]

But cadres could push back, as was captured in a 1984 analysis by the CIA:

> Although Deng [Xiaoping] and his allies have placed supporters in key central and provincial positions, their political and economic reforms remain controversial and have been implemented unevenly. In Beijing's analysis, the main locus of resistance is at the middle and lower levels of administration. Through political connections and long, undisturbed tenure in office, many local officials are immune to central discipline; consequently, they often defy Beijing without

fear of retribution. Unless local officials are absolutely certain that the national leadership is united behind a measure, they often respond to central initiatives in ways that suit their own personal interests.[39]

The PLA, which served as a constant thorn in the side of reformers throughout the 1980s, was also unenthusiastic about the side effects of these reforms. As new opportunities in the countryside emerged, many existing soldiers wanted to return to their hometowns to help their families work the land. Likewise, recruiting new soldiers became more difficult as economic opportunities expanded. Those rural households with children serving in the military were similarly disadvantaged relative to those without any serving members, and thus the pressure on sons to leave the low-paying PLA was great. As one PLA political commissar remarked in 1980, "The new rural policy has caused consternation in the ranks."[40]

This was also the case in the realm of ideology, where the party's grip on propaganda was challenged by an influx of books and magazines imported from Hong Kong and Taiwan. Open letters, translated English publications, and a surge of newly established journals began to shape how Chinese people saw not only the outside world, but more importantly, their own country and its political system. Foreign movies and music became widely available on the streets of Chinese cities, supplanting the role of traditional (i.e., socialist) cultural productions. Abstract art and avant-garde theater were making inroads, and as they explored themes of individual identity and historical reckoning, they provided alternatives to the ideologies the party had spent decades building and maintaining.

Foreign companies flooded into the market, bringing a new ethos of conspicuous consumption. Nothing was sacred, not even *Red Flag*, the CCP's arch-conservative theoretical journal, which announced in 1980 that it would henceforth accept advertisements from foreign companies (Coca-Cola, inexplicably, being the sole exception).[41] As one official told a visiting journalist in 1984, "Most people today don't care whether something is capitalist or socialist. They just want their lives to improve. The details are a matter of the theoreticians."[42]

But even the professional theoreticians had a hard time making sense of it all, and as the economic reforms deepened, the party's ability to defend (or even plausibly articulate) its socialist credentials became increasingly strained. Hu Yaobang, at one point the General Secretary of the Communist Party, conceded, "Some cadres ask: Can you give a ready definition for 'socialism with Chinese characteristics'? We say that there is no pre-prepared, ready definition. It is impossible to have one."[43] The liberal Marxist philosopher Su Shaozhi pointed out in 1984: "There are no Marxist quotations for what we are doing now."[44]

As new opportunities arose outside of the old planned economy, and as official ideology waned in its appeal, young Chinese began ignoring the CCP altogether. One official survey found that student support for "communism" dropped from 38.1 percent in 1986 to just 6.1 percent in 1988, while support for "socialism" decreased from 16.4 percent to 5 percent during the same time period.[45] Communist Party membership among students experienced a similar decline, from 10.8 percent in 1978 to just 2.9 percent in 1988.[46] Other surveys reported that students no longer cared who was in power, just so long as they delivered growth and rising living standards.[47] Numerous studies by party-affiliated researchers concluded that students in the 1980s lost faith in the party owing to a failure of education, the influence of "Western" ideologies, and the impact official corruption was having on the party's legitimacy.[48] In a reforming China, lamented *Red Flag*, "ideals are far away, politics is meaningless, but cash is real."[49]

But if concerns over the party's diminishing ideological control mainly bothered the political establishment, the negative side effects of China's rapid economic transformation and the dismantling of its social safety net resonated more widely.

Beginning in 1981, crime in China's cities began to soar. While for the first few years after 1978, the spike in crime could be blamed on the "pernicious influence of the Gang of Four," this excuse began to tire as the years went on, forcing even pro-reform officials to admit that not all was right. Hu Yaobang warned in 1982 that "vile social evils which had been stamped out long ago by New China" had now "cropped up again."[50] The Minister of Public Security argued that "Abominable phenomena . . . eliminated since the founding of New China [in 1949] are beginning to surface."[51] An editorial appearing in the New Year's Day edition of the *People's Daily* declared that combating economic crime was one of the two main tasks for the government in 1982.[52] Serious crimes rose 21 percent in 1987 and increased by another 34.8 percent in 1988.[53] In July 1988, the head of China's People's Supreme Court reported that felony crimes (including murder, robbery, and rape) increased 36.4 percent from the year before.[54] The return of crime and the "old ways" marked a drastic reversal of the gains won during the Mao era.

As crime proliferated so, too, did official corruption. During the Mao era, rent-seeking opportunities had been limited by the lack of resources to pilfer in the first place, but as private enterprise and opportunities for market arbitrage multiplied, corruption did as well. Few benefited more than the sons and daughters of high-ranking party officials, known as the *gaogan zidi*, who leveraged family connections to build vast fortunes and to secure their own cushy positions in the party-state. In one of the more well-known cases from the 1980s, several officials and *gaogan zidi* on the southern island of Hainan were investigated for illegally importing 89,000 Toyota automobiles, nearly three million TVs, and 250,000 video cassette players. In another case, party corruption authorities in Beijing uncovered nearly two hundred million RMB in evaded taxes, and hundreds of millions more RMB in illegally obtained funds.[55] In response, 300 cadres were kicked out of the party and 89 were tried in civil courts.[56] Bo Yibo, whose son Bo Xilai would become a populist hero to neo-Maoists two decades later and himself fall afoul of the authorities, worried that "the principle of commodity exchange has permeated the political life of some Party organs."[57]

Few threw themselves into the business of rent-seeking with quite the same gusto as the offspring of Deng Xiaoping. His son-in-law, He Ping, secured a seat on the board of Poly Technologies, which, among other things, sold weapons and missiles to Iran and Saudi Arabia.[58] Deng Pufang, Deng's first-born son, who had been paralyzed during the Cultural Revolution after being defenestrated by Red Guards, formed the Kanghua Development Corporation in 1984 as an offshoot of his China Welfare Fund for the Handicapped. Despite being billed as a company by and for those with physical disabilities, within a matter of years it had effectively morphed into an ATM for the children of the elite, with more than two hundred sons and daughters of high-ranking party officials working for the company.

This rampant corruption had a significant impact on public perceptions of the CCP. "Corruption is an inevitable accompaniment of social progress," declared the *People's Daily* in the summer of 1988. "But we should limit it as far as possible and no leniency should be allowed in dealing with corruption cases, otherwise it will not only harm the reform but will also lead to domestic disturbances."[59] A poll conducted by CASS in 1988 found that more than 80 percent of urban residents reported official corruption as among their top concerns.[60]

These reform side effects became powerful ammunition for conservative pushback, and they never tired of reminding their opponents of their earlier warnings. For the reforms to be considered successful, a good deal had to go right; whereas for reform opponents, even a seemingly small, isolated incident could be used to exaggerate their cost. As the dissident journalist Liu Binyan put it:

> Conservatives could use economic reasons to attack the reforms, saying, "Look! The majority of people are suffering from inflation while a minority who benefit from the market reforms lives well!" That approach might be effective because people are upset about the new social inequality and what they perceive as a falling standard of living.[61]

In 1980, Chen Yun effectively stalled the economic reforms under the banner of "comprehensive balance" over concerns about rising trade and budget deficits, as well as a decline in household purchasing power. As Chen remarked that December: "An unstable economy leads to an unstable political situation."[62] In 1983, party propagandists (with the support of Deng Xiaoping) launched a campaign to combat "spiritual pollution," which according to hardliner Deng Liqun, included, "efforts to seek personal gain, and indulgence in individualism, anarchism, and liberalism."[63] According to one China-based foreign correspondent, the campaign "created more problems than it sought to solve, as die-hard Maoists seized the opportunity to strike out against changes wrought by the recent economic policy shifts, including the so-called open door policy of commerce with the West."[64] Government officials, fearing accusations of "Western contamination," backed off from new deals with foreign companies. In 1987 hardliners used a campaign against "bourgeois liberalization" to put pressure on liberal party leader Hu Yaobang, who, with Deng Xiaoping's support, was unceremoniously sacked.

Of course, by the end of the 1980s, it was undeniable that "Reform and Opening" had created dramatic improvements in the living standards of the majority of Chinese people. But when looked at more closely, the progress of reform throughout the 1980s was far more volatile than popular historical retrospective lets on. Scholar Harry Harding described China's first decade of reform as a "wavelike pattern" where "periods of consolidation or retreat have followed periods of advance."[65] Harding saw this advance-retreat dynamic stemming partly from the tendency of the reforms to produce negative side effects, including "inflation, budget deficits, excessive investment, and surges in imports."[66]

When these problems gave rise to social tensions, conservatives within the leadership were emboldened to call for a retrenchment, or at least a pause, in the reform process. "The cycles of reforms have . . . reflected an interweaving of a struggle for power within the reform coalition with attempts to remedy the problems that reform has produced," Harding wrote[67] The cycles of opening and retrenchment defined the politics of the 1980s, and the outcome was by no means as inevitable as is often portrayed. While the depth and longevity of these pendulum swings varied, throughout the 1980s China never went more than a year of opening before the forces of orthodoxy mounted a counterattack.[68]

By early 1992, Deng worried that the pendulum had swung too far to the left, and with his failing health, he would soon lack the strength to control the pendulum swings as he'd done so effectively for more than a decade. The events of 1989 and 1991 were decisive because they seemed to confirm the fears of orthodox conservatives that the abandonment of the planned economy would inevitably lead to social and political chaos. Since the Theory Conference in 1979, they'd warned of the "sugar-coated bullets" of market reforms and the danger of allowing Western capitalist ideas to infiltrate and colonize China. The student protests in 1989, with their makeshift statues commemorating democracy and their direct criticisms of party leadership, appeared to be irrefutable proof that these fears were prescient.

The open and inevitable talk of a "post-Deng" era and the planned Fourteenth Party Congress that fall further convinced Deng that he had one final chance to save the economic reforms before his health failed him. There was also the matter of his legacy, which had been tarnished by his support for the violent suppression of the Tiananmen Square protests. Although unapologetic about this decision—it was, after all, a matter of national survival in Deng's mind—this was not the way he wanted to be remembered. He was also concerned that the man he had installed to lead China for the next decade, Jiang Zemin, didn't have the power, the prestige, or the relationships needed to salvage— let alone advance—the reform agenda through the millennium. "If I am the only one to speak in favor of reform and opening up, it won't be enough," he lamented in early 1991.[69]

So, in early 1992, Deng took his message on the road.

Stopping in Wuhan, he warned cadres: "Whoever is against reform must leave office."[70] In Changsha, he demanded officials "speed up economic development." Channeling Mao Zedong, Deng exhorted, "We must not act like women with bound feet." In Guangdong, he instructed the assembled, "Revolution means the emancipation of the productive forces." Upon reaching Shenzhen, a symbol of China's economic modernization, he proclaimed, "We've been poor for thousands of years, but we won't be poor again."[71] He was asked to explain how China wasn't capitalist despite having a market economy. Socialism had markets, too, was his terse reply. Was China at risk of regime change? "Why have other nations collapsed within one night? It's because the people's living standards had not improved," he responded.[72] He dismissed criticisms of foreign investment: "We levy taxes, our workers are paid, and we learn new technology and management. What's wrong with that?"[73]

Provincial leaders soon began echoing Deng's pro-reform statements. Beginning in mid-February, and after two years of hardline rhetoric, the tone of the official pro-reform propaganda noticeably softened. *Guangming Daily* filled nearly two-thirds of its February 22 edition with a call to "liberate our thinking, deepen reform, open the door more widely." The *People's Daily* approved of using an "appropriate capitalist economy" as a "supplement to the socialist economy." The paper added, "As our country is in only the preliminary stage of socialism, it is impossible to wipe out capitalism completely, and some exploitation will linger for a long while."[74] On February 28, the Central Committee issued "Document No. 2," a collection of Deng's statements during his trip south, including his soon-to-be famous invocation, "Reform is liberation of the forces of production, as was revolution."

On March 20, Premier Li Peng attempted to save face for the retrenchment program, declaring that it had been successful in its attempt to "rebalance" the economy and therefore was no longer needed. In April, a bootleg recording of a speech by Vice Premier Tian Jiyun scorning leftists became a hit around the country. If the planned economy was so good, Tian asked, why not just let these conservatives create their own special economic zone for leftists? "Salaries would be low, prices of goods would be low, you would rely on coupons, you would have to stand on line to buy everything and suffer everything else that goes along with leftism," Tian mocked. "If we actually set up a place to do this, would anybody want to go?"[75] The Fourteenth Party Congress in October further cemented the gains from Deng's Southern Tour, including the adoption of "Deng Xiaoping Theory of Building Socialism with Chinese Characteristics" and the official change in designation of China's economy from a "planned socialist commodity economy" to a "socialist market economy."

It seemed like a total victory for Deng, but there was still work to do before he could finally retire: specifically, stopping the "conservative-reformer" pendulum that had persisted in swinging policy back and forth since 1978. While still in southern China, Deng had made a bold—and ultimately prophetic—declaration: "At present, we are being affected by both Right and 'Left' tendencies," he said, utilizing the traditional scare quotes to denote nonsanctioned varieties of leftism. "But it is the 'Left' tendencies that have the deepest roots." Henceforth, Deng argued, "China should maintain vigilance against the Right but primarily against the 'Left.' "

This was a remarkable statement from a nominally Communist regime, one that publicly declared its economic and political system as socialist. But after a decade of reform and retrenchment, Deng was convinced that economic growth was the only way to ensure the survival of the party. "Development is a hard truth," he declared. That, Deng believed, was the only way to ensure the party remained in power. What was the point of all this ideological prattle if you couldn't hold on to power? From now on, Deng proclaimed, party leaders would stop bickering, and China would stick to the path of reform and opening. "Not to engage in debates," Deng would later brag, "this was an invention of mine. Not to debate—this is in order to get more time to accomplish things."[76]

Deng's concern over the "deep roots" of leftist critiques was well founded. China was still nominally a socialist nation with a socialist market economy overseen by the Communist Party. Even as it continued to pursue capitalist policies, it was still required to justify them in socialist terms, a feat that became increasingly difficult as its economy opened to foreign investment and private enterprise. And beginning in the mid-1990s, China began to restructure its sprawling state-owned sector, leaving tens of millions of workers without the protection of their "iron rice bowl."[77] How could the party abandon workers to the vagaries of the market *and* simultaneously claim to represent the proletariat?

For many, 1992 marked the year when the debate indeed stopped, and Deng's Southern Tour was soon memorialized as a definitive inflection point in China's ongoing journey from Mao to market. "From the beginning of Deng's reforms in 1978, until his Southern Tour, China had continuously debated political ideology," wrote Robert Lawrence Kuhn in his book *How China Leaders Think*. "After 1992 the debate was over: the path was clear and the pace was swift."[78]

But this wasn't quite true. Despite Deng's exhortation that the Chinese people become "economic animals and political vegetables," in the words of scholar Feng Chen, the debate was far from over.[79] While Deng's personal prestige and leadership style kept party factionalism and ideological debates in check, his demise permitted a proliferation of new and existing "isms" that sought to challenge his Southern Tour consensus. "During the 1980s, you had a left-wing and a right-wing, but they both listened to Deng Xiaoping," said Wang Xiaodong, one of the young nationalist writers to emerge in the 1990s.[80] This was no exaggeration, and it's a useful illustration of how the system functioned while Deng was physically able to govern. But his "date with Marx" was approaching (he would make one final public appearance in 1994 and finally pass away in February 1997), and Jiang Zemin was still in the midst of consolidating power.

Into this temporary political vacuum poured new ideas, fueled by growing social, political, and economic contradictions.

In September 1991, intellectuals associated with the *China Youth Daily* met with several princelings (including Chen Yuan and Bo Xicheng) in a Beijing hotel to produce "Realistic Responses and Strategic Choices for China after the Soviet Upheaval," the founding manifesto of what became known as "neo-conservatism," the prefix "neo" to indicate that it shared many of the same base sympathies with the conservatism that had developed during the 1980s. Yet it called for the CCP to ditch Marxism (which few seemed to believe in anyhow) and instead anchor its legitimacy to more primal forces—nationalism and the ability to deliver a stable political environment. "We must realistically accept that, among a certain section of the masses at least, the appeal of ideology of the past has declined, and all that boosting the old-style ideological education arouses is rebelliousness," the "Strategic Choices" report argued.[81]

Neo-conservatism traced its intellectual roots to neo-authoritarianism, which had developed in the mid-1980s in reaction to Beijing's gradual loss of control over local governments as a result of the economic reforms. The doctrine held that political stability provided the foundation for economic development and that considerations such as democracy and individual liberty should be postponed until conditions were appropriate. As Fudan University political scientist Wang Huning (who now sits on the Politburo Standing Committee) wrote in 1993, "The formation of democratic institutions requires the existence of specific historical, social, and cultural conditions. Until these conditions are mature, political power should be directed toward the development of these conditions."[82] One of the doctrine's most forceful advocates was Wu Jiaxiang, an economist at the CCP Central Committee General Office. "Before democracy and freedom 'get married,'" he observed, "there is a 'flirtation period' between autocracy and freedom. If one says democracy is the life-long partner of freedom, then autocracy can be seen as freedom's 'lover' before marriage."[83]

One additional source of inspiration for the neo-authoritarians were the other fast-developing East Asian nations (Taiwan, Singapore, and South Korea), which appeared to prove that economic modernization necessitated (or at least could coexist with) an iron-willed political system. Fudan University's Wang Huning visited Singapore in 1993 along with the university's debate team and he returned to China with glowing impressions of the city-state. Residents were "industrious" and "hospitable," had outstanding manners, and spoke "impeccable Chinese." The city's infrastructure was "first-rate," its airport on par with many cities in the US. Its office buildings and shopping centers were well-planned and aesthetically pleasing. And Singapore was rich— "exceptionally prosperous" in Wang's words. Its stores were brimming with bright colors and exotic goods. So advanced was its economy that people from surrounding countries all made pilgrimages to its many shopping centers. For Wang, the lesson was clear: there was a path to wealth that didn't have to travel through the West. As he later wrote of his time in the city, "[Singapore] has encountered many challenges posed by Western culture and is searching for methods to deal with them. This process is enlightening for all Chinese communities."[84]

Moving to such a system was not, the neo-authoritarians argued, a return to China's authoritarian past but rather represented a transition phase, wherein an enlightened governing elite with reformist tendencies would oversee the development process in the belief that the "masses," if left to their own devices, would wreck the entire project. In other words, modernization needs stability and order, but all in the name of good governance and, ultimately, some form of democracy.

By early 1989, neo-authoritarianism was one of the hottest intellectual trends around, as many came to question the direction and speed of the economic reforms. So hungry were people for answers that in April 1989, nearly two thousand students, intellectuals, and faculty crammed into a lecture hall at People's University in Beijing for a four-hour debate on the topic. One account from Hong Kong reported that Zhao Ziyang told Deng Xiaoping, "There is a theory about neo-authoritarianism in foreign countries, and domestic theoretical circles are now discussing this theory." To which Deng replied, "This is also my idea."[85] After the June 4 crackdown and the purge of Zhao Ziyang, however, neo-authoritarianism needed a brand makeover. Its call for a "transition" to a more democratic form of political system (albeit vaguely outlined) was jettisoned, leaving only the call for a strong and unchallenged leviathan in the form of the CCP.

But neo-authoritarianism lived on, reborn as neo-conservatism. Writers such as Wang Xiaodong (writing under the nom de guerre Shi Zhong) and Shanghai Normal University's Xiao Gongqin further developed the theory in the journal *Strategy and Management,* which was founded in 1993 with backing from the PLA. Xiao's 1994 article "Nationalism and Ideology During China's Transformative Period" argued, "When any country and nation face external pressures and crises, so long as the political leader appeals to the glorious history, culture, courage and wisdom of the nation and the people, he will ensure the regime's legitimacy."[86]

Not everyone was convinced. While more traditional conservatives agreed with the neo-conservative emphasis on nationalism, they scorned their willingness to abandon the party's traditional emphasis on ideology and their tolerance for the market economy, even one highly circumscribed.

Also emerging in the 1990s was the "New Left," which originally comprised a group of brilliant and largely US-educated academics who returned to China and began applying the methods of Western intellectual criticism to China's development model.[87] Like other new "isms," the New Left was born in reaction to externalities of the economic reforms, the 1989 student protests, the collapse of the Soviet Union, and the demise of the global communist movement. While there was no one central text or creed, the New Left sought new modes of socialist modernization that would restrain what they saw as the brutal realities of globalization and capitalist reforms on China's workers and peasants. While heterogeneous in their beliefs, they shared a general criticism of the party's unwillingness to explore more heterodox—and socialist—forms of development that placed equity and collective interests at the core of its agenda. "The common objective of China's new left is to create an understanding of the full implications of China's current policies," said Wang Hui, one of the movement's founding intellectuals.[88]

The arrival of new "isms" did not mean the demise of the original conservatives (or the "Old Left" as they were increasingly called). In China's highly personalized political system, these retired cadres, some of whom had previously held top positions in party-state bureaucracy, remained connected and influential, even if their ability to directly impact policy from the inside diminished. As they watched the consolidation of Deng's Southern Tour consensus, they, too, grew alarmed.

Beginning in the mid-1990s, a series of anonymous critiques of the market reforms began circulating within domestic intellectual and party circles and in overseas publications. They were dubbed "10,000-word manifestos" (*wanyanshu*), a nod to Wang Anshi, a Song dynasty-era mandarin who delivered his reformist dissent to the emperor in the form of a lengthy political tract. These modern-day incarnations lamented the erosion of the socialist social contract with Chinese workers, the privatization of China's state-owned assets, and the breakdown of traditional socialist morality.

The first manifesto was published in late 1995 under the title "Several Factors Affecting China's State Security" and was rumored to be the work of Deng Liqun or his close associate Li Yanming of the CASS Institute of Political Science. Since being passed over for a seat on the CCP Central Committee in 1987, Deng had grown increasingly caustic as his influence in elite political circles waned. With his *wanyanshu*, if it was indeed his, he was not only questioning a specific policy but also attempting to undermine the socialist credentials of the party's leadership, including General Secretary Jiang Zemin. He argued that China's national security was imperiled by the hollowing out of state-owned enterprises, which, he argued, formed the core of China's economic stability. Under Jiang, he claimed public wealth in the form of the SOEs was being siphoned off to corrupt cadres and capitalists. The piece concluded with a direct challenge to party leadership:

> If these things are not rectified now, the number of people supporting the party and government will probably fall, while the number in opposition or taking a neutral stand will be bound to rise. When a political storm comes, and we find ourselves in an unfavorable position, it may be too late to reverse the situation.[89]

Reformers blasted the tract. Writing in *Economic Work Monthly*, reformist lawyer Cao Siyuan claimed the piece "completely negates China's ten years of reform and opening."[90] Cao also accused Deng Liqun of seeking to "turn back the clock to the Cultural Revolution."[91]

Six months after Deng's article was released, another *wanyanshu* appeared, this one reportedly the work of Wu Yifeng, a Marxist economist at Beijing's People's University. Entitled "A Preliminary Inquiry into the Major Threats to the National Security of Our Country in the Next One to Two Decades," it warned of "peaceful evolution" (i.e., regime change) smuggled into China through economic, ideological, and cultural integration with Western economies, particularly the United States. Further, opening the domestic economy to foreign capital and investment in strategically sensitive industries, such as finance and telecommunications, was an existential threat to China's sovereignty. Only with "real Marxists" in power could China combat "bourgeois liberalism" and stave off a Soviet Union–style collapse.[92]

This burgeoning intellectual pluralism was set against the backdrop of growing uncertainty in the external environment, with not only the disintegration of the global Communist movement to contend with, but an increasingly fractious relationship with the United States. This deteriorated rapidly in 1996, when the USS *Nimitz* sailed through the Taiwan Strait, and reached its nadir in May 1999 with the NATO bombing of the Chinese embassy in Belgrade, which many Chinese saw as a deliberate attack, despite US insistence that it was accidental and President Clinton's apology to Jiang Zemin.

But perhaps the most wrenching and consequential shift during this period was the government's 1996 announcement of a deep restructuring to China's sprawling state-owned sector, which would result in the decimation of entire local economies and tens of millions of workers losing their livelihoods. The plan to "grasp the large and release the small" would consolidate and support those firms believed to have strategic significance, while those seen as nonessential—roughly a thousand small- and medium-sized firms—would be left to fend for themselves. The advocates for the plan argued that China could no longer afford subsidies for loss-making, unprofitable, and highly indebted SOEs. But to the plan's opponents, the party was hollowing out its industrial core, and in furthering a policy that would eventually lead to millions more layoffs, it was also tearing up the socialist social contract on which its legitimacy rested.

In response, the editorial board of *Contemporary Currents of Thought* (what one academic called the "bimonthly of frustration") released a third and fourth *wanyanshu* immediately prior to and following Deng Xiaoping's death in early 1997.[93] The first piece warned, "if public ownership loses its dominant position, there will be serious class polarization, the entire working class will be reduced to mere wage labor, the CCP will lose the economic basis of its rule . . . and the country as a whole will change its socialist character and become an appendage of international capitalism."[94] The fourth piece, entitled "The Trend and Characteristics of Bourgeois Liberalization Since 1992," was a collection of thirty-nine remarks made by public figures deemed to be ideologically suspect, including those who had made disparaging remarks about the party's revolutionary history, had "negated" socialism, or who had called for the abandonment of Marxism.[95]

If the impact of the *wanyanshu* were to be judged by their effect on Beijing's policy line, they would have to be considered complete failures. The leadership team of Jiang Zemin and Premier Zhu Rongji not only held the line on reform but also took a series of actions that just a few years earlier would have seemed unthinkable.

The most controversial of these was Jiang's "Three Represents" proposal, which called for allowing capitalists to join the Communist Party, a proposal he first raised while touring Guangdong in February 2000 and then formally announced on July 1, 2001, during a speech celebrating the eightieth anniversary of the CCP's founding. Jiang argued that as China's private sector expanded, the party had to ensure it was assimilating "productive elements" into the political system. Private entrepreneurs, he argued, should join workers, farmers, intellectuals, cadres, and PLA soldiers as "worthy people . . . who are loyal to the motherland and [to] socialism."[96]

Even throughout the heady days of Reform and Opening in the early 1980s, the party had viewed the private sector and entrepreneurs with a mix of political and ideological skepticism. While select individuals were lauded for their contribution to China's modernization efforts, as a class, capitalists were blamed for the "evil winds" blowing into China, including crime, corruption, and the deterioration of socialist values. Official recognition of the private sector was hemmed in by a long ideological tradition of treating the private sector as "exploitative." Through 1988, private firms had been prohibited from hiring more than eight workers, a limit that purportedly came from a passage in Marx's

Das Kapital.[97] That year, the National People's Congress amended the constitution to include language that read, "The private sector of the economy is a complement to the socialist public economy." After the Tiananmen Square protests, conservatives blamed the private sector for its role in inciting social instability, and a ban on recruiting capitalists into the party was put in place.

The period after Deng's Southern Tour saw a renewal of official support for the private sector, this time under the increasingly enthusiastic leadership of Jiang Zemin. On May 29, 1997, Jiang gave a speech at the Central Party School in which he declared China to still be in the "primary stage of socialism," a phrase the purged Zhao Ziyang had used in 1987 to justify the increasing prevalence of capitalist activity. In 1999, the constitution was again amended to further elevate the private sector as an important component of the "socialist market economy."

While conservatives were largely sidelined from power, they were not entirely helpless as the party moved to embrace the market economy. As with the *wanyanshu*, they published a series of scathing critiques of Jiang's plan to welcome private entrepreneurs, primarily in two official journals: *Pursuit of Truth* (*Zhenli de Zhuiqiu*) and *Midstream* (*Zhongliu*). While their circulation was small, they were highly influential in official circles and were two of the only remaining publications willing to publish conservative attacks on the reform agenda. Both publications had powerful backers (called "*houtai*"), including former premier Li Peng; Wang Zhen, a former general and one of the Eight Immortals of the CCP (elite party cadres who played a substantial role in the founding of the PRC); and most importantly, Deng Liqun.[98]

In article after article, the two journals savaged Jiang's capitalist amnesty plan when it was still being formulated.

Among those writing articles protesting the decision to bring capitalists into the party was Zhang Dejiang, who served with Xi Jinping on the Politburo Standing Committee between 2013 and 2018. In a 2000 article for Party Building Research which was excerpted in *Pursuit of Truth*, Zhang declared, "We must be clear that private entrepreneurs cannot join the Party."[99] As a vanguard political organization, Zhang said, the party must not allow individuals who would alienate the party from the masses, or weaken the party's ideological convictions.

Yu Quanyu, a longtime party propagandist who was appointed editor-in-chief of *Pursuit of Truth* in 1999, called Jiang's proposal an "international joke." He added:

> Over the past few years, owing to the selling-off of SOEs, the shrinking of the collective economy, the huge development of the private sector, and corrupt elements in the Party and government, the masses of this country, especially those who are unemployed, have been laid off, and those public officials who do not receive their wages on time are brimming with dissent, complaints, and emotion.[100]

More controversially, in the spring of 2002, Deng Liqun and sixteen other former high-ranking officials addressed an open letter to the Central Committee, nominally Jiang Zemin's boss, accusing the General Secretary of "political misconduct unprecedented in the history of our Party." The letter argued that his proposal to allow capitalists into the party was a violation of Marxist theory, violated the basic statutes of the party, and was in opposition to the will of the people. As punishment, "Comrade Jiang Zemin needs to carry out serious self-criticism within the Party regarding his misconduct in order to remove ideological confusions that have been caused by his misconduct and to undo its negative consequences."[101]

The *wanyanshu* of the mid-1990s had always been careful to avoid direct attacks on specific leaders and had framed their criticisms as differences over ideology, not politics. Now, however, conservatives felt their old tactics weren't working, and the pace with which the CCP was "changing its colors" necessitated new methods of dissent. "The open challenge to the party leader by a group of senior party members acting as a group appears unprecedented," observed Boston University's Joseph Fewsmith in early 2002.[102]

Jiang's reaction was swift and severe. He shuttered *Midstream* and *Pursuit of Truth*, ordering future leftist opposition to be "exterminated at the budding stage."[103] Conservatives fiercely protested the closing of these two remaining vehicles for voicing disagreements on official policy, but there was too much at stake for Jiang to back down. The next year was a leadership transition year, always the most sensitive period for China's political system. "The decisions have already been made, and opposition is futile," an editor at one party magazine said of Jiang's actions.[104]

As China approached the Sixteenth Party Congress in late 2002, the prospects for socialism in China appeared dim. After two decades of harassing the reform agenda, it seemed as though the strong-arm tactics of Deng Xiaoping and Jiang Zemin had finally broken the back of leftists and conservatives. The small number of publications willing to print their reform critiques had largely been decimated by government censors. Opposition to Jiang's plan for capitalists to join the party had failed. Under the leadership of Premier Zhu Rongji, painful reforms were being made to China's state-owned sector, leaving tens of millions of workers unemployed and billions of dollars in state assets in the hands of private investors. In late 2001, China joined the World Trade Organization, a move that seemed to many to portend a fundamental political transformation for the country.

After decades of challenging the reform agenda, the "moral left," in the words of scholar Michael Schoenhals, "does not pose a threat to stability—and by extension the current Party leadership—in organizational terms, as it lacks even a semblance of cohesion."[105]

But as the open letter calling for Jiang Zemin's sacking had shown, a new type of opposition politics was in the making.

3

Storm

In China, a socialist country led by the Communist Party, it is not normal
for students to laugh at Marxism.

—Economist Liu Guoguang, July 15, 2006[1]

IN EARLY MARCH 2001, a young university student named Jin Haike
approached his old high school classmate Fan Erjun with a warning: the
Beijing police were planning to arrest several of their friends, perhaps
even the two of them. A nervous Fan sought out a Communist Party
official at Beijing University of Aeronautics and Astronautics ("Beihang
University"), his alma mater and where he was working as a tutor.
That night, the party official called Fan back to his office, where three
members of the Ministry of State Security (MSS), China's most powerful intelligence agency, were waiting. At 3 a.m., after several hours of
questioning, he was released. "I tried to explain everything to them, but
I couldn't remember a lot, and they weren't satisfied," he told journalist
Philip Pan.[2]

The MSS was interested in the "New Youth Study Group," which
Fan had co-founded the previous year. The group was a loose affiliation
of current and former university students who shared a commitment
to social justice and a general dissatisfaction with China's economic
development model. According to one early member, "We all had a
sincere goal of doing something for our country, especially disadvantaged groups and the weakest among us."[3] Almost half of the group's
members belonged to the Communist Party. Yet for all its lofty goals,

the New Youth Study Group was a decidedly amateur operation. They never had more than ten members and only met sporadically in the few months the group existed. It was more of a club than a fully fledged organization.

But good intentions and Communist Party memberships couldn't protect the group from Chinese authorities. For the country's security apparatus, no potential threat, even a disorganized band of idealistic college students, could be ignored. This extreme caution was in the DNA of the party, which, since its founding in 1921, had survived by viewing outsiders as suspect and independent groups as potentially hostile. Having been formed by just one dozen delegates in a house in Shanghai, the party understood that big things start small. Or to quote Mao Zedong, "A single spark can start a prairie fire."[4]

Adding to the cloud of suspicion was the group's use of a new form of communication technology that was slowly spreading in China: the Internet. The New Youth Study Group had started posting essays extolling political and social reform on a website created by member Yang Zili called the "Yang Zili Thought Garden." This wasn't mere paranoia by the CCP. Outside observers were proclaiming that with the arrival of broadband to China, "the party's future looks even shakier as technological developments, such as the Internet, gradually erode its command over the flow of information."[5]

On March 13, Jin Haike's warning proved prescient. Along with group members Yang Zili, Zhang Honghai, and Xu Wei, he was detained on suspicion of "state subversion." The charges were extreme, considering the informal, even slapdash, nature of the group. But what the four defendants didn't know was that Fan Erjun was spying on them and passing along reports to state security claiming that they had denounced the CCP, even calling for its overthrow. Two months later, the court sentenced the four men to between eight and ten years in prison.[6]

The case sent a chill throughout China's intellectual community. It was a clear warning from the party to the burgeoning online community that the same unwritten rules that applied offline were applicable in cyberspace as well. Politics, both online and offline, was the sole dominion of the party.

Thanks to his cooperation with the authorities, Fan Erjun was spared prosecution, and one might have imagined he would forswear politics for good. But for Fan, the journey had just begun. Sometime between the arrest of his friends in 2001 and the fall of 2003, he changed his name to Fan Jinggang and co-founded Utopia, an organization that challenged the way the Communist Party ruled China.

One of Fan's early mentors while at university was Han Deqiang, a young economist from Zhejiang Province. As a child, Han idolized Lei Feng, the model PLA soldier celebrated for his unquestioning devotion to Mao and the "masses." Yet in 1984, when Han was seventeen, he read the party's "Decision of the Central Committee of the Communist Party of China on Reform of the Economic Structure," which redefined China's economy as a "planned socialist commodity economy," with "commodity" being a thinly disguised euphemism for "market." Han later said the document left him devastated. If this was true, he thought, and if China's economy was governed by material incentives, "Why the heck would [China's revolutionary leaders] have been tramping through the mountains and valleys conducting guerrilla warfare?"[7]

At school, Han dreamed of a career studying particle physics—"I wanted to explore new sources of energy for the nation"—but with the dramatic changes of the 1980s, he found himself increasingly drawn to social issues.[8] After graduating from university in 1989 with a degree in management engineering, he became a full-time political supervisor and deputy party secretary at Beihang University, where he would later meet a young Fan Jinggang (then still known as "Erjun").

In 1991, Han took his first step toward a career as an intellectual-activist, writing a lengthy article entitled "Where Is China Going?," which he mailed to all of the country's provincial party leaders. He wanted them to understand that China was in the midst of a crisis of values brought on by its market reforms and its dismantling of the planned economy. The following year, Deng Xiaoping embarked on his Southern Tour to revive the economic reforms and declare the left as the main ideological threat to China's modernization. Han said he was disappointed, "even to the point of despair."[9]

As it became clear that Jiang Zemin would take up the Southern Tour mantle, and as Han became more disillusioned with the direction the party was taking the country, his intellectual focus shifted to economics. In particular, he was increasingly concerned about China's planned accession to the World Trade Organization (WTO), which he worried would leave the country's private and state-owned firms exposed to unfair competition by stronger multinational corporations. It was also, he believed, a Trojan Horse for smuggling capitalism into China for the benefit of the country's economic elite. "We are told 'Join the WTO, so that reform and the opening up policy won't be reversed,'" he said in a speech to the European Parliament. "This could be translated as 'Join the WTO, so that the wallets of the rich won't be under threat.'"[10]

In January 2000, he published *Collision: The Globalization Trap and China's Real Choice*, a broadside against the WTO and what he believed was China's submission to a US-dominated global trading system.[11] "The belief that globalization is irreversible and must be welcomed by humanity is a belief forced by the minority onto the majority," Han wrote. "The truth is, with the intensification of globalization, more and more people are being pushed into an abyss of unemployment and poverty."[12] The book was heavily influenced by the 1997 Asian Financial Crisis, which Han believed demonstrated the risks of opening China's capital markets to the global economy. Han was also outraged by the 1999 NATO bombing of the Chinese embassy in Belgrade, proof, he thought, of the West's contempt for China. The Chinese government's own admission that the WTO would necessitate deep structural changes to China's economy also worried Han. As China's lead trade negotiator declared, "China's economy must become a market economy in order to become part of the global economic system."[13]

Statements like these, which in many ways were intended to convince foreign audiences that China was indeed becoming a country they could do business with, also had the effect of galvanizing anti-reform voices back in China. Just before the release of Han's book, several young nationalists published *China's Path Under the Shadow of Globalization*, which argued, "It is time to wake up. For the third world, economic globalization offers more risks than opportunities and greater costs than benefits."[14] In May 2000, CASS researcher Yang Bin had published *The Covert War Threatening China*, which framed the WTO as part of a "soft war" waged by Western powers, particularly the United States and the United Kingdom, to pry open China's markets for the benefit of Western corporations, and ultimately, to "advance neo-colonialism and to control the entire world."[15]

In the end, these protests were not enough to block China's accession to the WTO, which was formally completed in late 2001. But the sense of powerlessness felt by many leftist intellectuals by the end of the 1990s had the unintended effect of creating a sense of unity, born of marginalization. By the early 2000s, an embryonic pan-leftist movement was taking root, and for all its ideological differences (and they were many), it was held together by a common lament—that the Communist Party was abandoning socialism and embracing economic growth at all costs. This was, they argued, to the benefit of an elite few and at the expense of the majority, especially China's workers and peasants.

But if marginalization was drawing leftists together, technology was enabling them to communicate and to share their message with a wider audience.

Like the New Youth Study Group, disenfranchised intellectuals and activists were turning to the Internet to share and develop ideas, as well as to experience a sense of participation in a political system that discouraged and punished activism. From just 26.5 million users in 2001, within a year this number had jumped 72.8 percent to nearly 46 million.[16] As China's online population expanded, so did their options. Through admittedly crudely designed, new websites and bulletin boards (BBS) allowed users to experience a degree of freedom unthinkable in the real world. Liberal or socialist, there was an intellectual home for everyone. Left-leaning websites such as China Workers Net, Socialist Countryside, Peasant-Worker World, and Patriots' Alliance explored topics such as the impact of SOE reforms on urban workers, the environmental impact of economic growth, and the future of China's agricultural sector.[17]

The editors of *Pursuit of Truth* saw the development of the Internet as a possible solution to their closure, detailed in the previous chapter, on the orders of Jiang Zemin. Had Jiang taken this action just a few years earlier, it's quite likely that the journal's brand of orthodox leftism could have withered, absent an alternative platform. But in the early

2000s, there were new options, and the editors began exploring the Internet as a possible home for the continued struggle against the party's embrace of market economics and globalization.

Creating a website made sense. Indeed, it was likely the only avenue open to them given the current political climate. The real question was, could they create a platform for leftist voices that wouldn't immediately suffer the same fate as *Pursuit of Truth*?

One thing was clear to them: as the economic reforms deepened and created new social tensions, Mao Zedong had become a symbol of a more equitable time. "I wish we could go back to Mao's day," a Shanghai worker told a foreign reporter in the late 1980s. "At that time, we had no inflation and we were guaranteed a certain living standard. Now I can hardly afford to feed my family."[18] The editors of *Pursuit of Truth* understood this, and in late 2003 they launched Maoflag (maoflag. net) with the support of old left stalwarts Ma Bin, Deng Liqun, Zhang Quanjing, and Li Chengrui. They hoped that by wrapping themselves in the flag of Mao Zedong, the party would be reluctant to shut their website down, but more importantly, that by appealing to the country's founding ideals, they could nudge the party back onto the path of socialism.[19] "As Party members, we must support Marxism," one of the website's founders told me. "This is why we started the website. The slogan of Marxism is still with the party. We don't need to leave the party, as it's still in theory Marxist."[20]

If the Internet was breathing new life into the left in China, such developments weren't being reported in the West, where a new and confident narrative was emerging: the World Wide Web was universal acid for destroying outdated ideologies such as those espoused by the newly established Maoflag website. "Let me put it in plain, blunt terms," presidential candidate George W. Bush declared in 1999, "If the Internet were to take hold in China, freedom's genie will be out of the bottle."[21] In a 2000 speech, US president Bill Clinton famously compared trying to control the Internet to "trying to nail Jell-O to the wall."[22]

Techno-utopianism wasn't just an American affliction. Many liberal-leaning intellectuals in China agreed. CASS political scientist Liu Junning argued, "The Internet and IT are [an] unprecedented technological force that empowers China's march toward globalization, a free market, and an open society."[23]

Of course, to an extent Liu Junning was correct. The Internet *did* make it easier for liberal values to spread, and it did contribute to China's integration into the global economy. And while it may not have resulted in quite the degree of freedom George W. Bush had in mind, the Internet undoubtedly "expanded the information horizons" of hundreds of millions of Chinese.[24]

But it also helped sustain voices advocating increased state dominance of the economy and for a return to more rigid ideological control. Individuals who were increasingly alienated from the party as it embraced globalization and privatization saw the Internet as one of the only venues where they could freely discuss the plight of workers, the social costs of capitalism, the fate of socialism, and the future of the Communist Party.

This included Han Deqiang, who was an early and frequent contributor to Maoflag. As he saw the potential of the Internet to sustain more heterodox political opinions, he looked for new ways to bridge the online and offline worlds. In the lead-up to the US invasion of Iraq in 2003, he circulated an electronic petition opposing the war that garnered 1,500 signatures, which he then delivered to the US Embassy in Beijing.[25] Start-up online media companies gave widespread coverage to this new type of online civic activism. In an interview conducted by the popular online portal Sina.com with the nationalist writer and co-signatory Wang Xiaodong, Han praised the Internet as a democratic tool for expressing the "will of the people."[26] Also signing the petition were New Left scholars Cui Zhiyuan and Wang Hui, "neo-statist" intellectual He Xin, playwright Huang Jisu, and Peking University professor of literature Kong Qingdong.[27]

Among those expressing public opposition to the Iraq War was a young economist named Yang Fan, who Han first met at a conference in 1999. Yang had grown up in Beijing, where his father taught at the Central Party School, a training ground for high-ranking party cadres. His father's status afforded Yang the opportunity to attend the elite Beijing No. 4 High School along with the other sons and daughters of party aristocracy. In 1982, Yang graduated from Jilin University with an undergraduate degree in political economy and a master's degree in world economics three years later. After a brief stint at Central University of Finance and Economics, Yang went to work for the Bank of China in Shenzhen, later transferring to the Tianjin Development zone, where he worked as a researcher.[28] In 1994, he joined the macroeconomic research center at CASS in Beijing, where he also completed his PhD.

In 1991, Yang published *The Republic's Third Generation* at the urging of his old classmate Bo Xicheng, the son of party elder Bo Yibo and brother of Bo Xilai (who will be discussed in detail later in this book). *The Republic's Third Generation* described the political and economic development of the generation of princelings who were in elementary and middle school during the Cultural Revolution and were now mapping out their own paths to power and riches. The book also described an elitist "new political program" that would help ensure the princelings could successfully transition into power given their lack of revolutionary credibility. Rather than following the old Maoist "mass line," he wrote, "We must absolutely not think that any regime can remain separate from politicians, thinkers, and entrepreneurs, that it can reject intellectuals and 'rely directly on the broad masses.' Quite the contrary, policies that truly represent the popular interests can only be produced when the ruling is made scientific."[29]

By the time Yang met Han in 1999, he was a remarkably prolific author, writing dozens of articles each year on topics including exchange rate policy and inflation. Like Han Deqiang, Yang had grown disillusioned with the direction of China's economic policy, which he increasingly described as "neoliberal." An influx of translations of Western economists in the mid-1990s, such as the libertarian Nobel Prize–winning economist F. A. Hayek had, in Yang's opinion, shifted the intellectual climate to the right. He was also alarmed at the pace with which the Chinese government, under the leadership of Premier Zhu Rongji, was dismantling China's state-owned sector with little regard for the social costs to the millions of laid-off workers.[30]

And like Han, he was beginning to see the potential of the Internet. In the summer of 2003, the two men decided to create their own pan-leftist platform, one that would unabashedly explore alternative paths for China's development and provide a forum for diverse views.[31] They would start with a "book bar," a physical meeting space for lectures and for selling socialist and left-leaning books and magazines. At Han's urging, their website would carry original articles and promote up-coming events.

Han also knew a promising former student named Fan Jinggang who could help with the day-to-day administration.

On September 6, 2003, the Beijing Utopia Cultural Communications Corporation Limited opened its doors in northwest Beijing, just next to Beihang University's west gate. The name "Utopia" was Han Deqiang's idea. The State Administration for Industry and Commerce didn't ap-prove his first choice, "wutuobang," a direct phonetic translation of the English word "utopia," so he changed it to "Land of Utopia" (*wuyou zhixiang*). "Utopia is unrealistic, and I admit that I'm unrealistic," Han said. "But isn't it OK for unrealistic people to dream? This dream is called 'Land of Utopia.' "[32]

Utopia declared humble intentions, aiming to become "a small plat-form through which social progress can be facilitated by pursuing a fairness-first society and the formation and expansion of a responsible middle-class. The book bar wishes to become a meeting and discus-sion site for pan-Leftist scholars, cultural personnel, white-collars, entrepreneurs, university students and government officials."[33]

Yang Fan presided over the inaugural event on September 14, 2003, a four-hour lecture on wealth disparities and the rise of China's nou-veau riche.[34] One week later, Utopia held the first of its regular salons, which were open to the public for a charge of $3.75 per person ($1.80 for students). The events covered a plethora of topics: from discussions of China's agricultural policy to the impacts of neoliberalism in Latin America to Mao Zedong's role in World War II. These early events fea-tured an impressive array of current and former officials, academics, writers, artists, and intellectuals, including influential international relations scholar Pan Wei; legal scholar Gong Xiantian; *Dushu* co-editor Huang Ping; Xu Xiaoqing, a researcher at the State Council's Development Research Center; National Reform and Development Commission researcher Gao Liang; Yu Quanyu, the former chief editor of *Pursuit of Truth*; Zhou Enlai's niece Zhou Bingde; Marxist academic Cheng Enfu; and New Left scholar Cui Zhiyuan.

Guo Songmin, a former air force pilot turned freelance writer, visited Utopia for the first time in the summer of 2004. Guo was then writing articles on political topics for a variety of small websites, and Utopia had started to repost them.[35] Curious about this new organization, he went to one of their events, where he met a "short and chunky" young man with a strong Henan accent named Fan Jinggang. The speaker that day was Tong Xiaoxi, an academic at China Agricultural University, who discussed issues affecting China's agricultural sector. Utopia's upstairs lecture hall was jammed with university students and the audience spilled onto the staircase leading to the first floor. There was no air conditioning, Guo remembers, and everyone was dripping with sweat. But this was the first time many in the audience, including Guo Songmin, had heard these issues discussed so openly and with so much passion. And perhaps more importantly, they were part of a community—the name "Utopia" would come to represent a shared intellectual home for concerned and committed activists, scholars, retired party officials, laid-off workers, artists, students, and young professionals.

For Guo, the experience was enthralling, and he would later describe these early years as Utopia's "golden age."[36]

By the time Utopia opened its doors in the fall of 2003, something unexpected was happening: China appeared to be undergoing what one scholar called a "left tilt."[37] The previous December, Hu Jintao traveled to Xibaipo in Hebei Province for his inaugural outing as the party's general secretary. The city served as the CCP's headquarters during the final phase of its bloody civil war with Chiang Kai-shek's KMT, and it was here, in March 1949, that Mao Zedong warned his fellow party members that victory over the KMT was just the beginning of their struggle, for "the road after the revolution will be longer, the work greater and more arduous." The real battle, he declared, was to win and maintain the support of the people, and to do this, the party must "remain modest, prudent and free from arrogance and rashness in their style of work. The comrades must be taught to preserve the style of plain living and hard struggle."[38] Hu's choice of Xibaipo was, according to University of California economist Barry Naughton, an "implicit rebuke to the style of Jiang Zemin, with his unrestrained celebration of elites, wealth, and fame."[39]

The trip marked the beginning of a clear policy shift to confront some of the wrenching social costs from China's decades-long pursuit of brute economic development.[40] From environmental to rural policy, the Hu administration began addressing many of the long-standing social and economic inequities that had accumulated throughout the reform period. Taxes for rural residents were slashed or abolished, most notably 2,600-year-old agricultural tax. New initiatives for health care and environmental protection were announced, as was a plan for a "new socialist countryside," which sought to modernize China's rural areas to ensure the country's economic growth was more evenly distributed.

Driving this policy shift was a growing degree of unrest in the country's rural areas and in its industrial heartland. Reforms were exacting costs on these two constituencies, and they were exacerbated by local-level corruption and widespread abuse by party cadres. As one analysis from 2002 described the problem, "China now confronts the most massive scale of unemployment and peasant labor migration in the history of the People's Republic."[41] An open letter from one rural official addressed to Premier Zhu Rongji declared, "The peasants' lot is really bitter, the countryside is really poor, and agriculture is in crisis."[42] Crucially, news of the crisis was making its way across the country. In 2004, the husband-and-wife team of Chen Guidi and Wu Chuntao published an explosive book, *An Investigation of Chinese Peasants*, which provided an exhaustive account of the everyday corruption, injustice, and economic insecurity experienced by peasants in rural Anhui Province. Despite being banned by the Propaganda Department, underground versions of the book sold an estimated seven million copies, and Premier Wen Jiabao's top advisor on rural issues stated in a 2004 interview that he had a copy of the book on his bedside table.[43]

As the Hu Jintao administration took steps to address these concerns, signals were being sent to academics and intellectuals that new space for research, dialogue, and debate opening up.

In 2003, CASS, with the strong support of academy president Chen Kuiyuan, established a task force to investigate the impact of neoliberalism on China's political and economic system. They released their findings the following year in a book entitled *Neoliberalism: Commentaries and Analyses*, a blistering—if uneven—attack on many of the same policies that the country had been pursuing for the better part of two decades. The CASS report set off a wave of criticisms of neoliberalism in the press and online. In June 2004, *People's Daily* published an article titled "Beware of the Influence of Neoliberalism," which used language redolent of the conservative attacks on "bourgeois liberalism" in the 1980s. It described neoliberalism as "the theoretical expression of the international monopoly capitalist class on globalization," and called on Chinese intellectuals to "actively mobilize themselves to counteract the challenge that neoliberalism has posed for Marxism, so as to consolidate the guiding role of Marxism in the ideological and social sciences domains."[44]

Utopia took notice and began reposting excerpts from the CASS report on its website, along with the various critiques of neoliberalism that were appearing in newspapers and magazines across the country. More importantly, several of Utopia's "advisory scholars" were invited to attend the official CASS event announcing the publication of its final report on neoliberalism.[45] The book's release was "just the beginning of China's formal reflection on, and criticism of, neoliberalism," Utopia wrote on its website. Still, the group argued that the CASS project didn't go far enough in linking the negative consequences of neoliberalism to China's experience with Reform and Opening: "This is the direction we need to earnestly work toward with our next steps."[46]

This opportunity came on August 9, 2004, when an American-trained economist named Lang Xianping (known to his English-speaking friends as "Larry") delivered a speech at Shanghai's Fudan University on the subject of SOEs privatization. Specifically, Larry Lang's speech accused some of the country's best-known entrepreneurs and companies of appropriating state assets under the guise of a completely legal process known as a "management buyout" (MBO). Dating back to the SOE restructuring of the late 1990s, an MBO occurred when the existing management at an SOE purchased a significant (or complete) equity stake in the company, often times through a newly established private firm. This allowed China to reform its SOE sector through de facto privatization, while avoiding having to explicitly refer to it as such. Strictly speaking, MBOs weren't governed by the market, and the sale of SOEs often went for bargain-basement prices to political insiders or their proxies.

Lang's primary target was Gu Chujun, one of the most adept practitioners of MBOs, and according to *Forbes*, one of China's wealthiest entrepreneurs.[47] A native of China's Jiangsu Province, Gu moved to Hong Kong in 1996, where he founded Greencool Group after inventing a new type of chlorofluorocarbon-free refrigeration coolant. In 2001, Greencool purchased significant equity stakes in Kelon Electronic, a state-owned producer of household appliances. Gu became Kelon's chairman, and in 2002, he completed the full purchase—and thus privatization—of Kelon.

In his August speech in Shanghai, Lang claimed that after three months of investigation into Gu's business activities, he'd determined that four companies Gu recently purchased, Kelon included, had inaccurately reported significant losses prior to their sale to Gu in order to justify a lower sale price. In short, this was a giveaway to Gu at the expense of the ultimate owners of these companies: the Chinese people.[48]

Lang's speech was the opening shot in what would become known as the "Larry Lang Storm" (郎咸平旋风). It would last nearly a year and result in the arrest and eventual conviction of Gu, one of China's most famous entrepreneurs, on charges of embezzlement. It would also prompt Chinese regulators to eventually outlaw SOE privatization through MBOs. But most importantly for Utopia, the public debate provoked by Larry Lang's speech proved the power of the Internet to facilitate and channel public dissent and, crucially, to effect real policy change.

The 2004 scandal over MBOs "broke the taboo," said Utopia's Fan Jinggang.[49]

After receiving a bachelor's and master's degree in his native Taiwan, Larry Lang went to study in the United States, obtaining a PhD in finance from the University of Pennsylvania's Wharton School in 1986. But even with a degree from one of the world's best business schools, Lang had trouble finding a permanent position, and he spent the remainder of the 1980s and most of the early 1990s bouncing from school to school, including stints at Michigan State University, Ohio State University, and finally New York University. Lang later told a Chinese journalist that he'd written more than enough academic papers to have been granted tenure if he'd been interested in settling down.[50] He left the United States for Hong Kong in 1994, and in 2000 he relocated to China and began teaching at Peking University and the Cheung Kong Graduate School of Business.

Lang's academic interest faded soon after arriving in China. He'd already told former colleagues that most academics were "doing research for the sake of doing research," and because most fields were monopolized by a few big names it was harder for younger academics such as Lang to "become famous."[51] Instead, Lang found relative fame in writing company profiles for Dapeng Securities, an investment research and securities firm. In 2001, he wrote a blistering exposé of D'Long Investment for *New Fortune* magazine, accusing the firm of illegal stock trading. The story sent D'Long's stock into a tailspin, and in 2003, after Lang told a journalist that the China Securities Regulatory Commission had opened an investigation into D'Long, the company went bankrupt.

As Lang's public profile began to rise, so too did rumors that he was using his platform to extort payments from firms in return for his silence, as well as claims that firms were approaching Lang to write hit pieces on their rivals. A former colleague at Dapeng Securities, Wu Dingjie, later claimed that Lang carved out a profitable niche by pressuring financial firms to compensate him for his cooperation. Highly exposed to investor sentiment, Wu said that many firms would pay Lang rather than risk the negative market fallout.[52] Gu Chujun later claimed that it was his refusal to pay a "public relations fee" that led to Lang's public denunciation of his company in August 2004.[53]

Lang's public accusations provided a rallying point for the disparate anti-reform voices. Although they disagreed on issues of ideology and tactics, many anti-reformers were in agreement that Lang's accusations provided a window of opportunity to publicly debate issues surrounding the pace of SOE restructuring. They also saw the narrower issue of MBOs as a wedge to discuss the much wider and more fundamental questions surrounding the future trajectory of China's economic and political system.

On August 28, the ideological divide between left and right on these issues took on a geographical dimension. In Shenzhen, in the south, several of China's most famous reformist economists, including Wu Jinglian (known affectionately as "Market Wu"), Xu Xiaonian, and Zhang Weiying gave speeches in support of the reform process and further restructuring of China's SOEs. While some of the speakers at the conference chose to avoid speaking directly about the Lang-Gu controversy, Zhang Weiying, a Cambridge-trained economist at Peking University, accused Lang of "sensationalism" and "lacking credibility."[54]

Back in the north, in Beijing, Lang and his supporters held an event on "State Asset Loss and the Development of the State-Owned Economy" at the Chang'an Grand Theatre, just three kilometers from Tiananmen Square and the leadership compound at Zhongnanhai. Yang Bin, author of *The Covert War Threatening China*, was there, as were Utopia's Yang Fan and Han Deqiang, and the New Left economist Zuo Dapei, a longtime friend of Yang Fan's and a researcher at CASS. When it came time for Lang to speak, he thundered, "I want to criticize the neoliberal school that has dominated China's property rights reform for 20 years. . . . This neoliberal school believes that reform is the complete withdrawal of state-owned enterprises from the economic arena." Lang announced that he'd invited Wu Jinglian and Zhang Weiying to speak at the event, "but they refused to participate." He continued, "I am replying to Zhang Weiying's remarks now: I represent small and medium shareholders in encouraging professional managers to assume their fiduciary responsibility."[55]

That same day, Han Deqiang, Yang Fan, and Zuo Dapei released an open letter addressed to "the relevant leading comrades" in which they declared, "We believe that Professor Lang Xianping's analysis is objective and fair." They called on the leadership to open investigations into the companies Lang had implicated, including Gu's Greencool, to stop all future MBOs, to ensure that all previous MBOs were carried out with appropriate valuations, to require the *People's Daily* to publish the results of the investigations, and to "accept the people's supervision and comments on the supervision process." The letter ended with a plea and a warning: "The day SOEs are fully privatized is the day when the social function of SOEs disappears, and it will also be the time when China's troubled autumn comes. . . . We hope, and we're willing to believe, that the new leaders of the party and the government . . . can revitalize the glory of the SOEs."[56]

Emboldened by the previous day's event, Lang gave an interview to *Shanghai Bund* magazine in which he stated, "It doesn't matter how many scholars support or oppose me. What's more important is that even more scholars start paying attention to problems with the SOE reforms."[57] Few took up Lang's call with more alacrity than CASS's Zuo

Dapei, a prominent New Left economist who, like Han Deqiang, had also campaigned against China's accession into the WTO. In addition to the open letter, Zuo issued his own statement, declaring, "I resolutely stand with [Lang Xianping]." It went much further: "Whomever allows the loss of state assets behind the back of the people has committed a crime." This statement, a direct charge of criminal behavior by the government, was carried on business websites, including the financial website of the *People's Daily*.[58]

Online (and unscientific) polls appeared on popular Internet portals Sina and Sohu showing lopsided support for Lang, with 90 percent of the forty thousand respondents declaring their support for him over Peking University economist Zhang Weiying. Regardless of their accuracy, the poll results were quickly exploited by sympathetic websites and journalists.[59] On September 6, ten academics, including Zuo Dapei and Marxist economist Cheng Enfu, issued yet another public statement supporting Lang, this one citing the polls as proof of overwhelming public support for the campaign against MBOs.[60]

The Larry Lang Storm coincided with a string of large-scale anti-privatization protests that reinforced the sense for the left that Lang's campaign was having an impact outside of meeting rooms in Beijing and Shenzhen. In one city in Shaanxi Province, six thousand workers at a former textile SOE went on strike in September 2004 to protest the loss of wages and benefits after the firm was privatized. At a former military factory in Chongqing, thousands of workers protested the sale of the company to a private entrepreneur for under fair value. One firsthand account of the Chongqing factory privatization, published on gongnong.org (Worker and Peasant), declared, "Chongqing is under the control of dark forces" and appealed to the CCP Central Committee for direct intervention on behalf of the workers. An open letter to the party leadership posted on the leftist website China and the World, declared, "The Privatization of State-Owned Enterprises Will Eventually Lead to Revolution."[61]

Despite the growing intensity of debate over SOE reforms, the Chinese government remained quiet, clearly hoping to carefully guide the debate through its control of a vast network of newspapers and magazines. In December, it finally weighed in and did so on the side of Larry Lang and his now-legions of supporters: MBOs would no longer be allowed for large SOEs, and the rules for acquisitions for smaller SOEs would be dramatically tightened. The following May, the China Securities Regulatory Commission began investigating one of Gu Chujun's companies, and just a few months later, Gu and eight other executives from Kelon and Greencool were arrested on charges of falsifying documents and misallocating company assets.

Lang's victory, or the perception thereof, made him a genuine star. His public campaign to name and shame China's most successful magnates was immensely popular with a Chinese population that was increasingly fed up with corruption and backroom deals. Lang was rewarded with a weekly TV talk show, *Larry Lang Live* (财经郎闲评), which aired Friday nights at 10 p.m. on a Shanghai TV station. "I have been told by female viewers that there are three new fashions in Shanghai: to carry a Louis Vuitton bag, to have a Cartier watch and to watch *Larry Lang Live*," Lang boasted to the *Financial Times*.[62] On air, he continued to hammer the issue of SOE privatization: "Russia needed two years for privatization whereas China will need 20. But the outcome will be the same," he warned.[63]

Lang's victory was also a triumph for the loose network of intellectuals, writers, activists, and academics who supported him and (thanks to the Internet) had amplified his voice. Few did more for Lang than Utopia, which published dozens of articles on its website written by a who's who of leftist academics and intellectuals. It hosted events to give the burgeoning online community an offline home. Zuo Dapei, who had been writing for Utopia since its founding, was quoted on the Lang-Gu affair in some of China's largest newspapers, including *China Youth News* and *Beijing Morning Post*. In the twelve months since its founding in 2003, Utopia could credibly claim to have achieved its mission "to become a meeting and discussion site for pan-Leftist scholars."

The controversy was also good for the organization. In an increasingly crowded field of leftist websites, Utopia was able to break away from the pack by aggressively promoting Larry Lang and using his popularity to drive the conversation toward more fundamental political and economic questions. And now, with the government's recent decision limiting MBOs, there was a discussion within the organization about what should come next. No one in the broader pan-left movement (and certainly not Utopia) wanted to waste the momentum that had been achieved through the campaign against SOE privatization. There were even bigger issues to tackle.

Despite the government's acquiescence on limiting MBOs in December 2004 (or perhaps because of this), Premier Wen Jiabao rang in 2005 by calling it the "year of reform." But by year's end, it was clear this wasn't going to be the case. The debate opened by Larry Lang didn't stop with the decision on MBOs. In fact, anti-reform voices were gaining strength, thanks to the networking power the Internet provided them, and they were bolstered by a newfound confidence that they could actually impact national-level policy.

In March, *China Youth Daily* published an interview with economist Liu Guoguang, who, like Wu Jinglian, had also earned the nickname "Market" for his early support of Deng Xiaoping's reforms. In it, he argued that China's economy had drifted too far from government planning. "At present, there is a misunderstanding that is widely circulated throughout the country, which is that the word 'plan' is completely derogatory," Liu said. He continued, "Some people advocate that everything should be market-oriented and that there is no need for planning, no need for macro-controls, and the government should only act as a 'night watchman.'" Liu argued that while he had originally supported market reforms in the 1980s after witnessing the damage done to China under Mao's planned economy, the slow accumulation of economic problems and social tensions during Reform and Opening necessitated a rebalancing back toward planning.[64]

Just days later, Liu, Wu Jinglian, and two other economists were presented with the inaugural Chinese Economics Prize, jointly awarded by the China Society of Macroeconomics (中国宏观经济学会) and the China Society of Economic Reform (中国经济体制改革研究会). During his acceptance speech, Liu again returned to the topic of the planned economy. "Some people think that the dust has settled; that the market has the upper hand while the plan is no longer fashionable. I don't see it this way. The planned economy has played a glorious historical role in the former Soviet Union and in China," Liu remarked. He wasn't calling for the complete abandonment of a market economy, as he repeatedly stressed, but rather he thought that China's socialist market economy had ignored the word "socialist" for too long. Serious issues such as income inequality and environmental degradation had been exacerbated by markets, Liu argued, and a rebalancing toward government control was needed.[65]

But he still wasn't done. On July 15, his remarks at a small gathering at the Ministry of Education were recorded and released online under the title "Liu Guoguang Discussed Some Problems in Teaching and Studying Economics." Unlike the more careful arguments against what he believed was China's overreliance on the market economy, his July comments were infused with language reminiscent of the ideological debates of the 1980s. In particular, Liu was concerned about the supplanting of Marxism in academia by "Western bourgeois ideology," which he believed had "penetrated both economic research work and economic decision-making." To combat this, Liu called on the Ministry of Education to ensure that all leadership positions at educational institutions were "in the hands of Marxists."[66] Liu later claimed that his remarks were shared with Politburo Standing Committee member and Propaganda Department head Li Changchun, and that, prompted by Liu's concerns, a Ministry of Education investigation team was sent to a "famous" Beijing university.[67]

In August, Utopia "special advisor" and Peking University law professor Gong Xiantian denounced a newly released draft property law in an open letter addressed to National People's Congress chair Wu Bangguo. Gong's letter, provocatively titled, "A Law That Goes Against the Principles of Socialism and the Constitution," denounced the draft law for failing to recognize and protect public property, "which is the foundation of socialist legislative work." Gong's letter concluded, "The 'Communist Party' formed by the people has become a 'private property party'!" This was not a fine-tuned argument based on a careful legal reading of the draft law text, but rather a public accusation of ideological betrayal by the CCP.[68]

Gong Xiantian had been a true believer since university. In October 1966, while still a student at the Peking College of Political Science and Law, he and his classmates set out for the old party stronghold of Yan'an, the "revolutionary holy land."[69] They spent New Year's Day exploring Yan'an's system of caves, where the party leadership, including Mao Zedong and Zhou Enlai, had spent more than a decade beginning in the late 1930s. Gong soon joined the CCP, and after graduation in 1968, he took up a series of party positions in Inner Mongolia, Heilongjiang, Guangxi, and as a party secretary of a people's commune in Shandong Province. Keen to continue studying law, he spent five years at the University of Sarajevo in Yugoslavia, where he received a juris doctorate in 1987. He was offered a position at Peking University at the rank of associate professor, and he joined the university's party committee, where he supported student "ideological teaching." After Deng's 1992 Southern Tour, however, Gong quit this position, blaming the "confused" ideological thinking of the student body.[70] He remained an ardent opponent of the economic reforms throughout the 1990s and 2000s, alienating many of his colleagues. "I never conceal my opinion, for true Communists will not hide their views," he would later state.[71]

Coming off the back of the Lang-Gu controversy and Liu Guoguang's comments on the planned economy, Gong's open letter caused a sensation. In September, he was invited to meet with officials at the Commission of Legislative Affairs of the NPC Standing Committee, which lasted eighty minutes. Two weeks later, Wu Bangguo declared that the law's drafting team should pay particular attention to China's own practical circumstances and avoid copying Western law. Still later, the NPC announced that it would not consider the law at its upcoming meeting in March, delaying a vote until it could complete further study and revisions.

"I know that my open letter is working," Gong told a reporter. "But it's not my work alone."[72] This was true. In February, Gong pointed a reporter from *Southern Weekend* to the Utopia website where he'd posted a detailed criticism of the draft law.[73] The website hosted dozens of articles on the controversy and helped organize forums around Beijing. The rapidly expanding ecosystem of leftist websites, particularly Utopia, were now important platforms for amplifying Gong's critique, as they had done for Larry Lang and Liu Guoguang.

The period between 2004 and 2006 was marked by an explosion of open intellectual and ideological debate in China. Beginning with Larry Lang's speech at Fudan University, problems associated with China's ongoing economic transformation received unprecedented media attention, and for a while, at least, direct government response. Leftist voices marginalized in the wake of Deng's 1992 declaration of "no debate" were now proliferating thanks to the expansion of online communities, lively intellectual forums, and salons in cities such as Beijing and Shanghai.

News of this newly assertive and unabashed left wing began to make its way into the pages of Western media. After Gong Xiantian's campaign to block the draft property law, the *New York Times* reported,

> Those who dismissed [Gong's] attack as a throwback to an earlier era underestimated the continued appeal of socialist ideas in a country where glaring disparities between rich and poor, rampant corruption, labor abuses and land seizures offer daily reminders of how far China has strayed from its official ideology.[74]

But if the left was beginning to feel confident, its hopes would soon be smashed. China and the Communist Party were about to enter a period of extreme turbulence, and many of the left's recent victories would be rolled back.

And for Utopia, a radical transformation was imminent. From its origins as a "small platform through which social progress can be facilitated by pursuing for a fairness-first society," the organization was about to make an abrupt turn toward paranoia, internal feuding, and open calls for revolution.

The result would be the birth of the neo-Maoist movement.

4

Unhappy China

Anyone wanting to overthrow a political regime must create public opinion and do some preparatory ideological work.

—Mao Zedong, 1962

ON MARCH 4, 2006, reform-minded intellectuals met in Beijing's Western Hills at the Xinglin Mountain Village at the invitation of the government-affiliated China Society of Economic Reform and its chairperson Gao Shangquan.[1] Attendees included free-market economists Wu Jinglian and Zhang Weiying, sociologist Sun Liping, and outspoken legal scholar He Weifang. The meeting was designed to provide the twenty influential participants with an open forum for frank discussions on sensitive policy issues. Zhang Weiying quipped that the meeting's lack of journalists made it a "safe place" where it was "easy to raise issues."[2] But the focus that day was not on narrow policy discussions. Instead, they weighed in on the future of China's economic and political reform trajectory.

Li Shuguang, the dean at China University of Politics and Law, declared at the meeting: "The period of economic reform has ended."[3] Events of the previous twelve months, including the Lang-Gu controversy, Liu Guoguang's call for increased planning of the economy, and Gong Xiantian's campaign to block the draft property law, convinced the assembled that leftist voices were on the ascendant and were increasingly influential with the government. This sentiment had been captured in an op-ed by *China Reform* magazine editor Xin Wang the previous fall, which despaired, "The trend of opposing the market and opposing reform has gone from the grassroots all the way to the top."[4]

For many of the participants at the March 4 conference, it was the accompanying leftward shift in public opinion that worried them the most. "Leftists in our society are saying absurd things," said Sun Liping. "But as elite intellectuals, we cannot deny that they have a solid basis for saying them."[5] He Weifang worried that "people on the left [who] often take a clear-cut stand under the banner of socialism, calling for, among other things, a return to the legislative tradition pioneered by the Soviet Union."[6] Because of the current ideological environment, he believed that the "common goal" of conference participants—a multiparty political system, freedom of the press, and a "true democracy"— were off limits from public advocacy. "We are all of the belief that this is the direction China should go, but for now we cannot express this belief openly."

Two weeks later, the entire meeting transcript was leaked and published on the overseas website Huayue Forum, and days later in China on the Utopia and Maoflag websites. In response, the China Society of Economic Reform issued a "formal" transcript, but it had been significantly altered, including the deletion of large sections from He Weifang's remarks.

The meeting was a turning point for Utopia and the broadening coalition of leftist voices in China. For years, they had spoken of shadowy forces working on behalf of the capitalist class to influence, and eventually overthrow, the Communist Party. Jiang Zemin's "Three Represents," which welcomed private entrepreneurs into the party, was taken as prima facie evidence of the conspiracy at work. With the leaked minutes from the "New Xishan Meeting," as they came to call it ("xishan" meaning "western hills"), they had concrete proof that the cabal was real.

From this point on, Utopia and an increasing cohort of competitors and copycats would embrace a paranoid worldview that saw global conspiracies of Western domination, the infiltration of China and the party by traitors and "hostile forces," and a belief in an inevitable and unavoidable conflict with the United States.

As they prepared for this coming struggle, they saw Mao Zedong as their magic weapon.

A "paranoid style" in Chinese politics dated back to the country's founding.[7] In January 1953, US secretary of state nominee John Foster Dulles said during his confirmation hearing that America "must always have in mind the liberation of these captive peoples [living under communism]." This "liberation," Dulles added, did not necessarily mean war, and could include the "weight of propaganda," "moral pressure," and "psychological force."[8] While Dulles's remarks were intended to refer to the Soviet Union, they resonated in Beijing, where Mao Zedong was already beginning to fear that the United States would use a strategy of "peaceful evolution" to infiltrate China and eventually overthrow the CCP.

Similar remarks by Dulles throughout the 1950s coincided with what Mao perceived to be threats to his personal authority by forces both internal and external. In February 1956, Soviet leader Nikita Khrushchev delivered his famous "secret speech" at the 20th Congress of the Communist Party of the Soviet Union denouncing the deceased Joseph Stalin, which Mao viewed as veiled criticism of his own burgeoning cult of personality.[9] A popular uprising against the Communist regime in Hungary later that year exacerbated Mao's fear that his regime was at risk from what he would call "hostile forces." At a meeting with senior party and government leaders in 1959, he raised the issue of a Western plot to overthrow his regime through methods of "peaceful evolution," and from this point on, according to one senior party official, he would "repeatedly alert the whole party on the issue."[10]

"Hostile forces" had been on Mao's mind for much longer than "peaceful evolution," even if he didn't put his name to it until 1948, when the term first appeared in the *People's Daily*. As scholar Michael Dutton has pointed out, the "first line of the first page of the first volume of Mao Zedong's *Selected Works* posed the question, 'Who are our enemies, who are our friends? That is the question germane to the revolution.' "[11] After Chiang Kai-shek's KMT betrayed its alliance with the CCP and murdered thousands of party members in 1927, the "friend" and "enemy" distinction took on a life-and-death importance. From then on, the fear of outside infiltration remained a mainstay of party ideology and practice. A decade after the KMT massacre, Mao delivered a lecture on guerrilla war tactics in which he urged the creation of a new "political director" position in the party to "guard against the infiltration and activity of reactionary elements."[12]

These threats had been a consistent theme from the early years of the revolution. In 1938, Mao warned, "There must be no slackening of vigilance against infiltration by enemy agents."[13] And from the founding of the PRC in 1949, this vigilance became a mainstay of the party's political culture. After the Great Leap Forward, Mao blamed the starvation on local government officials corrupted by KMT subversion. Films such as *Track the Tiger Into Its Lair* (1956) told tales of fifth column spies, saboteurs, and traitors. The "anti-rightist campaign" in 1956 sought to ferret out rogue intellectuals whose *true* purpose was to sabotage the revolution and attack the leadership.

After Mao's death in 1976, warnings of foreign infiltration were tamped down as China courted foreign investment and Deng Xiaoping sought to de-radicalize political culture. Yet the references never completely disappeared: between 1980 and 1988, "hostile forces" appeared in seventy-two articles in the *People's Daily*, mostly clustered around political campaigns, such as one against "Spiritual Pollution" in 1983, and later, during the purge of Hu Yaobang in 1986–1987.

After June 4, however, "hostile forces" and warnings of "peaceful evolution" returned with a vengeance. In 1989 alone, the *People's Daily* ran nearly a hundred articles that referred to "hostile forces," and by 1991, the term appeared more than five hundred times in the paper.[14] In a speech that same year, party leader Jiang Zemin warned, "International hostile forces will never stop using peaceful evolution against us for a single day."[15]

But once the party felt it had regained a partial hold on political stability after 1992, it returned its focus to developing its economy, which included attracting foreign investment and initiating negotiations on membership in the WTO. Phrases such as "hostile forces" and "peaceful evolution" were bad for business. Jiang Zemin spoke less and less of foreign plots, and the phrases largely disappeared from official press such as the *People's Daily* and the speeches of Jiang and other senior leaders.[16]

Below the surface, however, these concerns never went away. In response to the Tiananmen Square protests and the collapse of the Soviet Union, China launched a massive "patriotic education" campaign aiming to inculcate Chinese youths with national pride, and more importantly, party loyalty.[17] "Colleges and universities are a key component in the field of ideology, and so they are also a key objective for the international hostile forces seeking to engage in peaceful evolution," wrote party researchers in Liaoning Province.[18] The head of the Shandong provincial Department of Justice argued that universities needed to construct "iron Great Walls" to combat peaceful evolution. "We need to cultivate the builders and successors of socialism who are both red and expert, completely implement the party's educational line, and place moral education as our top priority," he wrote in 1992.[19]

External events, most notably deteriorating relations with the United States since 1989, convinced many young Chinese that the party's perennial warning of "hostile forces" might not be just propaganda after all.

For the young nationalist writer Song Qiang, the change in attitude by the United States in the early 1990s was jarring. "In the 1970s, China had a massive human rights problem, but the US was friendly and came to China with a smile," Song said. "Yet in the 1990s, the smile faded even though our overall human rights condition had improved."[20]

That the US smile was fading was undeniable.

News reports from the Tiananmen Square crackdown in 1989, including the searing images of fleeing protestors and PLA tanks in the streets of Beijing, outraged the US public and forced a reluctant George H. W. Bush to place sanctions on China. In 1992 the United States announced the sale of F-16 fighter jets to Taiwan, despite a preexisting agreement prohibiting such actions. (China's Foreign Ministry said it was "shocked and outraged" by the sale but did nothing in response.[21]) In September 1993, China lost its bid to host the 2000 Summer Olympic Games, a decision that many Chinese, Song Qiang included, saw as the underhanded work of the United States. That same year, the US Navy detained a Chinese shipping vessel in international waters for twenty-four days, believing (incorrectly) that it was carrying chemical weapons.

In May 1994, Lee Teng-hui, the president of Taiwan (formally the "Republic of China") requested permission from the Clinton administration to stay overnight in Hawaii on his way to Costa Rica. This was no small request, for allowing the democratically elected head of Taiwan on US soil would entail "serious consequences," according to the Chinese ambassador.[22] The United States reacted cautiously, permitting

Lee's plane to spend a mere two hours at the Honolulu airport to refuel and dispatching the chairman of the American Institute of Taiwan (the de facto US embassy to Taiwan) to greet him. A furious Lee refused to leave the plane, telling the US diplomat, "I can't get too close to the door of the plane, I might slip and enter America."[23] Congress wasn't pleased either, and facing mounting pressure, President Clinton agreed to issue Lee a visa the following May to speak at his alma mater, Cornell University, during a June graduate school reunion. (Lee received a PhD in agricultural economics in 1968.) The Chinese government was apoplectic, and to register its disapproval, the PLA conducted a series of missile tests just sixty kilometers north of Taiwanese territory. The United States, in turn, sent the aircraft carrier USS *Nimitz* sailing through the Taiwan Straits, effectively calling China's bluff.

These perceived indignities were accompanied by a rising American triumphalism that, from the perspective of an insecure Communist government, appeared to be directly aimed at overthrowing Beijing. They could read all about it in the American press. Charles Krauthammer argued for "universal domination" in the winter of 1989–1990 in an essay in the *National Interest*, writing, "After having doubly defeated totalitarianism, America's purpose should be to steer the world away from its coming multipolar future toward a qualitatively new outcome—a unipolar world whose center is a confederated West."[24] Krauthammer followed this with a 1995 *Time* magazine piece entitled "Why We Must Contain China." In 1998, journalists Richard Bernstein and Ross Munro published *The Coming Conflict with China*, in which they warned, "China is seeking to replace the United States as the dominant power in Asia."

Paradoxically, just as the new "China threat" orthodoxy typified by the Bernstein and Munro book was gaining popularity, so was the argument that China was on the brink of disintegration or was otherwise irrelevant. *Foreign Affairs* published "The Coming Collapse of China" by Jack Goldstone in the summer of 1995, in which he argued, "China shows every sign of a country approaching crisis."[25] Gerald Segal, again writing in *Foreign Affairs*, declared, "Only when we finally understand how little China matters will we be able to craft a sensible policy toward it," in a piece entitled "Does China Matter?"[26]

These opinions made their way back to China, where they shocked many intellectuals previously disposed to greater emulation of the West, America in particular. For others, the hardening stance of the United States toward China had only been a matter of time.

"I have never believed that the US is really all that concerned with the human rights of the Chinese people," wrote Wang Xiaodong, one of the new breed of self-confident nationalists who emerged in the post-1989 intellectual milieu. "The reason that the US does not like us is because we are strong; we have the possibility of developing and then could be an obstacle to America's special place in the world."[27] In the inaugural issue of the conservative journal *Strategy & Management*, Wang took on Samuel P. Huntington's "clash of civilizations" thesis, which had just been published that summer in *Foreign Affairs*. A conflict with the United States was coming, Wang argued, but it would not come because of incompatible civilizations—for the Chinese generally welcomed US values, he said—but because the two nations would come to have conflicting economic interests.[28] In another piece, he celebrated the "glorious isolation" that would develop as China's "growing political and economic strength begins to penetrate other areas of the world," thus increasing the country's strategic space to make decisions without the interference of American hegemony.[29] On the economic front, he criticized those looking to make "fundamental reforms," writing that "previously we made the mistake of 'cutting off the tail of capitalism,' now do we want to make the mistake of 'cutting off the tail of socialism'?"[30]

International relations scholars Yan Xuetong and Li Zhongcheng warned, "A few Western countries do not want China to become powerful too fast and inevitably will plot in many ways to divide China."[31] In his mid-1990s tract *The Revitalization of China and the Future of the World*, neo-conservative intellectual He Xin wrote,

> On the surface, the United States encouraged China to establish a democratic government with political pluralism. But its real intention was to see a politically soft and weak and internally loose and divided government in China, one that would not be able to rely on its own strength to resolve complicated economic and social problems, mirroring the situation in the current Soviet Union.[32]

The most famous nationalist tract of the 1990s was published in May 1996 under the title *China Can Say No: Political and Emotional Choices in the Post–Cold War Era*, with an afterword by Yu Quanyu, an Old Left conservative and ally of Deng Liqun. The book comprised essays individually written by five authors, covering a variety of topics: from the corrosive influence of Hollywood movies on Chinese values, the activities of the CIA in China (both real and imagined), and the necessity of unifying Taiwan (by force if necessary). It carried chapter titles such as "US Diplomacy Is Dishonest and Irresponsible," "I Will Never Ride on a Boeing 777," and "How the Pro-American Plague Spreads." The book was brimming with pride and argued that China's best days lay ahead. The country was a "colossal nation," and in the twenty-first century it would become "the sole force leading human thought." But in order to fulfill this potential, the Chinese people must first "say no" to outside powers determined to block China's rise.

The *New York Times* accused the tract of "Yankee bashing" and concluded that it "is not so much political analysis as a handbook for anti-American and anti-British slogans, conspiracy theories and satire."[33] Former US ambassador to China James Lilley dismissed *Say No* and its numerous copycats as "propaganda tracts."[34] In *The Coming Conflict with China*, Bernstein and Munro called *Say No* an "anti-American manifesto." Another review slammed it as "a shallow work, reflecting little sophistication about either China or the West," and what's more, the "chief motivation [for writing the book], although the authors deny it, appears to have been to make money, and perhaps to make a splash on the social scene."[35] One academic review inferred that the authors were "more intent upon making a buck and venting their emotions than formulating a scholarly argument."[36] Even Japanese nationalist politician Ishihara Shintaro, whose 1989 essay *The Japan That Can Say No* originally inspired the book, dismissed it as "naive" and "infuriating."[37]

The initial print run of fifty thousand copies was gone within twenty days, and in total it sold more than two million copies.[38] It was translated into eight languages and spawned an industry of other "say no" books, including *China Still Says No*, *China Can Still Say No*, and *Why Does China Say No*. For foreign governments, the book provoked fears of a rising nation powered by revanchist popular nationalism. For China's own government, the surprise popularity of the book reinforced the potential for nationalism to buttress an increasingly ideologically confused Communist Party but, at the same time, provoked deep concerns about an increasingly raucous public square.

Official scrutiny of the book was justified, for when stripped bare of its many pro-party platitudes and its outward support of Beijing, the authors of *China Can Say No* were delivering a threat: stand up to the West—militarily, economically, culturally—or else you will lose the support of the people.

Populist nationalism continued to grow throughout the late 1990s and early 2000s, despite attempts by the party to channel it, or at times, to marginalize or stifle it. The accidental NATO bombing of the Chinese embassy in Belgrade in May 1999, which killed three journalists, sparked fierce protests through the country. Two years later, the Chinese government suppressed popular protests in response to a PLA Navy jet colliding with a US spy plane off the cost of southern China.

A rising sense of nationalism provided critical fuel for Utopia's development. For the first several years of its operation, the group was less concerned with global events and the presence of "hostile forces" in China than it was with issues such as rural taxation, the rights of migrant laborers, and with the erosion of the state-owned economy (as discussed in the previous chapter). But the presence of this "paranoid style" of politics was always just below the surface. One of Utopia's first events, held two months after its founding, featured nationalist writer Wang Xiaodong speaking on the topic "Is the US Using SARS as a Weapon to Target China?" An outbreak of severe acute respiratory syndrome (SARS) had occurred the previous year, and some intellectuals, including Wang Xiaodong saw "hostile forces" at work. "Whether SARS is a genetic weapon of the United States, I have no research and I don't dare say. I just want to talk about the possibility of genetic weapons," Wang prefaced, before going on to say, "the United States has collected a lot of blood samples in China. . . ."[39]

In the wake of the Xishan Conference in 2006, the paranoid style of nationalism that could be traced back to the Mao era, and had been on the rise since the 1990s, suddenly subsumed all other themes to become dominant on the leftist agenda. This was a pronounced turn toward paranoid xenophobia and the belief that a fifth column was actively working to infiltrate, and eventually, destroy the Communist Party in order to thwart China's rise. This transformation coincided with Utopia's increasing popularity and influence. "Our numbers are better these days," Han Deqiang told a US academic in 2007, "as is our ability to coordinate with each other."[40]

Few embodied this shift more completely than Zhang Qinde, a former official at the party's Central Policy Research Office and a long-time Maoist intellectual. At the start of the reforms in the late 1970s, Zhang worked as an editor for the Heilongjiang provincial party committee magazine, *Struggle* (奋斗), which was founded in 1958, just as China was careening toward widespread famine from Mao's Great Leap Forward. In 1989, he was elevated to the Central Policy Research Office, an internal think tank providing policy research and advice to China's top leaders. After the collapse of the Soviet Union, Zhang wrote a series of articles for CCP journals arguing that party leaders must not relinquish political control as they pursued economic reform. In a 1992 article for *Theoretical Exploration*, a bi-monthly publication of the Shanxi provincial party committee, Zhang argued that the essence of China's reforms must remain socialist, otherwise the country was susceptible to "peaceful evolution" through policies that were capitalist in nature.[41] As Zhu Rongji's SOE reforms gained momentum in the late 1990s, Zhang wrote long (and occasionally turgid) defenses of the state-owned economy on ideological and efficiency grounds. His 1999 book on the subject argued that SOEs could overcome lagging profitability by increasing worker participation in management decisions.[42] After Utopia and Maoflag were founded in 2003, he was a regular contributor to both websites, and unconstrained from often suffocating censorship that writing for official party publications entailed, an entirely new and more radical voice emerged.

His response to the Xishan Conference was published on April 30 under the title "Three Warnings from the 'Xishan Incident.'" In it, Zhang accused the attendees of being "agents of Western hostile forces," who were pushing for "privatization, comprehensive marketization, minimizing government functions and a multi-party system" under the rubric of "gradual Westernization." Domestically, they represented "vested interests" composed of the "foreign comprador class," the "old bourgeoisie" and "old landlord" classes, "right opportunists within the

Party," and "corrupt elements within the cadre [ranks]." Even more controversially, Zhang accused conference participants of "intending to seize the highest leadership authority through 'color revolution,'" a reference to the recent popular protest movements in the former Soviet Union. "In order to seize the supreme leadership in this 'color revolution,' [the attendees of the Xishan Conference] openly accused and attacked current top leaders at this meeting," Zhang wrote. "The 'color revolution' carried out by hostile forces at home and abroad may take the form of street politics and economic turmoil, or through a court coup or even a reign of terror."[43]

In response to these charges, Zheng Shengli, a senior attorney at the Northern Tianjin Law Firm, wrote a lengthy rebuttal accusing Zhang of libeling conference attendees, characterizing his writing style as being "deeply influenced by the legacy of the Cultural Revolution," with his penchant for "insulting others" as reminiscent of Yao Wenyuan and Zhang Chunqiao, two members of the Gang of Four.[44] Attacking what she called the "Zhang Qinde Phenomenon," Zheng wrote that the "shadow of the Cultural Revolution" has "warped" those over the age of fifty and negatively influenced the so-called angry youth, a reference to a growing chorus of young nationalist voices.[45] To rectify the situation, Zheng Shengli called on Zhang to "publicly apologize to the victims [the conference participants] before they file a lawsuit . . . and apologize to the majority of netizens."

Needless to say, Zhang Qinde did not apologize, and the letter by Zheng Shengli only served to further intensify the belief that the Xishan Conference was part of a larger conspiracy for "peaceful evolution." Leftist websites like Utopia believed they had uncovered the proverbial smoke-filled room where the real decisions on policy were made by "elite intellectuals" such as He Weifang and Sun Liping. The fact that the conference organizers released a redacted version of the speeches given at Xishan, coupled with the eventual censoring of any mentions of the event online, further fueled the conspiracy narrative.[46]

Few took up the mantle of conspiracy with more alacrity than Zhang Hongliang of Minzu University of China in Beijing. Zhang was an obscure academic until he began associating with Utopia in the summer of 2006. In August, he wrote a blistering attack on the lawyer Zheng Shengli for the Utopia website in which he called her a shill for "international capital" and accused her of aiding "developed countries to plunder developing countries."[47] The only problem was that Zhang was attacking the wrong person, believing that the Zheng Shengli in question was a professor at Peking University Law School rather than Zheng Shengli from the Northern Tianjin Law Firm. After receiving calls from colleagues asking if he was the same person implicated in Zhang Hongliang's article, Prof. Zheng issued a statement clarifying that he had nothing to do with Zhang Qinde or the Xishan Conference.[48]

Zhang Hongliang was unchastened by the mistake, and in the coming years, he played an outsized role in pushing Utopia to the extremes.

Just weeks after his erroneous attack on the Peking University legal scholar, Zhang Hongliang published a lengthy manifesto entitled, "The Current Struggle Between China's Leftists and Rightists."[49] Released thirty years to the day that Mao Zedong died, the article marked the beginning of the modern neo-Maoist movement.

The piece began by noting that the year 2006 was an "important year for China's political and ideological development." It was the seventieth anniversary of the Red Army's fabled six-thousand-mile Long March, one of the key founding myths of the Communist Party. It was the fortieth anniversary of the beginning (and thirtieth anniversary of the end) of the Cultural Revolution, during which, Zhang argued, "the Chinese people carried out an unprecedented reform of the political system" by creating, "for the first time in human history, the establishment of a model of mass politics." The year 2006 also marked the thirtieth anniversary of the death of Mao Zedong, "the great leader of the Chinese people and the soul of the Chinese nation."

Not all anniversaries in 2006 were reasons for celebration, however. It was the twentieth anniversary of what Zhang called the "China liberalization movement," when "some Chinese intellectual elites, now active in the US, began publicly holding up the banner of 'complete Westernization.'" It was the tenth anniversary of the SOE reforms, which Zhang estimated led to the layoffs of sixty million workers.

These events formed dual narratives, Zhang argued, one leading to the salvation of the Chinese nation, the other to its betrayal and submission. The road to salvation required a fundamental realignment back to China's own unique path, one first discovered and traveled by Mao Zedong. The path to defeat began during the Opium Wars of the mid-nineteenth century, when foreign powers occupied and nearly destroyed the country. This continued through Deng's Reform and Opening right up to the present day. "The threats to ancient China came mainly from the West," Zhang wrote. "The threats during modern times came from the east [Japan], and now we are surrounded by threats."

Zhang held there were three groups vying for power of China's political system in order to determine which road the country would travel.

"Rightists" worked on behalf of "bureaucratic compradors" and other "vested interests." Under their influence, trillions of dollars in state assets were "stolen," while "international anti-China forces," with the help of "US state terrorism," tried to destroy China and the Communist Party. They were "fabricating political rumors" about the Mao era, including "lies" about mass famine during the Great Leap Forward and "chaos" caused by the Cultural Revolution.

The second group in Zhang's taxonomy was the "Old Left" comprised of the "old privileged class" who controlled the party-state bureaucracy prior to the start of the economic reforms in the late 1970s. While initially sympathetic to the reform agenda, they gradually turned against the reforms as they saw social, economic, and political problems manifest. Another distinguishing feature of the Old Left was their condemnation of the Cultural Revolution and their aversion to the Mao-era politics of mass campaigns. While Zhang does not list names, it's clear here that he's referring to "conservatives" like Chen Yun and Deng Liqun.

Both the Rightists and the Old Left emerged out of the Cultural Revolution, and, Zhang argued, their power remained relatively balanced during the Deng era. Zhang highlights as evidence Deng's "four cardinal principles," which supported economic reforms but only within a framework of political and ideological guardrails. These two groups likewise supported the party's official judgment that the Cultural Revolution was a disaster not to be repeated.

Zhang saw both groups as now undermining China's progress. What the country needed, and now had, was a third group—a "new left"— that would oppose Deng-style economic reforms and embrace the Maoist legacy—all of it—including (indeed especially) the Cultural

Revolution and its great innovations in "mass democracy." And this was relevant today, Zhang concluded, because China was threatened by a wave of "color revolutions" incited and supported by the United States. "If the Rightists launch a 'color revolution' [in China], it is only the New Left which has the power to transform this color revolution into a second Cultural Revolution to completely bury the Rightists."

Zhang's article, with its open reverence for Mao Zedong and its revisionist account of the Cultural Revolution, opened the floodgates for similar paeans to the Great Helmsman and his past campaigns.

On December 26, Ma Bin, a member of the Communist Party since 1935 and one of the signatories to the 2002 open letter opposing Jiang Zemin's proposal to admit capitalists into the CCP, published *Commemorating Mao Zedong* (纪念毛泽东). "It's been almost 30 years since the initial stages of the first Cultural Revolution," Ma wrote, "and it's time that we begin planning and actively preparing for the next stage of the first Cultural Revolution, or what we can call the Second Cultural Revolution." Bringing to mind Thomas Jefferson's 1787 letter to James Madison, in which he stated, "a little rebellion now and then is a good thing," Ma Bin believed China should wage a cultural revolution every seven to eight years in order to prevent a "capitalist restoration."

At a Utopia event commemorating Ma Bin's book, writer Qiu Shike praised Ma for his "correct and thorough" understanding of the Cultural Revolution. "Recently, many older comrades have begun to reflect on the history of the Cultural Revolution . . . and have affirmed [it] to varying degrees."[50] When compared to the near-wholesale condemnation of the Cultural Revolution throughout the 1980s and '90s, to have a public declaration of support from a figure of Ma Bin's standing was significant. Zhang Hongliang concurred: "We look forward to the day when even more cadres like Teacher Ma will emerge."[51]

The year 2006 was a turning point for Utopia, for it was no longer a gathering place for pan-leftist voices. Despite Zhang Hongliang's use of the label "new left" to describe his third political force, there was diminishing common ground between groups like Utopia and the New Left thinkers like Cui Zhiyuan and Wang Hui. Instead, it was a conspiratorial, openly Maoist, and aggressively nationalistic style of ideological agitation that would dominate. The organization was rapidly morphing into an overtly political organization, one that saw a direct connection between its work in the ideological realm and actual changes to policy.

Crucially, Mao Zedong was becoming an essential feature of the group's identity, both because they genuinely believed that Mao Zedong Thought offered solutions for China, but also because they saw the "banner of Mao" as the most effective means of spreading their message.

Despite the 1981 "History Resolution," which pinned much of the blame for the excesses of the Cultural Revolution on Mao, all subsequent party leaders were careful to ensure that core features of Mao's personal and historical legacy remained intact. This symbolic immunity made Mao a powerful totem for marginalized figures who could attack the party leadership simply by quoting Mao's words or evoking (admittedly rosy) memories of the Mao era. C. K. Lee, in her powerful study of labor unrest in the 1990s and 2000s, reported that widespread nostalgia for Mao was common among China's workers. One retiree told her, "Openness and reform work only for those with ability, culture, and knowledge and for those who are sneaky. For honest, ordinary, and mediocre people like us, Mao's egalitarianism was much better."[52] Such nostalgia was not unique to China and could be found in varying degrees in almost all post-Communist systems.[53] In the former German Democratic Republic (GDR), it was known as "Ostalgie," or "nostalgia for the east." As novelist Fritz Stern has written, "The older generation began to cleanse its memory of the oppressive aspects of the GDR and remember gratefully the parochial privacy, slowness and predictability of its 'socialist' life."[54]

What was unique to China, however, was the ability to channel Maoist nostalgia and co-opt Maoist symbolism as a political weapon. Utopia, and the growing number of websites and organizations comprising what was increasingly known as neo-Maoism, believed Mao Zedong's legacy possessed instrumental, as well as symbolic, power. This was something similar to what the Tea Party in the United States had done with the legacy of the Founding Fathers. "If you don't use the banner of Mao, you're nobody. Who would believe in you?" Yang Fan said.[55] With Mao on their side, the neo-Maoists believed they had the power to crush their political enemies and ensure that the party returned to the path of true socialism.

On October 3, 2008, Zhang Xiaobo, Song Qiang, and Wang Xiaodong, three of the authors of the 1996 bestselling nationalist tract *China Can Say No*, gathered on the outskirts of Beijing to take stock of recent developments in China. They were joined by current affairs commentator Liu Yang, Marxist playwright and frequent Utopia contributor Huang Jisu, and former PLA Navy officer-turned-state-TV-commentator Song Xiaojun. While China had experienced more traumatic years in its history, by any reckoning, 2008 had been an extraordinary year.

In March, demonstrations erupted in Tibet's capital, Lhasa, which proved the most serious unrest in the area in decades. In response to the Chinese government's subsequent crackdown, demonstrators in Paris attacked a twenty-seven-year-old Chinese Paralympic athlete named Jin Jing as she carried the Olympic torch on its journey to Beijing for the Summer Olympic Games, which were scheduled to start later that year. The event outraged many Chinese and made Jin a folk hero. "I would die to protect the torch," she told state media.[56] On May 12, Sichuan Province was rocked by a massive earthquake that killed nearly seventy thousand people and left nearly five million homeless. In August, China successfully hosted the Summer Olympics, which foreign media dubbed China's "coming out party."[57] The following month, the US financial services firm Lehman Brothers collapsed, sparking the most severe global financial crisis since the Great Depression.

For three days in October, the six individuals discussed the state of China and the world. Wang Xiaodong believed that the global financial crisis "showed that the Chinese people shouldn't copy the West" and that "those who thought we should travel the US road no longer had any right to speak."[58] Song Qiang argued that the West was "facing a crisis," which only strengthened the thesis that China should "say no" to the US-dominated global order.[59]

Co-author Zhang Xiaobo made an audio recording of their discussions, and in March 2009 the edited transcripts were published in book form under the title *Unhappy China: The Great Time, The Grand Vision and Our Challenges*. If the message of *China Can Say No* was that the country sought to remain free from foreign meddling as it charted a path to economic and political modernization, *Unhappy China* had a different message: China was ready to rule the world. "With Chinese national strength growing at an unprecedented rate, China should stop debasing itself and come to recognize the fact that it has the power to lead the world and the necessity to break away from Western influence," its authors declared.

The book was immediately controversial. As with *China Can Say No*, it was criticized for being a salacious cash grab. Others, like international relations scholar Shi Yinhong, believed the book was counterproductive, telling the *International Herald Leader*, "I think these individuals have a distinctive feature: they have lots of criticisms, but very few constructive suggestions."[60] Former liberal party propagandist Wu Jiaxiang argued that the book carried a "virus" that could infect the "psychology of the nation."[61] Neo-authoritarian scholar Xiao Gongqin told *Xinmin Weekly*, "There is no question that what the authors of this book are promoting is a high-pitched, vainly arrogant and radical form of nationalism."[62] One co-author of a book-length criticism of *Unhappy China* argued, "If we reject the West, the result will be a closed nation. The further we lag behind, the more we will suffer indignities and China will never be able to stand up."[63]

This outraged reaction was precisely what the authors of *Unhappy China* were hoping for, especially if it helped their message reach the United States. "Our book is meant to make people uncomfortable with the status quo and think about changes," Song Qiang told one newspaper. "Our role is like a flea and we want the US government to know about our existence," he added.[64] Wang Xiaodong's message for the US was less subtle: "If you don't respect us we will beat you up."[65]

But what was the message for Beijing?

Its success clearly unnerved Chinese officials, who had long seen grassroots nationalism as a double-edged sword.[66] On the one hand, an increasingly nationalistic population offered the party a powerful source of legitimacy, especially when faced with external challenges, both real and imagined. Yet this nationalist support carried corresponding risks. As Cornell University's Jessica Chen Weiss has argued, "Nationalism promotes love of the nation, not love of the government, meaning that nationalistic protest can easily escalate to demands for revolution if the public feels that the government has failed to defend the nation from foreign deprecations."[67]

Both Song Qiang and Wang Xiaodong claimed that portions of the manuscript dealing with Mao Zedong, democracy, and other domestic political issues were removed by government censors for being too con-troversial.[68] Rumors circulated that the Propaganda Department had instructed that the book receive negative reviews, although the fact that the book was still allowed to be sold indicated that there were some in the party who supported its message, or at least found its existence helpful insofar as it staked out a more radical extreme. Wang Xiaodong and Song Qiang stated that the book was displayed in the back of bookstores rather than in the front, and reports from *Xinhua* seem to confirm this point: "Major book retailers . . . have stocked the book on inconspicuous shelves labeled with 'Chinese politics.' "[69]

One can understand the party's concern over *Unhappy China* and the possibility that it might further incite a populist nationalist movement, one which was already fueled by a cocktail of legitimate grievances, conspiratorial paranoia, and an ever-expanding online ecosystem that appeared to operate outside the normal rules of Chinese politics. As in the mid-1990s, the period beginning in 2006 saw an explosion of new voices in print and online pushing new demands on the party leadership.

Some of these voices called on China to play a more assertive role in protecting and advocating its national interests. Others made even more radical claims. In 2007, financial analyst Song Hongbing published *Currency Wars* (货币战争), which argued that the West, the United States in particular, was controlled by a group of international bankers who made massive fortunes from currency manipulation. Song believed that Jewish people (especially the Rothschilds) played a central role in this global plot, although he later denied charges of anti-Semitism.[70] In 2009, he followed up with *Currency Wars 2*, which predicted that this same cabal of Jewish bankers would successfully establish a new global currency by 2024, which they alone would control.

In 2010, writer Mo Luo released *China Rises: Our Future, Destiny, and Spiritual Independence*, which criticized a "cult of the West" that had "infected" the Chinese people since the May Fourth Movement in 1919. If China truly wanted to become a great nation, it should cease worshipping foreign cultures and begin respecting its own iden-tity. "There are some well-known elite in China who play the role of thought police on behalf of Western colonial forces," Luo wrote. "As soon as there are signs of an ideology that the West does not like, these individuals grab the fire extinguisher."[71]

Utopia was eager to capitalize on the ensuing debate.

At an event in April 2009, nominally to discuss the impact of *Unhappy China*, co-author Wang Xiaodong used the book's surprise success to issue a call to action. "I thought if we sold 50,000 copies and a few people read it, that would be all right," but now that it had "aroused such a big debate, let's not waste it, let's not limit it to this book," he said.[72]

Su Tieshan also spoke at the event. His father, Su Jin, was a legendary military commander who had been on the Long March with Mao and fought against both the Japanese in World War II and against the KMT in China's civil war. This made Su Tieshan a princeling, a "second-generation red," and an influential backer of the neo-Maoist movement.

"Everyone knows I'm a descendant of the Red Army," he said in his remarks, "and recently I've been thinking about the crisis facing the Communist Party." China was facing a crisis that needed to be addressed, he warned. There were three major problems, Su argued, including a moral crisis born of the party's abandonment of its close relationship with the people. Second, the party was becoming ideologically confused the more it departed from Mao Zedong Thought. "The political logic of the first three decades [of the PRC] was complete, powerful, and consistent with social practice," he said. But now, "the internal political logic is very chaotic and is deeply inconsistent with social practice." Finally, the Chinese people were increasingly dissatisfied with the direction of the country, owing to the breakdown of an economic order that once provided health care, education, and a high degree of social equity.

"Why do I say these things in such a public place today? I just hope someone can pass these words along to the ears of [Beijing]."

He needn't have worried, for the authorities were already paying attention to Utopia and groups like it.

In 2005, the government briefly closed Utopia's website due to the group's activism on behalf of Wang Binyu, a young migrant laborer who was executed for murdering his boss and three others after his wages were illegally withheld for two years. On September 12 of that year,

Utopia joined the websites Workers Online (中国工人网) and Left Bank (左岸) to issue an online petition calling for judicial authorities to give Wang a reprieve from the death penalty and for his brother to be compensated for the years of wage nonpayment. After sympathetic accounts of the case in national newspapers garnered public sympathy for Wang's case, Utopia organized several events at their bookstore to discuss Wang's treatment and the plight of migrant workers throughout China. A gathering on September 21 drew 120 participants, with speeches by well-known legal and human rights activist Teng Biao, now exiled in the US. In his remarks, Han Deqiang claimed that the heads of several private firms in Ningxia Province (where Wang was being tried) had warned the local court that if they didn't sentence Wang to death, companies would lose control of their employees. This was an extraordinary claim and one that Han asserted without offering any evidence. Utopia's website was blocked the same day and didn't reopen until the following month.

Authorities shuttered the websites of China Workers' Net and Communists Net the following year, ostensibly because the websites had failed to comply with legal requirements for a minimum of registered capital. In an interview, China Workers' Net administrator Yan Yuanzhang described his website as a "stick of dynamite" for the CCP. He explained, "From [the government's] vantage, our discussion list has made available information about workers' strikes in China, right? Right-wing websites that are declared enemies of the CCP then take that information and transfer it to their sites. This is detrimental to the image of the Party since foreign media will pick up on such information and use it to attack the CCP."[73]

According to a leaked US embassy cable, Zhang Xiaojin, the associate dean of international studies at People's University, told American officials that Chinese authorities were increasingly nervous about "ideological" and "protest" websites and had implemented "more aggressive monitoring" over sites of "special concern." According to Zhang, "the State Council and Beijing Information Offices recently convened a meeting of Internet monitors to discuss tight control of seven websites," among which were "two ultra-left sites, Utopia and Maoflag."[74]

But it was a lengthy piece circulating on neo-Maoist websites in March 2009 that likely proved most concerning for party authorities.

The anonymous report claimed that on December 26, 2008, the 115th anniversary of Mao Zedong's birth, citizens from cities around China formed a new political party: the "Mao Zedong Communist Party." Their online manifesto called for the realization of Mao's vision of a true and workable socialism, one that would restore the people's communes, establish "people's supervisory councils" to oversee state-owned firms, and guarantee housing and employment to all citizens. In order to realize this vision, the party demanded that the "counter-revolutionary ruling bloc resign voluntarily," and if that failed, then the "proletariat" should overthrow them through a "revolutionary baptism through blood and fire."[75]

Utopia denied any involvement with the fledgling party, but that didn't mean they were going to avoid direct involvement in China's political system. Since 2003, the organization had grown from obscurity into the leader of a genuine political movement, neo-Maoism. It combined grassroots popularity with deep connections to current and former party officials, including the offspring of the country's political aristocracy. But there was only so much the neo-Maoists could accomplish through bookstore events and online activism. What the movement needed was a leader, someone to propel their cause onto the national stage.

In Bo Xilai, the charismatic party secretary of the southwestern metropolis Chongqing, the neo-Maoists believed they'd finally found someone to continue Mao's revolution.

5

Bombard the Headquarters

And beneath the surface of an ever more sophisticated society what dark passions and inflammable credulities do we find, sometimes accidentally released, sometimes deliberately mobilized!
— Hugh Trevor-Roper, *The Crisis of the Seventeenth Century*, 1967

GOVERNMENT PRESS CONFERENCES IN China aren't usually dramatic affairs. But Premier Wen Jiabao's final appearance before stepping down from office was different.

During a three-hour Q&A session on March 14, 2012, marking the conclusion of the annual National People's Congress and the Chinese People's Political Consultative Conference, together known as the "two meetings," a Singaporean journalist asked Wen about political reform in China.

His response, although clearly prepared, was nonetheless remarkable for its directness: without future reforms "such historical tragedy as the Cultural Revolution might happen again."[1]

Since Ma Bin's call for a "second Cultural Revolution" in 2006 and the normalization Mao-era "class struggle" discourse by neo-Maoist organizations such as Utopia and Maoflag, liberal-leaning intellectuals had stepped up their warnings of a populist threat to China's Reform-era gains and the country's political and economic stability. While party propaganda organs regularly intervened to contain both sides of the debate, statements from China's top leaders remained confined to platitudes about the importance of reform to China's modernization and the need for "harmonious development." They had rarely, if ever, weighed directly into political controversy or aired the party's dirty laundry in public.

Until now.

Within minutes of Wen's remarks, traffic to Utopia's website exploded.[2] The next morning, the website was blocked, as were nearly one dozen other neo-Maoist websites. Those who could circumvent China's "Great Firewall" to access the sites were greeted with a message of defiance, and a warning for Wen Jiabao and the party's leadership in Beijing: "Fake Communists Have Seized Power in New China."[3]

One month before the National People's Congress, Wang Lijun, the police chief of the southwest metropolis of Chongqing, reportedly disguised himself as a woman and drove to the US Consulate in nearby Chengdu. He brought with him rumors of intrigue at the highest reaches of the party—including infidelities, corruption, and even murder—and he wanted the Americans to protect him. After thirty-six hours of questioning, US diplomats calculated that sheltering Wang wasn't worth angering Beijing, and he was unceremoniously turned over to security officials from Beijing. (The State Department claimed he'd "left of his own volition.") A party investigation was quickly launched, and state media reported that Wang would undergo "vacation-style medical treatment" for mental stress.

For Wang's boss, Chongqing party secretary Bo Xilai, a precipitous fall from power was imminent, and for a time, it seemed as though he would take the entire neo-Maoist movement down with him.

The son of the legendary party "immortal" Bo Yibo, Bo Xilai was raised as a member of China's red aristocracy. After the outbreak of the Cultural Revolution in 1966, however, elite bloodlines could be a curse as well as a blessing. In 1966, Kang Sheng, the head of internal security and intelligence, presented Mao Zedong with an old newspaper clipping that contained an anti-party comment purportedly made by the elder Bo in order to secure his release from a KMT prison in 1936. This was enough for Bo, who'd been a Communist Party member for forty years, to spend the next decade in jail. His wife, and Bo Xilai's mother, Hu Ming, died in 1967 while being transported by Red Guards from Guangzhou to Beijing. The Red Guards claimed she had committed suicide, but rumors of her murder persist to this day. Despite this, Bo Yibo still kept his faith. "Even though I have no freedom, I still worship Mao," he once said.[4]

As the children of a disgraced party leader, Bo Xilai and his brothers were subject to frequent abuse by the Red Guards. As one sinister playground rhyme went, "The father's a hero, the son's a brave lad; the father's a reactionary, the son's a bastard."[5] But in the chaos of the Cultural Revolution, victims could also be tyrants, and Bo's classmates would remember him participating in the violence as a member of the "United Action" Red Guard faction.[6]

After Bo Yibo was rehabilitated in 1978, his son's fortunes improved. At age thirty, he was admitted to Peking University, where he studied world history and journalism. Even then, Bo stood out. "Bo Xilai was the biggest figure in my class," remembers one classmate.[7] Rather than pursue a career in journalism, Bo turned to politics. During the early 1980s, Bo worked in the party's Central Secretariat and in its General Office before being assigned to Dalian, a coastal city in Liaoning Province, where he served as the deputy party secretary.

From the beginning, he was a different type of party official, more retail politician than bland apparatchik. In a system that rewarded quiet competence and discipline, Bo conspicuously lacked both. He wore expensive suits, hired his own biographer, and enjoyed speaking to the media. His second wife, Gu Kailai, shared his instincts for self-promotion: After winning a legal case in the United States, she cashed in on the victory, writing a book and producing a TV show called *Winning a Lawsuit in America*.

Having grown up in the inner sanctum of the party, Bo also understood how the system really worked. After his promotion to become the mayor of Dalian, he erected a five-story display of the General Secretary Jiang Zemin in the city's main square. This was one of the "nauseating displays of loyalty," in the words of political scientist Victor Shih, that helped ambitious cadres climb their way up the party hierarchy.[8]

Yet this was a selective loyalty that didn't extend to his immediate superiors. In Dalian, Bo frequently made important decisions without consulting his boss, the municipal party secretary. In response, he failed to receive enough votes to be selected as a local delegate to the Fifteenth Party Congress in 1997. But this didn't deter Bo, and in 2002, he secured a seat on the party's Central Committee and two years later was promoted to become the Minister of Commerce. This new position gave him prominence in Beijing and internationally, and rumors circulated that Bo's next objective was a seat on the Politburo and one day, its Standing Committee—the pinnacle of power in China's one-party system.

Despite his obvious political skill and undeniable charisma, Bo Xilai was still riding on the coattails of his powerful father. Despite having long since retired from his formal positions in the party, the elder Bo was still incredibly influential in political circles, his status as one of the party's "eight immortals" continuing to shield and strengthen that of his son. In January 2007, however, at the age of ninety-eight, Bo Yibo passed away. Bo Xilai lost both his father and his most important political benefactor. He was now on his own.

That November, the party sent the newly politically exposed Bo mixed messages. On the one hand, he was granted a seat on the twenty-five-member Politburo, yet at the same time, he was being reassigned from his high-profile role at the Ministry of Commerce in Beijing to the southern-central city of Chongqing, some one thousand miles inland, as its next party secretary.

Chongqing was by no means a backwater. It served as China's capital during World War II and is one of only four cities directly administered by the State Council in Beijing. For most party officials, a stint leading Chongqing would mark the pinnacle of their career.

But Bo wasn't like most party officials. He was an ambitious man in a hurry, and he had no intention of quietly marking time. Instead, he quickly set about transforming the city into a staging ground for his political assault on Beijing.

Since at least Deng's Southern Tour in 1992, China's economic development model had been relatively straightforward—growth at all costs. This emphasis on what the watered-down Marxists in the CCP leadership called "productive forces" created a cascade of social and economic maladies, from environmental degradation to rampant corruption. This wasn't a bug of the system either: Officials were evaluated and promoted on their ability to drive GDP growth. And by the time problems emerged in a given locality, cadres were often already in some new location preparing to repeat the process. In addition, capricious local officials were abusing their positions to extract unsanctioned taxes from citizens (primarily rural peasants), and to use their power to confiscate land at below-market prices and sell it to developers for commercial and residential projects.

Around the time of Bo's arrival in Chongqing, a series of scandals added to the growing sense that China's economic and political system, while delivering on increased national prestige, was unable to meet the basic needs of its people. In one of the more egregious cases, children were abducted and sold into slavery to work in brick kilns. After growing frustrated with the inaction of local police departments, groups of parents began traveling across China's countryside looking for their missing children, prompting sympathetic coverage from local media and public outrage on the Internet.[9] In another scandal, first reported in 2008, six infants died and an estimated three hundred thousand were poisoned by baby formula and milk spiked with melamine, a chemical used in the production of plastics and adhesives, which had been added to boost the protein content.

The anger felt by many Chinese was captured in an essay on the Utopia website in 2011 that's worth quoting at length:

> [The] contradictions and conflicts in Chinese society have sharply intensified: a small spark of discontent can start a great fire of social unrest. In the eyes of bureaucrats, compradors, and traitors, they see China in a time of peace and prosperity. However, in the eyes of ordinary people, we see corrupt officials, one after another, shamelessly and insatiably stealing and plundering the wealth of our nation in order to send it abroad. We see officials who have sent all of their families abroad, who abuse their power for personal gain, colluding with businessmen and local gangs, who speak and behave hypocritically and shamelessly and squander trillions of RMB of public money. We see the wealth of China concentrated in those who "got rich first," none of them by honest means. We see slave labor in illegal brickyards and coalmines, and countless rural migrant workers beaten to death or to disability just because they want to recover unpaid wages from employers. They are even willing to have a thoracotomy just to show that they have [black lung] and get compensated from the [mining] company they work for. We see rivers polluted

and natural resources depleted, and our complete industrial system set up during Mao Zedong's era now purchased and controlled by foreigners. We see local governments selling off land for money, and there is almost no cutting-edge technology in our GDP. We see a marketized educational system, in which treacherous professors and experts sell their theories that turn Chinese people into slaves of foreigners, and secure public money for their research projects by cheating. We see a wicked marketized healthcare system, vulgar mass media, declining moral standard in our society, and resurgence of prostitution, gambling, and drug using. We see China, once famous for its cleanness and fairness, now even worse than India in terms of the gap between the rich and the poor. We see corruption in every corner of our society. This is why we miss Mao Zedong and his era.[10]

Bo Xilai stepped into this cauldron of anger and saw an opportunity. His response was a series of policies aimed at addressing issues of long-standing importance to migrants, farmers, and young workers in Chongqing, including the availability of affordable housing, land-use rights, and urban residency permits. He also set out to tackle the city's flagging state-owned enterprises, which had slumped in productivity and profitability but, Bo argued, needed revitalization rather than privatization. He also pledged that between 2010 and 2020, Chongqing would build more than forty million square meters of public housing, with rent controlled at 40 percent below the market price. His announced property reforms would ensure that agricultural land was not sacrificed for urban expansion (which typically benefited developers at the expense of farmers). Finally, he promised a relaxation of the city's residency permit system for migrants, the much-loathed *hukou*, that would greatly expand access to social services and give legal standing in the city.[11]

In a February 2009 cover story, Hong Kong's *Asia Weekly* dubbed this the "Chongqing Model" and celebrated Bo's "innovative new thinking," which had become a "brand-new engine for China's economic transformation and a new model leading China out of the [2008] financial crisis."[12]

The city's mayor and Bo's number-two, Huang Qifan, argued that Chongqing's policies were both good for the people *and* for business, and that the Chongqing Model could be described as "Marx Plus Reagan."[13]

Chongqing soon attracted support from a wide array of leftist intellectuals who viewed it as having the potential to shape a new economic development model for China, one that put "common prosperity" and social equity above the growth-at-all-costs development model that had predominated since the early 1990s.

The New Left scholar and Tsinghua University academic Cui Zhiyuan traveled to Chongqing eight times to research what he called the "Chongqing experience," and he later accepted a one-year leave of absence from his teaching duties to serve as special assistant to the agency that oversaw the city's SOEs. Cui believed Chongqing was exploring "the reform and innovation of the socialist market economy in order to realize socialist values driven by the people's livelihood."[14]

Famed political scientist Wang Shaoguang dubbed Bo's experiment "Chinese socialism 3.0" and argued that it showed China's continuous exploration for new and improved modes of economic, social, and political development.[15]

Li Xiguang, the co-author of the mid-1990s bestseller *Behind the Demonization of China*, which argued that the US was leading an international plot to contain China, saw in Chongqing the realization of China's national goal of "strong nation, prosperous people." More than this, Li argued, "Chongqing's experience has not only broken the Washington consensus, but has also surpassed the Japanese and East Asian models."[16]

Larry Lang told a journalist from the *Nanjing Daily*, "I personally think that under the current real estate situation, only the Chongqing Model can save Chinese real estate. If the Chongqing Model is promoted, China's real estate market will gradually stabilize, and our stock market will gradually rise."[17]

International media descended on Chongqing, both reflecting Bo's increasing prominence and simultaneously inflating it. "New Party Boss Brings Hope to Chongqing," declared the *New York Times* in February 2008. CNN included him in its list of "Who Mattered Most in Asia 2009," declaring that Bo "had a year so good that he's now projected to succeed Hu Jintao."[18] Henry Kissinger, the architect of US-China relations, met with Bo in Chongqing in June 2011 and came away impressed: "Chongqing is completely beyond my imagination. Chongqing today benefits from the great imagination of the leaders and the hard work of the people of Chongqing. The vitality of Chongqing makes me feel excited."[19] Kissinger said the Bo effect was inspiring a new generation of would-be cadres, telling historian Simon Schama, "One of my associates who has been in China tells me that university graduates who 10 years ago all wanted to be Goldman Sachs executives now want to be government officials [because of Bo]."[20]

Coinciding with the local popularity and national acclaim for his Chongqing Model, Bo undertook a widespread and ruthless anti-crime campaign named "strike black," a reference to organized crime, which is known in Chinese as the "black society." Ostensibly aimed at breaking the back of the city's mafia, the campaign utilized rough-hand tactics and a flagrant disregard for legal procedure. Under the leadership of police chief Wang Lijun, thousands were arrested, including Wen Qiang, the head of the city's justice department. Wen's sister-in-law, Xie Caiping, was also arrested: she oversaw a vast network of illegal casinos, including one situated across the street from the Supreme Court building. Li Zhuang, a lawyer who was imprisoned for more than five hundred days on trumped-up charges of perjury, told journalist Carrie Gracie, "Wang and Bo were very similar. Both of them liked to do things on an epic scale, they liked to make headlines. Put them together and it was an explosive mix."[21]

As a university journalism major, Bo understood the power of the soundbite and courted the media to bolster the campaign's popularity. "The Triads are chopping up people, just like butchers killing animals," he told local reporters.[22] After the sentencing of Xie Caiping, dubbed the "godmother of the underworld" despite being only forty-six years old, Bo exclaimed: "This kind of behavior wouldn't have been tolerated even under the Qing dynasty!"[23]

While Bo's crackdown on crime and corruption proved popular with Chongqing residents, it also had the benefit of highlighting problems that had accumulated under the watch of Wang Yang, his predecessor in Chongqing and the then-current party secretary of Guangdong Province. Like Bo, Wang was gunning for higher office and using his own unique mix of policy and panache to get there. Unlike Chongqing, with its emphasis on what Bo had begun to call "shared prosperity" and a heavy reliance on state intervention and subsidies, the Guangdong Model preached a gospel of market-driven wealth creation and the rule of law. In the media, the competition between the two models was quickly dubbed the "cake debate" (蛋糕论), after the two party leaders made remarks about whether it was best to enlarge the economic cake (Wang) or to share it more equally (Bo). "Some cadres subconsciously think the only cake worth talking about is one that's big," Bo told the *Chongqing Daily* in November 2010 in a clear reference to Wang. "But a cake with no justice is not just a bad cake, but even its maker won't find it interesting."[24] Under Bo's "strike black" campaign, the more crime and corruption Bo could unearth, the louder the implicit point—this is what you get with Wang in charge.

It was a rare public spat between two rapidly rising party officials, and as the debate played out in public, space opened up for (limited) political participation and ideological debate. Reformers and liberals rallied in support of Wang Yang, while China's left-leaning intellectuals cheered on Bo. And for a time, Beijing appeared content to simply spectate, likely a reflection of uncertainty as to which side to support. While Wang's Guangdong Model was pitched as carrying forward the spirit of Deng Xiaoping's economic reforms, Bo's emphasis on social inclusion and shared wealth made it difficult for a nominally socialist government to ignore or oppose him.

The ferocity and extra-legality of Bo's "strike black" crackdown sent chills through China's community of lawyers and human rights advocates. After visiting Chongqing in April 2011, He Weifang, the outspoken law professor who attended the 2006 Xishan Conference, published an open letter addressed to his "colleagues in the legal world in Chongqing." He had graduated from the city's Southwest University of Political Science and Law in 1982 but "thirty years have passed, and so many things have happened in this city with which we are so intimately familiar, things that cause one to feel that time has been dialed back, that the Cultural Revolution is being replayed, and that the ideal of rule of law is right now being lost."[25]

It wasn't just Bo's unabashed use of state violence in the "strike black" campaign that evoked comparisons to Mao's Cultural Revolution. In June 2008, Bo initiated a "red culture campaign" with an "Ode to the Dear Party" singing contest for municipal employees and the promotion of thirty-six newly written "red songs" that glorified the party and the nation. The campaign quickly expanded to include red text messages—some reputedly from Bo himself—red concerts and galas, and red TV shows. According to one report, there had been more than 148,000 "singing red" performances, reaching a total audience of eighty-seven million by the end of 2010.[26] Together with the crime crackdown, Bo's project became known as "strike black, sing red."

By the standards of the actual Cultural Revolution, Bo's red revival was relatively tame. There were no open gun battles between opposing Red Guard factions, the songs were devoid of calls for global revolution and class struggle, and all group events were highly regulated affairs. This was the era of stability maintenance, after all. But the open celebration of Mao-era culture and imagery was deeply unnerving to those who worried that the political and economic gains China had made since Mao's death were still too fragile to withstand such a campaign.

Bo dismissed such criticisms, calling them "complete nonsense."[27] During a 2011 speech to mark the ninetieth anniversary of the Communist Party's founding, Bo said, "There's a strange phenomenon nowadays: people sing obscene songs, and no one takes notice. But we sing a few red songs, and suddenly people start to criticize us, saying we're leftists, or that we're returning to the 'Cultural Revolution.' " To Bo, the people tossing around accusations of extreme leftism "loathe the Communist Party's ideology."[28]

Chinese politics, much like politics in modern democracies, makes ample use of what political scientists call the "dog whistle effect," a term that arose from US election polling in the 1980s to refer to coded references that only certain groups or constituencies could understand. Bo Xilai understood the dog whistle, as evidenced by his July 1 speech, which, although it mocked those who warned of a second Cultural Revolution, also avoided any direct criticism of the Cultural Revolution. Zhang Hongliang heard the coded reference loud and clear. "This is the only such speech in more than 30 years that hasn't specifically celebrated Reform and Opening or criticized the 'Cultural Revolution Error and the Extreme Left Line,' " Zhang wrote on the Red Song Society website. What Bo understands, Zhang speculated, is that "[criticism of the] Cultural Revolution has become a sharp blade for extreme right-wing forces at home and abroad to butcher the Chinese nation."[29]

For the neo-Maoist movement, this was the first time in a long time that an alternative development model had been openly promoted by a Politburo member. Since 1992, if not before, they'd felt like political and ideological outcasts, marginalized as their core convictions clashed with Beijing's increasingly eclectic mix of socialist rhetoric and capitalist policies. With Bo's political ambitions and the popularity of his Chongqing Model, they saw a path to power, if not for them personally, then at least for their ideas. While Bo—with his tailored suits and his Oxford-educated son—made for an unlikely Communist folk hero, for neo-Maoists it came down to the simple mathematics of choice: it was either Bo or the status quo. "Before we were just scholars, but now we have a political leader recognized by people both inside and outside the system," Han Deqiang told journalist Chris Buckley.[30]

Key members of the neo-Maoist movement began making pilgrimages to Chongqing. In November 2010, Liu Yang and Song Qiang (co-authors of *Unhappy China*), independent scholar Sima Pingbang, and playwright Huang Jisu met with Chongqing's top cop, Wang Lijun. Sima Nan did the same the following summer. Utopia co-founder Fan Jinggang and eighty supporters visited the city, where they were greeted by officials from the municipal Public Security Bureau. While Bo avoided direct contact with groups such as Utopia, by making key individuals such as Wang Lijun available, the neo-Maoists believed he was sending a message: I hear you.[31]

Back in Beijing, Utopia held conferences extolling the virtues of Bo, his Chongqing Model, and the "strike black, sing red" campaign. At a December 2010 event at Utopia's offices, attendees agreed that the appearance of Bo and the Chongqing Model was "inevitable" given the negative side effects of China's economic reforms. At a Utopia event in Chongqing, held on the 117th anniversary of Mao Zedong's birth, Sima Pingbang, by this point a frequent visitor to the city, reported that Bo Xilai not only openly admired Mao Zedong, but could even recite entire paragraphs of the Chairman's articles from memory.[32] At the third and final of Utopia's Chongqing events, the tone of discussion became more resolute. "So long as a person is patriotic and holds the masses in their heart, they should accept [the Chongqing Model]," the conference summary concluded.[33]

Online, Bo's legions of neo-Maoist supporters issued striking declarations of solidarity. Before Bo's anti-crime campaign, wrote Han Deqiang, "the daily life of the ordinary people in Chongqing was filled with fear," but now, "Chongqing people have their city back. They think Chongqing's days have once again become 'sunny days,' and they praise Bo Xilai, who is Chongqing's 'blue sky.'"[34] Guo Songmin, the hawkish former air force pilot, argued that the "great significance in the Chongqing Model lies in its rebuilding of the Communist Party's legitimacy." The Chongqing Model was a "turning point in history," wrote one netizen using the name "Culture Red Guard," adding that Bo had "saved the party and the government, saved the Chinese people, saved reform and opening up, and has an epoch-making revolutionary historical significance!"[35] Sun Wenhao, writing on the Utopia website, argued that Bo Xilai's experiment, while not corresponding with Western norms of legal procedure, nonetheless was a "new mode of thinking about eliminating social justice" and one that recognized a fundamental truth: "Freedom and democracy must yield to bread. What ordinary people want is simple and tangible. That is to say, stability overrides all else."[36]

Utopia co-founder Yang Fan was also an early and passionate supporter of the Chongqing Model. As discussed in chapter 2, Yang had been one of the "rebel" (造反派) Red Guards while attending school at No. 4 Middle School with Bo Xilai's brother, Bo Xicheng. While this put him on the opposite side from the "royalists" (保皇派), Yang remained in touch with the Bo family. In January 2011, Yang and two researchers from the Chongqing municipal Communist Party School published *The Chongqing Model*, a 295-page celebration of Bo's project. Yang's chapter on the "sing red" campaign attacked those who viewed it as a return to the Mao Zedong era, arguing that those who made such accusations "haven't moved on in their thinking from 20 years ago or even 40 years ago . . . [they] use old models on new problems."[37]

But was it that simple? Neo-Maoists, and Bo Xilai himself, had been quick to dismiss any connection between the "sing red" campaign and a return to the Mao era. And it's true that since the arrest of the Gang of Four, accusations of sympathy for the Cultural Revolution had been one of the most potent—and frequently used—rhetorical weapons against the left in China.

In April 2011, however, these denials would become more difficult to sustain, as the neo-Maoists waged their most public and vicious attack yet.

One night in the summer of 1957, Mao Yushi, a young engineer at the Beijing Academy of Railway Sciences, left work early for his one-hour bicycle commute home to the city's central Wangfujing neighborhood. As he made his way through the darkened streets of the capital, back at his office his colleagues rifled through his possessions, looking for evidence of political or ideological infractions. Mao Zedong had just launched his "anti-Rightist campaign," and the local party secretary had a quota for rightists to discover and report. In one of Mao Yushi's notebooks, they found what they needed: a short statement that read, "If there is no pork at the market, why don't we let prices rise?" This would have been uncontroversial to anyone familiar with the basic economics of supply and demand, but in the summer of 1957, this was evidence of capitalist tendencies.

After being branded a "rightist," Mao Yushi was sent to Hebei Province to lay railway track. He was forbidden from publishing research under his own name and had his salary slashed. In 1960, in the middle of Mao Zedong's Great Leap Forward, he was sent to Shandong Province with dozens of his colleagues from the Beijing Academy of Railway Sciences. As he would recount in a short biographical essay:

> I was able to survive only because I learned to catch grasshoppers. . . .
> I would walk through the fields collecting them in an envelope.
> After catching 7 or 8, I would toss the envelope into the fire, the grasshoppers roasting while the envelope burned away. I had to swallow them quickly, as their digestive systems contained a bitter green liquid, the result of their diet of grass. When you're hungry, however, you disregard such things.

Mao survived the famine of the Great Leap Forward, but the rightist label continued to haunt him and his family. On August 23, 1966—three months after the outbreak of the Cultural Revolution—ten Red

Guards came to his house. "They rounded up my wife, our two children, and my mother and forced us into the neighbor's bathroom while they ransacked our house looking for anti-revolutionary materials," according to Mao's autobiography.[38] Several weeks later, the Red Guards returned to demand that Mao and his father begin cleaning the streets. "As we swept," he wrote, "Red Guards began to whip us with their leather belts, the copper buckles drawing blood from our bodies."

Living through the Cultural Revolution was for Mao like "grasping the tail of the revolution as it swung me about."

With the death of Mao Zedong came a reprieve. Mao Yushi turned to the study of economics, and in 1984 took up a post at the Chinese Academy of Social Sciences. A decade later, he and five other economists founded the Unirule Institute of Economics, one of China's first independent think tanks and a strong proponent of a market economy and the rule of law. In early 2000, Mao was purged from CASS as part of a campaign to stifle liberal criticism of Jiang Zemin, but this only helped cement his reputation as one of China's preeminent thinkers. This was confirmed in 2004, when the liberal-leaning *Southern People Weekly* named Mao as one of China's fifty most distinguished intellectuals. In 2007, *China Newsweek* named him and Tsinghua University's Qin Hui as the most influential intellectuals of the decade.

In 2008, Mao was one of the original signatories of "Charter 08," a political rights manifesto drafted by Liu Xiaobo. After Liu's arrest on charges of "state subversion," Mao joined two hundred intellectuals, academics, and activists in signing an open letter that stated, "If Mr. Liu Xiaobo is to be prosecuted . . . then each of us is an integral part of his case, and the indictment of Mr. Liu Xiaobo is to put each of us on trial; if Mr. Liu Xiaobo is convicted, it is equivalent to condemn[ing] every one of us as being guilty. We have no choice but to bear punishment with Liu Xiaobo."[39] In December 2010, in the lead-up to the Nobel Peace Prize award ceremony for Liu, Mao was detained at the airport in Beijing and refused permission to travel to Singapore for fear that he would instead travel to Norway to accept the Peace Prize on Liu's behalf, as Liu had praised Mao in several articles.

All of this was more than enough to bring Mao Yushi to the attention of the neo-Maoists, who, by the mid-2000s, frequently singled him out for attack online, and increasingly, offline at his lectures, where

they heckled and even attempted to assault the octogenarian economist. In 2010, Mao was included as a "slave of the West" on the ultra-
nationalist website Progress Society, joining Liu Xiaobo, Qin Hui, and
the human rights lawyer Teng Biao, who, as discussed in the previous
chapter, had actually spoken at a Utopia event in 2005. In its profile of
Mao, the website described him as "an old monster, an evil doer," and
a "parasite [who] has been living as a tick on the body of the Chinese
people."[40] The case against Mao included his opposition to boycotting
Japanese goods and his support for the market allocation of strategic
natural resources.

But it was Mao Yushi's criticisms of Mao Zedong that would incite
the most outrage.

On the evening of April 26, 2011, Mao Yushi posted an article on
his personal blog entitled "Returning Mao Zedong to Human Form."
It was a lengthy review of the 2008 book *The Fall of the Red Sun: The
Achievements and Crimes of Mao Zedong*, by Xin Ziling, a retired official from China's National Defense University. Xin's book denounced
Mao's "horrendous atrocities" and argued that if China took seriously
its commitment to democracy, it should "remove Mao's portrait and
remove Mao's corpse [from Tiananmen Square]."[41]

Mao Yushi agreed with Xin Ziling but went further. Mao Zedong
was "a slave to his own lust for power." His methods of class struggle
"resulted in the deaths of an untold number of Chinese, and for this
he showed not the slightest inkling of remorse." He "sexually assaulted
an untold number of women" and was "devoid of any humanity." Not
only did he create chaos in China, Mao Yushi argued, he "exported his
theory to the world so that all could share in his cruelty." He concluded,
"Only when we strip away the mythology and superstition that once
surrounded him can he finally be judged."[42]

Mao's essay was reposted on the website of *Caixin*, an influential
business publication founded by the muckraking journalist Hu Shuli.
Within a day, the piece was scrubbed from both Mao's blog and the
Caixin website by the country's army of censors, but in Internet time,
twenty-four hours was an eternity, and by the time it was deleted, it had
already been re-posted on countless websites and blogs.

The neo-Maoist response was immediate and unprecedented. They'd
been emboldened by Bo Xilai's rise in Chongqing, especially the official

sanction his "sing red" campaign appeared to receive from Beijing. But, paradoxically, they also went on the defensive, forced into a corner by the perceived surge in open attacks on the CCP, its revolutionary history, and most importantly, the founding father of the PRC, Mao Zedong, by intellectuals such as Xin Ziling and Mao Yushi.

On May 23, the group delivered a petition to a Beijing police station calling for the arrest of Mao Yushi and Xin Ziling for the crime of state subversion. "[Mao and Xin] fabricated innumerable lies to slander Chairman Mao Zedong and denigrate the history of the Chinese Communist Party and New China," the petition argued. It added, "The fundamental purpose of these lies is to deny the legitimacy of the Chinese Communist Party in power and eventually overthrow the leadership of the Communist Party of China and the socialist system."[43]

Up to a point, the neo-Maoists were correct. Mao Yushi and his supporters clearly understood the connection between Mao's legacy and the legitimacy of the CCP. Chen Fengxiao, who, like Mao Yushi, had been labeled a rightist in 1957 before finally being rehabilitated in 1980, told a journalist in the summer of 2011, "If China wants to carry out genuine political reform, we cannot ignore a complete accounting of all of Mao Zedong's crimes. Without clearing this hurdle, China will be unable to carry out political reform, and there is no way for China to become a truly modern society. We must bring to light all of Mao Zedong's crimes."[44] The call for a full accounting of the Mao era by Mao Yushi and Xin Ziling was as much about contemporary politics as it was about remembering the past.

The petition against the two men circulated online and quickly amassed fifty thousand signatures, including from Liu Siqi (the widow of Mao Zedong's son Mao Anying), Ma Bin, Mao Xiaoqing (Mao Zedong's niece), and Han Zhong, the actor who had played Chairman Mao in a 2010 biopic of his son.

Utopia continued to escalate the campaign against Mao Yushi into the summer of 2011, urging supporters across the country to organize public events in support of the petition. At one rally held in Shanxi Province, organizers hung banners calling Mao Yushi a "traitor to the Han race." A report from the rally, later posted on the Utopia website, gave a flavor of the day's agenda:

The attendees all spoke out, angrily denouncing the vicious slanders, libels and attacks against Chairman Mao and the party by the race traitors and collaborationists Mao Yushi and Xin Ziling. Our glorious senior revolutionary comrades spoke first at the meeting, in an angry and trenchant speech, they denounced the exceedingly despicable, vicious, obscene, contemptible words and strategies used by the race traitors and collaborators Mao Yushi and Xin Ziling against the Great Leader Chairman Mao. . . . Each comrade expounded from all angles the greatness of the Party and Chairman Mao, and bitterly attacked the slanderous and despicable actions of the race traitors and collaborators Mao Yushi and Xin Ziling.[45]

On June 19, sixty students from universities around Beijing gathered to denounce Mao and Xin's "vicious attack and slander of Chairman Mao." One student accused Mao Yushi of being a "traitor" and a "gear in the chain of globalization" who "voluntarily serves the West." Another accused Mao of working with the US to "dismember" China.[46]

That same month, Utopia reprinted remarks by a high-ranking PLA official calling for the establishment of a research institute to investigate the penetration of China's political system by "race traitors" (hanjian in Chinese), a clear reference to Mao Yushi. Rear Admiral Zhang Zhaozhong, perhaps best known for claiming on national TV that China's smog was its best defense against a US laser attack,[47] argued the problem of treason had long plagued China's political system, and had undermined every dynasty and every era, reaching its apogee with the invasion of the Manchus in 1644 and Japan's conquest of the country in the mid-twentieth century. In the modern-day traitor, Zhang argued, "We have a type of person in China who, because they speak a foreign language, have been abroad, have eaten foreign fast food, or for some other peculiar reason like foreign people, speak in that foreign tongue and use the foreign perspective to evaluate Chinese issues."[48]

By the fall of 2011, Utopia's petition to imprison Mao Yushi and Xin Liling had signatories from nearly thirty provinces, and the group had organized events in dozens of cities. Emboldened by the grassroots support, Utopia released an open letter signed by its leadership calling for the PRC constitution to be amended to give the state the power to "punish all traitors," rather than merely "treasonable activities." The provision, which was included in the 1954, 1975, and 1978 versions of the Constitution, had been amended in 1982 to read: "The State maintains public order and suppresses treasonable and other criminal activities that endanger State security." Utopia wanted the original language restored and expanded to cover a broad range of political and economic opinions at odds with their own idea of socialism:

> Strategic sectors and resources such as finance, information, foreign exchange, oil, railroads, automobiles, aviation, and seeds have fallen into enemy hands; state lands and waters have been recklessly ceded away; foreign capital controls key economic departments; state-owned enterprises and state banks have been sold off on the cheap; and genetically modified staples that endanger national survival have been brought in. In politics, the peddling of Western universal values has deliberately misguided reforms of the political system and has shaken the foundation of our socialist country. In culture, the peddling of decadent Western capitalist culture has attacked socialist culture.[49]

This wasn't the first time the neo-Maoists had called for legislation to punish *hanjian* traitors. In 2007, former *Pursuit of Truth* editor Yu Quanyu submitted a proposal to the National People's Congress for a new "anti-traitor" law after reading an essay in *Freezing Point*, a publication under the *China Youth News*, that criticized the extreme nationalistic tone of middle school textbooks. The offending essay, written by Sun Yat-sen University philosophy professor Yuan Weishi, worried that young Chinese are "continuing to drink the wolf's milk" of the Cultural Revolution.

The backlash to Yuan's article was swift, with the CCP Propaganda Department ordering the closing of *Freezing Point*, which it charged with attempting to "vindicate the criminal acts by imperialist powers in invading China" and "seriously distort[ing] historical facts."[50] This wasn't enough for Yu Quanyu, however, who called for a new law that would hand a ten-year prison sentence to "anyone defending aggression against China since the Opium War" and twenty years for anyone defending Japan's invasion of China after 1931.[51] In an interview, Yu stated that he'd been influenced by the anti–Holocaust denial laws in Germany and Austria and the case of David Irving, the historian arrested in Austria in 2005 and sentenced to three years in prison for speeches he'd given in 1989, including one where he'd mocked the "gas chamber fairy tale." Yu saw parallels to China: "Since the Opium War in 1846, China has suffered more than 100 years of foreign aggression, especially Japan's occupation of our Chinese territory, and its massacres of the Chinese. We Chinese can't forget this history. Some people now want to reverse these cases and insult our soldiers."[52]

Yuan Weishi, the historian who had been the impetus for Yu's proposal, told *Southern Metropolis Weekly*, "If this were thirty-some years ago, when the Cultural Revolution had not yet finished, it would not be at all strange to make this proposal." He continued, "Today, angry youth label people traitors online at the drop of a hat; if Yu Quanyu's proposal actually becomes law, then a tide of investigating 'traitorous speech' will sweep over the whole country, and that's really frightening."[53]

Yuan's warning proved prescient.

Attacks on Mao Yushi and Xin Ziling increased after Utopia released its list of "Top Ten Traitors in China" in December 2011. Mao Yushi held the top spot, followed by the historian Yuan Tengfei, who'd spoken critically of Mao Zedong in his popular online lecture series.[54] In announcing the results, Utopia declared that the popularity of the 2011 poll proved that 2012 would be the "year of smashing China's traitors."[55] Angry netizens phoned in death threats to Mao Yushi's home in western Beijing, and while delivering a lecture at the Beijing Institute of Technology, a man attempted to physically attack Mao before being restrained.

When asked about the threats to Mao's life, Utopia's Fan Jinggang responded, "If there were no such threats that would mean China no longer has any patriots."[56]

By the summer of 2011, Utopia co-founder Yang Fan was having second thoughts about the organization he'd helped launch and nurture for nearly a decade. He was also rethinking his support for Bo Xilai and the Chongqing Model, doubts sparked by the arrest and trial of Li Zhuang, a lawyer who had crossed Bo Xilai and Wang Lijun by representing one of their main political enemies in April 2011.

Yang's falling out with Utopia actually predated the campaign against Mao Yushi and the rise of Bo Xilai, having begun in 2007 with the arrival of Zhang Hongliang to Utopia and the organization's overt turn to a more militaristic nationalism. He hadn't even been invited to Utopia's sixth anniversary in 2009, leading him to accuse Zhang Hongliang of "kidnapping" Utopia with his brand of "extreme leftism" and support for "continuous revolution."[57]

These ideological disagreements were aggravated by a clash of personalities. In later interviews, Yang would return to the sense of aggrievement he felt at being sidelined, first by Han Deqiang, whom he considered a pupil, and then by Zhang Hongliang, whom he considered an interloper.[58]

But the final straw, Yang claimed, came on July 10, 2011 when at a Utopia event at which Zhang Hongliang gave a speech on the ninetieth anniversary of the CCP's founding. A participant from Hebei Province repeatedly shouted, "Zhang Hongliang is the leader of the left!" Yang protested and departed the event to the jeers of the audience. "I told them they were leftist historical nihilists," he told journalist Xu Weiwen. That same month, Yang sought out Han Deqiang to discuss Zhang Hongliang's influence on Utopia and its drift toward extremism, but Han ignored him. "His mind had been made up," Yang told me.[59]

Publicly, however, Yang Fan framed his break from Utopia as a principled stand against extremism. "My bottom line is that you cannot revisit the Cultural Revolution and cannot use the language of class struggle," he said in March 2012. "In the bones of [Utopia] is the pursuit of a Cultural Revolution. At their events, they consciously adopt the Cultural Revolution mentality," Yang lamented.[60] He claimed that he'd turned on Bo Xilai for the same reason, accusing him of becoming a "mini-Mao," as he told journalist John Garnaut in August 2011. "Bo's problems in Chongqing will be exposed and it will become chaotic."[61]

But in private, Yang believed Bo's problems were largely political. By overtly signaling his intention to enter the Politburo Standing Committee, a position Yang believed Bo felt entitled to as a princeling, he unified opposition and forced Beijing to act. "Bo Xilai didn't leave the party any choice," Yang told me.[62]

The end for Bo was swift.

The rumors Wang Lijun brought to the US Consulate included a remarkable story: Bo's wife, Gu Kailai, had poisoned and killed a British citizen named Neil Heywood in Chongqing's Lucky Holiday Hotel. Beijing's patience with Bo was already wearing thin, as his brash style and overt campaigning for higher office violated core rules the party used to conduct its business. Wang's attempted defection gave them an excuse to act.

On March 15, 2012, one day after Premier Wen Jiabao warned of a second Cultural Revolution, state media announced that Bo had been stripped of his position as Chongqing party secretary.

Bo's purge was a remarkable end to what had been China's most consequential political scandal since the Tiananmen Square crackdown in 1989. For four years, Bo Xilai had run roughshod over the unspoken laws that governed China's political system. The scandal shattered the widely held illusion of unity and "collective leadership" the party had carefully cultivated since the 1990s. "They want everyone to believe that the top level has no problem—that there's no split and no struggle. But this is a false impression," said Jin Zhong, the publisher of the influential Hong Kong–based *Open* magazine.[63] Bo had given lie to this narrative by waging a public campaign to join the Politburo Standing Committee, openly feuding with a fellow party leader (Wang Yang), and flirting with the politics of the Cultural Revolution, his denials notwithstanding.

He was expelled from the party on September 28, and the following summer he was charged with corruption, abuse of power, and bribery. After a four-day trial in August 2013, he was sentenced to life in prison. Gu Kailai received a suspended death sentence for the murder of Neil Heywood. Wang Lijun was charged with taking bribes and abuse of power, and after a two-day trial in September 2012, he was convicted and sentenced to fifteen years in prison.

The party now wanted to move on and to sweep the events of Chongqing under the rug. They were looking ahead to the party's quinquennial power transition that fall, where Xi Jinping would replace Hu Jintao as the General Secretary of the CCP. There would be no public discussion about the lessons of the Chongqing Model or Bo's "sing red" campaign. No soul searching about his "strike black" campaign, or regarding the question of how Bo was able to remain in office so long if he was as corrupt as the party now claimed he was. The official version held that the Bo Xilai affair was nothing more than a story of individual greed and abuse of power.

But this wasn't convincing to many. Tsinghua University sociologist Sun Liping argued that regardless of Bo's individual deeds, his Chongqing Model policies were "formed in the deep social soil" of "growing polarization, disparities between rich and the poor, the problems faced by the people in real life, and the strong dissatisfaction formed because of [these problems]."[64] Mao Yushi agreed, stating Bo had tapped into a deep-seated sense of grievance and anger that wasn't being adequately addressed by Beijing. "If China undertook a nationwide election," Mao said, "Chongqing's Bo Xilai would likely win."[65]

Neither were the neo-Maoists convinced that the Bo saga was over.

That same day that Bo's sacking was announced, Utopia, Maoflag, Red Song Society, and virtually every other prominent neo-Maoist website was blocked or ordered by the government to temporarily suspend operations. Both Utopia and Maoflag posted notices stating they had been visited by the Beijing Municipal Network Management Office, the Beijing Municipal Public Security Bureau's Internet Security Group, and representatives from the State Council. In an interview with *Time Weekly*, Fan Jinggang said the website's problems might have been technical and related to the massive increase in traffic after the announcement of Bo's purge, or were the result of an outside attack, possibly the work of the US military or a specialized department in the Chinese government.[66] New Left scholar Wang Hui agreed, seeing in the closing of leftist websites the work of a secret alliance of "Chinese and US authorities" to revive "neoliberalism" in the wake of the global financial crisis. "The question here," Wang wrote, "is whether there is a single intelligence at work, or a network of forces collaborating to bring about a particular result."[67]

Conspiracy or not, for a time, Bo Xilai's demise appeared as if it was tearing down the neo-Maoist movement along with him. Articles on the "collapse" of Utopia soon began to appear, as did autopsies of the "extreme left." Yang Fan drove much of this narrative, but with a rare degree of honesty. "I'm one of Utopia's founders," he told journalists from *Time Weekly*, "and my goal is to close Utopia and to send Zhang Hongliang to jail."[68]

After Bo Xilai's precipitous fall from power in March 2012 and the shuttering of Utopia and dozens of other red websites, it seemed the neo-Maoist movement had run aground.[69] Their direct involvement in the winner-take-all world of elite politics had made them a target for retribution.

But by year's end, Utopia was back up and running with a renewed mission: to police the lines of permissible historical investigation and enforce narratives that strengthened the party's rule. As it turned out, seeing off the leftist challenge from Bo Xilai allowed the party to focus its ideological struggles even more firmly on subversion from the capitalist West and its perceived allies within China. On this front, the neo-Maoists were important allies of the party-state.

6

Forgetting History Is a Betrayal

The purpose of summing up the past is to encourage people to close ranks
and look to the future.

—Deng Xiaoping, 1980[1]

STRIDING TO THE PODIUM of the Qiqihar University Music Hall in
China's far northeast on a cold November day in 2014, PLA Air Force
Senior Colonel Dai Xu looked out on the packed audience of the 1,057-
seat auditorium. The majority of the attendees wore military uniforms
and had come to hear a pep talk from one of China's most outspoken
military propagandists, and a hero to the country's neo-Maoists.[2]

But by definition a pep talk means that all is not well, and indeed,
Dai had come with words of warning:

> As I deliver today's lecture, the farce that is the Occupy Central in
> Hong Kong still hasn't ended. This is but a dress rehearsal for a color
> revolution. Before Hong Kong, there was the shattering of Ukraine.
> Before that, Egypt, Tunisia, Libya, Georgia, Kyrgyzstan, Yugoslavia,
> the breakup of the Soviet Union. The mortuary of global politics is
> piled high with the corpses of socialist countries. This is war! A new
> type of war! China once again faces an enormous threat.[3]

But if China was at war, who was its enemy? Few in the audience needed
it spelled out, but just to be certain, Dai clarified:

"[America] has dispatched "student advisors" and "strategic misdi-rection advisors" to China, where they wear invisible cloaks and call themselves economists and entrepreneurs. In accordance with their cultural strategy, they've captured the Chinese people on a large scale, entering China's top think tanks and guiding the country toward low-skilled labor and economic colonization. This is an attempt to get China to enter the global economic system they themselves lead.[4]

Although his role in China's military was more focused on words than action, Dai Xu commanded a sizable popular following in China with his hawkish—and paranoid—statements about the United States. In a 2010 commentary, he intoned, "From a historical perspective, the US has continuously found enemies and waged wars. It has become part of its social formula. Without wars the US economy loses stimulus. Without enemies, the US cannot hold the will of the whole nation."[5] In the nationalist *Global Times* newspaper, Dai wrote, "Since we have decided that the US is bluffing in the East China Sea, we should take this opportunity to respond to these empty provocations with some-thing real." He continued, "This includes Vietnam, the Philippines and Japan, who are the three running dogs of the United States in Asia. We only need to kill one, and it will immediately bring the others to heel."[6] On his Weibo account, he warned his nearly five hundred thousand followers that the H7N9 avian flu was a US "bio-psychological weapon" that was being "deliberately deployed against the Chinese people."[7]

As he neared the end of his ninety-minute speech in Harbin, Dai told the crowd that the coming struggle was not only against ex-ternal enemies (i.e., the United States) but, perhaps more importantly, against internal foes: academics, researchers, and intellectuals who op-pose China's political leadership by espousing subversive ideas about the rule of law, democracy, and the free market. To Dai Xu, they "eat Communist Party meals, but they smash the Communist Party pot."

Unlike conflicts of the twentieth century that were fought in the air, on the sea, and on land, this new war would require a resolute de-fense of China's cyberspace. "For those who defend the nation and the Chinese people, the Internet is the new Shangganling Mountain," Dai said, referring to the long and bloody Korean War campaign known in English as the Battle of Triangle Hill. The Communist Party of China required the renewed vigilance of the military and propaganda organs in this new ideological struggle, where Chinese websites and blogs would be the new battlefront.

Dai saw the Internet as an important weapon for US efforts to manipulate public opinion, especially the views of Chinese youths, and he believed that American Internet companies such as Google and Microsoft were tools for a larger US strategy to "devalue the Chinese socialist system while suppressing and blocking the opinions of patriotic scholars and citizens," as he wrote in an earlier piece for the PLA's website.[8]

Dai was especially concerned about the use of the Internet to spread "historical nihilism," which he defined as the distortion—or minimization—of the achievements of the Communist Party and its leaders with the intention of eroding the support of the Chinese people. The United States, in conjunction with willing supporters within China, had formulated a long-term strategy employing "hundreds of millions of public opinion platforms" to "erase the political achievements of the Chinese people" through the conscious manipulation of historical facts and narratives.[9]

Dai's fear of the power of the Internet in the hands of "hostile forces" and its potential to spread subversive historical nihilism and provoke regime change wasn't entirely fanciful. The previous summer, leaked classified documents by former US intelligence contractor Edward Snowden detailed global surveillance efforts by the National Security Agency in cooperation with US technology firms. The protests in Tunisia and Egypt in 2011 and 2012, widely hailed as "Facebook revolutions" for the website's role in facilitating political activism, likewise reverberated back to China, amplifying the already heightened fears of foreign interference. This was incontrovertible proof, it seemed to many, that long-standing fears of American penetration of China's cyberspace were justified.

If the increasingly compromised Internet provided a platform for an external assault on China's political system, Dai Xu believed many of China's intellectuals were attacking the country from within by denying the achievements of the CCP and the nation's founding father, Mao Zedong. "Both history and reality prove that Mao Zedong is indispensable," he wrote in early 2013. "As the leader of the nation, Mao

Zedong's merits and demerits can be judged. But as [China's] spiritual leader, Mao Zedong's place in modern China's national soul is irreplaceable."[10] This meant that "smears" (抹黑) or "distortions" (歪曲) of Mao and the Maoist legacy were particularly serious offenses. Under the guise of conducting "objective" historical research on the Mao era, the enemies of China sought to weaken its foundation by undercutting national confidence in its forebears. "After generations of unremitting struggle, no nation can divide or invade China using military force, including nuclear weapons," Dai wrote. "But at the same time, China still remains under the threat of a 'soft' attack through the penetration of ideology and other realms of spiritual consciousness," he warned.[11]

Opinions such as these made Dai popular with the neo-Maoists, and Utopia reposted hundreds of his articles on their website beginning in 2007. Like Dai, they also believed the United States had long since resolved to overthrow the CCP by way of "peaceful evolution," and if not for the party's occasional bouts of fortitude, America, with its legions of compradors and fifth-column subversives, could have succeeded in "changing China's colors."

Dai Xu and the neo-Maoists also viewed research on China's contemporary history as a proxy battle for the country's political future. There is no such thing as neutral history, they argued, and every utterance about Mao Zedong or the party's historical legacy had the effect, intentional or not, of either supporting or attacking the regime. All works of history were thus inherently political acts.[12]

"Some people think . . . that as long as they can prove that tens of millions of people died in the Great Leap Forward, then the Communist Party . . . will never be able to clear itself," said historian Yang Songlin, whose 2013 book, *Someone Must Finally Speak the Truth*, sought to refute reports of mass starvation during the Great Leap Forward.[13] In 2009, Utopia general manager Fan Jinggang blamed "bourgeois liberalization thought" for attempting to "completely negate the Party's history by denying the Cultural Revolution, denying the history of the first 30 years of New China . . . [and] completely denying Mao Zedong."[14] Utopia co-founder Yang Fan believed that once the process of "negating" China's revolutionary history was given a toehold, the logical conclusion was regime collapse. "If you negate the Communist Party, Mao Zedong, and China's revolutionary history," he argued, "next it's Sun Yat-sen and the New Democracy movement. After this, what leg do you have to stand on?"[15]

By the early 1980s, the conventional wisdom held that the Communist Party's popular support was derived from delivering material prosperity as opposed to the Mao-era promise of radical equality. This appeared to be confirmed in the period following Deng Xiaoping's Southern Tour (discussed in chapter 1). From this point on, the *New York Times* declared in 1997, "the Communist Party's legitimacy arose from its ability to deliver economic growth and rising incomes."[16] Economists Wu Jinglian and Qian Yingyi asserted in 2000, "The proposition of economic development became even more compelling after the 1989 Tiananmen Square incident, because *it was the only source from which the government would gain its legitimacy* [emphasis added]."[17]

There is certainly some truth in this.[18] Since its inception, the CCP constantly retrofitted its value proposition to better secure popular support, including with pledges to deliver widespread material prosperity. Indeed, owing to the supposed superiority of a socialist economic system, Communist parties of all stripes had long been promising to significantly improve the material well-being of the people by virtue of a more efficient planning, production, and distribution of economic resources. In early 1934, on the eve of the Great Terror, Stalin proclaimed, "There was no point in overthrowing capitalism in October 1917 and building socialism for all these years if we do not succeed in enabling people to live in a state of prosperity."[19] Fifty-three years later, Deng Xiaoping put it more succinctly: "Poverty is not socialism."[20]

Yet the simplistic formulation that "economic growth = popular legitimacy" was not accepted by the party leadership. In a speech to the PLA just days after authorizing troops to mow down protestors in Beijing and across China on June 4, 1989, Deng Xiaoping lamented that the leadership had lost the support of many Chinese because "We didn't tell [the people] enough about the need for hard struggle, about what China was like in the old days and what kind of a country it was to become. That was a serious error on our part."[21] As Deng's quote hints, the political leadership has always viewed its legitimacy as a baroque cocktail, comprising historical narratives combining both victory *and* defeat, a credible mass-mobilizing ideology, the ability to protect territorial integrity and keep internal chaos at bay, and yes, the delivery of increasing prosperity, which goes a long way to quelling popular grievances. Depending on the challenges at hand, the party would lean more heavily on one narrative than another (class struggle in the 1960s, economic development in the 1980s, nationalism in the 1990s, etc.), but at no time in the CCP's nearly hundred-year history has it placed all its bets on economic growth as its primary legitimator.

This isn't to say that growth didn't matter. The rising tide of prosperity, or a belief that such prosperity was within reach of the average citizen, provided breathing room for the party as it navigated the disorienting ideological period after Mao's death. At the same time, party propagandists hoped a growing economic pie would obscure the mounting contradictions in China's economic and ideological development model.

In the wake of China's debt-fueled recovery from the 2008 global financial crisis, it became increasingly clear that the era of double-digit growth was coming to an end, and the domestic economy would never again soar into the stratosphere. This meant that yet another recalibration of the party's legitimating narrative was needed. There would still be regular invocations of China's economic "miracle" and Beijing's ability to "lift" millions of citizens out of poverty, but these boasts would now be embedded into a broader narrative of the party's glorious past achievements in casting off imperialism, subduing external enemies, and transforming China into a strong nation firmly on the road to prosperity. Put another way, "Performance mattered," writes the long-time China correspondent Ian Johnson, "but mainly as proof of history's judgment."[22]

This recalibration wasn't straightforward, owing to the thicket of unresolved and unexamined history that had accumulated since the PRC's founding. How much popular support would the CCP have today if the enormity of the Cultural Revolution and the Great Leap Forward was laid bare for a full and open public debate? How could the party lay claim to superior governance if it failed so spectacularly to constrain the excesses of Mao Zedong's whim and will? And what surprises would academics find buried deep in the official archives if they were finally and fully opened for academic scrutiny? Harvard University's Elizabeth Perry put the matter bluntly, asking, "Just how durable is [historical] legitimacy, especially when objective inquiry may contradict the official narrative of events on which the regime's legitimacy is purportedly based?"[23]

The link between historical legacy and regime legitimacy has long vexed the CCP and its defenders, a sensitivity borne from the party's own instrumental view of history as a tool for bolstering—or threatening—its ruling legitimacy. One way to maintain the "durability" of the historical legitimacy Professor Perry mentions is to insist upon a unity of perspective, to amplify "correct" understandings of China's past and forbid those that run against the official narrative. But getting the balance right between both raising historical awareness, and constraining this awareness to only "positive" events would require both carrots and sticks. The former included the full-fledged support of the propaganda apparatus, providing those willing participants with funding for academic research and the ability to publish their work in influential—albeit overtly political—publications. At their lightest touch, the "sticks" would simply deny these same benefits, but for many historians who dared to question the official narrative, the penalties could be severe.

China's recent history and the role of party historiography was to take on a new relevance after Xi Jinping's rise to power in 2012. As the son of a legendary party leader and having spent his entire professional career working for the party, Xi's investment in protecting the CCP's perpetual monopoly on power is total. Under Xi, the party's "glorious history" was to be emphasized anew and placed at the center of its perpetually evolving narrative about why it alone deserves the right to rule. Threatening these efforts, however, were individuals seeking to expose the darker chapters of China's recent history, both out of a sense of moral commitment to historical truth, but also, as many would admit, because they understood the political implications for China's rulers.

Here, the neo-Maoists were themselves in complete agreement with Xi Jinping, and in this they found common cause. After nearly a decade of raging against the faux socialists in the CCP, and out of the ashes of their failed campaign to bring Bo Xilai to Beijing, groups like Utopia now directed their rage toward combating historical nihilism. This would bring them some significant victories and a strategic truce with the CCP as the two sides worked hand in hand to purify the public square.

I first heard the name Sun Jingxian in the summer of 2015 during a visit to Utopia's offices in the north of Beijing. I'd been invited to a roundtable on the prospects for neo-Maoism in China, and as our conversation turned to historical questions of the Mao era (as such discussions invariably did), several individuals recommended I read the work of a "brilliant" academic and mathematician who had "debunked" claims of mass famine during the Great Leap Forward in a series of articles appearing in influential publications, including *Red Flag Manuscript*, and on websites of respectable organizations, including the Chinese Academy of Social Sciences. This work culminated in a 244-page manuscript entitled *Returning History to the Truth: A Research Report on Population Change During China's "Three Years of Hardship."*[24]

Professor Sun Jingxian, I would learn, played a role to neo-Maoists akin to that of MIT's Richard Lindzen to climate change deniers, the controversial atmospheric physicist known for his skepticism of anthropogenic global warming. While the overwhelming academic consensus may lean toward a given conclusion, having even one highly credentialed expert in your corner is enough to cast doubt, or even to outright dismiss, the views of the majority. Read Sun's work, the individuals around the table at Utopia told me, and one would understand the truth about the Great Leap Forward and the severity of the lies propagated about China's past by traitors to the nation.

Maoflag co-founder Li Dingkai said that Sun helped resolve his own doubts about the mass starvation narrative, which contradicted his own experience growing up in the countryside during the late 1950s. "I didn't see many people starve," he told me, "just a few old people and some children."[25] Now, Li had proof, and armed with Sun's writings, he would no longer need to rely on his own anecdotal memory to combat what he saw as slanders against the Mao era.

Sun's work also inspired Yang Songlin, a retired government official and amateur historian who had grown frustrated with "inflated" death tolls for the Great Leap Forward. In 2011, he began reading Sun's articles online and judged his "analytical logic and facts to be clear."[26] The two began corresponding over e-mail and met in several Chinese cities to discuss the idea of jointly writing a book on the topic of the famine.[27] In 2013 Yang published his own work of historical revisionism entitled *Someone Must Finally Speak the Truth*, which, according to one description, "dismantles the so-called 'authoritative experts' at home and abroad who miraculously expand the number of abnormal deaths by 10 times!"[28] Rather than tens of millions of deaths from starvation, Yang estimated the figure closer to four million.

Li Chengrui, the former head of the National Bureau of Statistics and an influential elder statesman of the neo-Maoist movement, was another fan of Sun Jingxian. Li wrote a glowing introduction to Sun's monograph, in which his telling of the Mao era reads like a morality tale, with heroic struggle, "glorious victory," and iron-willed leadership triumphing over imperialism, poverty, and internal divisions. The hardship faced during the Great Leap Forward, according to Li, was the result of "natural disaster," "Soviet revisionism," and problems within the CCP's rank and file. Li believed the cause of the famine—limited as he believed it to be—was almost certainly not the result of policy mistakes by Mao, as some scholars alleged. In fact, according to Li, as soon as Chairman Mao discovered problems with food distribution, he immediately took steps to rectify the situation.

"Correcting" the historical record of the Mao era from slanders, distortions, and lies had been a core concern of neo-Maoists for much of the 2000s, although the intensity of their efforts increased after 2006 in reaction to what they perceived was the increasing sophistication of elite "historical nihilists" like Mao Yushi and Xin Ziling. In July 2004, Utopia sponsored an event with Tian Liwei, more popularly known as "Old Field" (老田), on the tactic of "negating" any beneficial outcomes from the Cultural Revolution in order to undercut the continuing relevance of Mao.[29] "Studying the hot topic of [the Cultural Revolution's legacy] is not something I myself was initially interested in," he said at the opening of his remarks, "but rather it was the anti-Mao, anti–Cultural Revolution crowd that made this such an important topic [to me]."

Sun Jingxian claimed his journey began in much the same way. Before turning to the historiography on the Mao era, he was a successful mathematician at Jiangsu Normal University, where he published widely in dense mathematical publications like the *Journal of Mathematical Research and Exposition* on impenetrable topics such as "nonlinear integral equations of Hammerstein type."

His interest in the Mao era began after reading the 2008 book *Tombstone*, a two-volume, 1,208-page history of the Great Leap Forward written by former journalist Yang Jisheng.[30] Yang retired from China's state-run Xinhua News Agency in the early 1990s, whereupon he began conducting interviews and combing through provincial archives to understand the causes and consequences of Mao's rapid industrialization drive in the late 1950s. As he told journalist Ian Johnson, "I consulted twelve provincial archives and the central archives. On average I copied 300 folders per archive, so I have over 3,600 folders of information. They fill up my apartment and some are in the countryside at a friend's house for safekeeping."[31] After more than a decade of research, Yang reached an explosive conclusion: thirty-six million people died of starvation between 1958 and 1962 as a result of Mao Zedong's utopian impulses.

The origins of the Great Leap Forward date to the mid-1950s and Mao's unhappiness with what he perceived to be the slow pace of socialist development. As mentioned in chapter 1, he'd grown impatient with conservative economic planners like Chen Yun, who argued against "rash advances," and after a trip to Moscow in 1957, where Soviet leader Nikita Khrushchev bragged about some day overtaking the United States in per capita industrial output, Mao returned to Beijing with a renewed determination to push forward with China's own industrialization. He ignored his economic advisors, however, and argued that in order to boost industrial output, China's agricultural sector would need to produce vastly more grain to feed the country's heavy industry. Yet as Stanford University's Andrew Walder points out in his insightful study of the Mao era, the actual ideas Mao brought to the table were "distinctly old fashioned, and to those steeped in socialist economics, they were dogmatically narrow minded and twenty years out of date."[32] But as criticisms persisted, Mao went on the political offensive, arguing these were not merely policy disagreements, but rather they represented "rightist" attacks on China's socialist system. Those voicing disagreement were purged, most crucially Peng Dehuai, leaving behind only those who agreed with Mao and those who pretended to.

Starting in 1958, China's collective farms were further consolidated, giving cadres even greater power to mobilize the Chinese population toward Mao's single-minded goal of rapidly increasing agricultural output. Rural peasants were forced to turn their backyards into small-scale steel smelters to help boost steel production, although the resulting output was virtually useless owing to its poor quality. Rural life was completely transformed as Mao's vision of "politics in command" overtook the long-entrenched practices of rural and agricultural life. As Mao's vision began to gain traction, it obliterated food production, but owing to the bureaucratic incentives to please higher-ups, fake statistics reporting exaggerated output were passed up the chain of command. Food shortages and misallocations soon led to famine, which would only abate after Mao's colleagues in Beijing finally summoned the courage to pull back from his failing great leap.

One of these famine victims was Yang Jisheng's father, who died in 1959, and Yang hoped his 2008 book would serve as a "tombstone" for all the deceased. "Human memory is the ladder on which a country and a people advance," he wrote. "We must remember not only the good things, but also the bad; bright spots, but also darkness."[33]

By the time his book was published, Yang was already a well-known liberal within the party-state system (*tizhi nei*) and part of a group of reform-minded officials who gathered around the magazine *Yanhuang Chunqiu*, often translated into English as *Annals of the Yellow Emperor* or *China Through the Ages*. The magazine wasn't so much anti-party as it was committed to a political vision that included a more open and tolerant political system that welcomed open historical investigation and experimentation with democratic and legal institutions.

An early principle for the magazine was that it wouldn't "speak false utterances," one of its former editors told me.[34] This requirement pushed the publication into uncomfortable territory, including on some of the party's most sensitive political and historical issues, as well as sympathetic coverage of blacklisted officials, including former party leaders Zhao Ziyang and Hu Yaobang, both of whom were purged in the 1980s. Because of its high-level connections, the magazine managed to largely circumnavigate party censors, a feat Yang Jisheng also credited to a keen political awareness. As he explained in a 2010 interview, "We don't touch current leaders. And issues that are extremely sensitive, like 6-4 [the June 4 Tiananmen Square massacre], we don't talk about. The Tibet issue, Xinjiang, we don't write about them. Current issues related to Hu Jintao, Jiang Zemin, and their family members' corruption, we don't talk about. If we talk just about the past, the pressure is smaller."[35]

This calculation changed, or at least it should have, as the party under Xi Jinping came to view history as a key legitimator, and conversely, as a possible vector for attacking its right to rule.

The mathematician Sun Jingxian certainly saw it that way, and in Yang Jisheng's book *Tombstone*, he saw a direct attack on China's political system by way of "distorted" historical investigation. He called Yang's book "extremely deceptive," and he spent much of the next few years attempting to discredit Yang's underlying methodology and, thus, the book's conclusions.[36] His skepticism over the severity of the famine was, like many of the neo-Maoists I'd spoken to, informed as much by personal experience as it was political conviction. In Sun's case, Yang's conclusions in *Tombstone* just didn't accord with his own childhood recollections.[37] Frustrated with the success of Yang's book (despite it being banned in China), Sun began publishing a series of negative reviews in which he called the book faulty, inadequate, and even "fraudulent."[38]

The crux of his argument was that Yang had made serious methodological errors in his assumption that starvation deaths could be calculated by looking at the difference between the *average* number of deaths for a given period and the *actual* number of deaths for that same year. This was an "absurd" mathematical formula, Sun believed. "As a professional mathematician," he wrote in a piece for the *Chinese Social Sciences Weekly*, "we must seriously point out that from an academic point of view, [Yang's methodology] completely violates the basic principles that modern mathematics must follow when dealing with such problems."[39] According to Sun's own calculations, there hadn't been thirty million deaths, or even ten million, for that matter. Rather, he believed that 3.66 million had starved to death between 1959 and 1961, nearly thirty-three million fewer than Yang Jisheng's estimate.[40]

Sun expanded his criticisms to include other scholars using what he saw as equally flabby methods for calculating death tolls, including historian Cao Shuji and demographer Jiang Zhenghua, the former director of the Population Research Institute of Xi'an Jiaotong University. In the 1980s, Jiang conducted a series of population studies that concluded there had been seventeen million "abnormal deaths" during the Great

Leap Forward.[41] In an article published on the Utopia website, Sun, writing under the penname Sun Jingze, argued that this estimate failed to account for "re-reporting, false reporting and underreporting" that occurred as a result of a major change to the household registration system in 1960, as well as the statistical anomalies that resulted from "large-scale migration" within China.[42]

Sun's criticisms of such famine estimates might have remained at the margins of political discourse had it not been for Xi Jinping, who, more than any recent Chinese leader, believed that the link between the party's long-term legitimacy and its own historical narrative to be inextricable.

On January 5, 2013, less than two months after taking office as general secretary of the CCP, he declared, "Just consider that if Comrade Mao Zedong had been entirely repudiated . . . could our Party have stood firmly or could the socialist system of China have been tenable? No, they couldn't. Since they couldn't, the country would have fallen into chaos."[43]

Even before being elevated to China's highest political office, Xi warned of a corrosive effect of historical analysis that deviated from the party line. In a 2010 speech, Xi (then China's vice president and a member of the Politburo Standing Committee) called for vigilance against historical nihilism, which "fundamentally denies the guiding position of Marxism and the historical inevitability of China's path to socialism, and denying the leadership of the Communist Party of China."[44]

Once in power, Xi revived Maoist tools of governance, including a one-year "mass line" campaign to improve cadre work styles and bring the party "closer to the people." The campaign, which began in April 2013, called for cadres to rectify their behavior and pay closer attention to the demands of the people, or as Xi put it in more earthy tones, they should "take a long look in the mirror, groom themselves, take a bath and seek remedies."[45]

On April 22, 2013, the General Office of the Party's Central Committee released the "Communique on the Current State of the Ideological Sphere," more commonly known as "Document #9."[46] The communiqué was leaked to the US-based *Mingjing* magazine by the journalist Gao Yu, who was convicted of "leaking state secrets" and given a five-year sentence under house arrest for her actions. The document framed China's ideological environment as a "complicated, intense struggle" and listed seven "trends" threatening the party's hold on power, including the promotion of "universal values," "neoliberalism," and "Western" ideas about journalism. Number six, historical nihilism, was defined as utilizing the "guise of 'reassessing history' to distort party history and the history of New China."[47] The appearance of the document further confirmed what had become increasingly evident with a spate of articles in official newspapers and journals warning of historical nihilism's "infiltration" of China and the threat it posed to the country's socialist system. Historical nihilism wasn't abstract, the articles warned, but was a concrete manifestation of foreign plots to divide and conquer the country, and it could be found in middle school textbooks, in conversations with your neighbors, and in the writings of your favorite novelist or academic. "By negating the history of modern China and questioning the historical inevitability and rationality of socialism," wrote one academic in the *Journal of Ideological and Political Work Research*, "[historical nihilism] panders to the Western political strategy of peaceful evolution."[48]

There was another reason the party didn't see historical nihilism as an "abstract" threat to the nation.

In the aftermath of the Soviet Union's collapse in 1991, the CCP undertook a massive investigation into its demise, one that continues to this day. Among the many causes they identified, historical nihilism was seen as playing an important role in undermining the Soviet Union's political integrity from within.[49] This was a point Xi made early in his tenure as General Secretary: "To dismiss the history of the Soviet Union and the Soviet Communist Party, to dismiss Lenin and Stalin, and to dismiss everything else is to engage in historic nihilism, and it confuses our thoughts and undermines the party's organizations on all levels."[50]

To combat historical nihilism, then, the party under Xi set out to both crush deviationist historical interpretations and historians, and at the same time, rehabilitate historical figures who'd been maligned and marginalized through outright neglect by the party or worse, by their intentional dethroning for political purposes. While the campaign would penetrate into the deepest and most obscure reaches of party historiography, it would begin with the PRC's founding father, Mao Zedong.

To mark the 120th anniversary of Mao's birth on December 26, 2013, Xi gave a speech fusing the pre- and post-Mao eras into one single narrative, beginning in 1949 with the founding of the People's Republic of China, continuing through the Reform and Opening period, and entering its third phase under the leadership of Xi. For decades, ideological battle lines had largely been drawn around support for either the Deng era (pro-market reformers) or the Mao era (leftists, conservatives, and other heterodox critics of reform). Liberals could quote Deng chapter and verse to support further reforms, while leftists and, later, neo-Maoists could counter with their own choice selections from Mao's *Selected Works*. Xi wanted to erase these lines and their resultant political infighting. "One cannot negate the historical period before the Reform and Opening-Up by the historical period after the Reform and Opening-Up, nor can one negate the historical period after the Reform and Opening-Up by the historical period before the Reform and Opening-Up," he declared.[51] This was one grand story with very clear ideological battle lines, Xi was saying.

Of course, previous party leaders also celebrated Mao, and it had been standard practice to declare that the party would forever "hold high the banner of Mao Zedong Thought." This started with Mao himself and the "Resolution on Some Questions of History," a 1945 precursor to the 1981 Resolution discussed in this book's prologue. Like the 1981 Resolution, the 1945 document was overtly political, designed less to explain historical episodes than to impose consensus among the varying, and often warring, factions within the party.[52] The Resolution positioned Mao Zedong at the center of all major events, and as one Communist Party historian remembered, "studying Party history became identical with studying Mao Zedong Thought, studying Party history was studying the works of Chairman Mao. The history of the Party was no more than the red thread, the background for studying the works of Chairman Mao."[53]

With Mao Zedong's death, the party faced the dilemma of how to "sum up" the catastrophes of the Mao era, including the anti-rightist campaign, the Great Leap Forward, and the Cultural Revolution, while at the same time exculpating the Communist Party and Mao Zedong (and Deng Xiaoping, for that matter).[54] The Theory Conference in 1979, with its early calls for a complete and open accounting of the Mao years, was enough to convince Deng that a more constrained consensus was needed in order for the party to focus on modernizing China. In the best case, debates about the past would delay China's progress, and in the worst case, they would tear open old wounds and exacerbate political divisions. With the 1981 Resolution, Deng hoped that "the thinking of Party members and non-Party people alike will be clarified, common views will be reached and, by and large, debate on the major historical questions will come to an end."[55] Yet the wounds of the recent past were too fresh and the experiences too vivid for Deng's demand of consensus to work, and the 1980s would see an outpouring of writings and reflections on the Mao years. The party would try to hold the line on an official historical narrative, but poets, novelists, journalists, and academics created parallel narratives that, for a time at least, the party leadership appeared unable to stop.

The events of June 4, 1989, were quickly blamed on "hostile forces" who provoked ideological confusion among the people, and shocked the party leadership into recommitting to the importance of consensus. History—and public debate, for that matter—was too important to leave to the vagaries of an open and uncontrolled public square. From here onward, the boundaries of permissible historical exploration would be tightly policed, a point party propagandists made abundantly clear: "Research on Party history is not oriented to the past, but rather it is oriented to the present and the future," one CCP history journal stated in 1990.[56] That same year, Zhang Zhenglong was detained for his book, *White Snow, Red Blood,* which recounted the PLA's military campaign against the KMT in northeast China during the country's civil war in the 1940s. Among the offending contents was a devastating portrayal of the PLA's siege of the northern city Changchun in 1948, which resulted in the starvation of an estimated 150,000 civilians, and was a blow to the PLA's reputation as the "people's army." Even though the publisher was under PLA control, Zhang was forced to draft a self-criticism in which he claimed the influence of "bourgeois liberalism" over his writing.[57]

While the turn of the millennium marked a relative opening in China's cultural and historical space, China's leaders still policed the lines of permissible discourse. In 2004, the future Nobel Prize winner Liu Xiaobo and dissident writer Yu Jie were detained after the Chinese chapter of the free speech organization PEN awarded Zhang Yinghe a prize for her banned memoir on the 1957 anti-rightist campaign, *The Past Is Not Like Smoke*. Zhang's next book, *Past Histories of Peking Opera Stars*, was likewise banned after publication in 2006, prompting the author to write an open letter to the deputy director of the General Administration of Press and Publications in which she implored, "Is a rightist a citizen? In contemporary China, a rightist cannot speak or write?"[58]

These efforts to rein in historical pluralism were anything but systematic, and throughout the 1990s and 2000s there remained latitude for writing about Mao Zedong and the Mao era, so long as one didn't directly attempt to undermine the party's right to rule. This was aided by the proliferation of media sources and the rise of the Internet that, for a time at least, offered Chinese citizens unprecedented access to information, just as the techno-utopians had been predicting.

By the spring of 2013 and Xi's launch of a "mass line" campaign, Sun's writings turned more overtly political, as did his critiques of historians such as Yang Jisheng. A fellowship at CASS's World Socialism Research Center gave Sun an elevated profile, and the center's head, Li Shenming, gave him direct entreé into the world of elite ideological politics. Li, who also served as the deputy head of CASS, previously served as the secretary to the hardliner Wang Zhen, one of the CCP's famed "Eight Immortals." With his backing, Sun weighed forcefully into the debate over the Great Leap Forward, publishing pieces attacking Yang Jisheng in influential publications, including the *Global Times* and *Red Flag Manuscript*.

The debate carried over into 2014 and a remarkable conference in the southern city of Wuhan on July 5 to 7. The event was organized by Boston University's Cao Tianyu and Huazhong Science and Technology University's He Xuefeng, and was attended by a wide range of Chinese and international scholars. Conference attendee Anthony Garnaut recalled: "The general tone of most of the presentations at the conference and questions from the audience was sympathetic to the aspect of Sun's project that aimed to absolve collectivism from blame for having contributed to the largest famine in modern history."[59] Yang Jisheng agreed, later writing that the majority of the participants were sympathetic to Mao Zedong and denied any man-made famine during the Great Leap Forward.[60] One academic visiting from the United States even accused Yang of exaggerating the scope of the famine in order to raise funds from overseas organizations.[61]

When it came time for Sun Jingxian to present his detailed criticism of Yang, he asked a young colleague to read his prepared remarks on his behalf, claiming high blood pressure prevented him from speaking. Rather than offering new evidence, Sun simply repackaged his previous arguments on Yang's supposedly faulty methodology, ignoring that Yang's estimate was well within the range of academic consensus and was corroborated by other scholarly works that were published outside of China.

Yang Jisheng, for his part, used his speech to reiterate his critiques of Sun's own methodology, as well as to highlight the fact that even the Communist Party admitted widespread famine, including government officials like Jiang Zhenghua who estimated nearly twenty million had starved to death. Yang concluded his speech with a discussion on the lopsided nature of the public debate over the Great Leap Forward, noting that Sun had cast doubt on Yang's book—and more importantly, the historical truth of famine in China—in influential party publications such as *Red Flag* and CASS's *Studies in Marxism*. Yet Yang's rebuttals had been relegated to the margins of debate, and his book was still banned in China, meaning that Sun's accusations amounted to "trial in absentia."[62]

A summary of the conference appeared several days later written by a "Xian Tian," widely rumored to be jointly written by Sun Jingxian and Gong Xiantian, the legal scholar who challenged China's 2005 draft property law. "In his speech, [Yang] acknowledged that Professor Sun's doubts about *Tombstone* are correct," the summary claimed. Furthermore, Sun's criticisms of Yang were so devastating that the "pack of lies that claims 30 million starved to death was finally debunked!"[63]

In a profile of Sun Jingxian, Anthony Garnaut argued that irrespective of how successful Sun's attempt to rebut Yang's claims of mass famine might have been from an academic standpoint, his work triumphed in another sense:

In the booming left-leaning ideological marketplace of contemporary China, editors of leading ideological journals and managers of online opinion forums have supported Sun in the spreading of his ideas, and as a result, the Chinese language Internet is now saturated with radical critiques of the notion that there was a massive famine during the Mao era. Internet users who avail themselves of Baidu or Google to browse the Chinese-language Web for information about the famine will now find two contesting views: one that there was a massive famine (thirty million deaths) and one that there was only a moderately large famine (three million deaths). The intervention introduced a sense of credible doubt to a sound and scientific analysis of those events, much as climate change sceptics have generated public confusion about a theory that is well established within scientific circles.[64]

Seeding doubt about the dark chapters of the Mao era was just the first of many victories for the neo-Maoists in the Xi Jinping era.

Over the coming years, several academics, party researchers, and high-profile public figures lost their careers owing to remarks deemed derogatory toward Mao Zedong or the Mao era. Organizations and publications that had long vexed Mao loyalists were shuttered or financially strangled. New legislation was passed that would criminalize perceived "slanders" of China's revolutionary "heroes and martyrs." Educational materials were revised to expand the length of China's "War of Resistance Against Japanese Aggression" from eight years to fourteen.

In 2015, popular CCTV presenter Bi Fujian was suspended after he was secretly recorded at a private dinner mocking Chairman Mao while singing the revolution-era song "Taking Tiger Mountain by Strategy." In early 2017, the deputy director of a municipal film and TV regulator was fired for a "serious violation of political discipline" after he called Mao a "devil" on a personal social media account.[65] That same month, Shandong Jianzhu University removed professor Deng Xiangchao after he wrote a post on Weibo claiming, "If [Mao had] died in 1945, China would have seen 6 million fewer killed in war. If he'd died in 1958, 30 million fewer would've starved to death. It wasn't until 1976 when he finally died that we at last had food to eat. The only correct thing he did was to die."[66] After posting comments supportive of Professor Deng, a producer for a Henan provincial TV station was suspended and forced to make a public apology for "having hurt the feelings of the public."[67]

After taking a pounding online by critics and censors, He Weifang, the liberal-leaning law professor discussed in chapter 3, closed his popular Weibo account (1.9 million followers). "The past five years have been really, really stifling," he told a journalist in a 2018 profile.[68]

Historian Yuan Tengfei, who rose to fame through his popular online lectures, was blocked from Weibo in the fall of 2017 after posting a comment that appeared to cheer the death of Mao Zedong.[69] Yuan had long been a target of Utopia's vitriol, having repeatedly denounced Mao, even calling him "a butcher whose hands are covered with the blood of the people."[70]

Also in 2017, the novel *Soft Burial*, which chronicled the brutal land reforms of the early 1950s, was banned after a vocal campaign by Utopia against the book and its author, Fang Fang. Zhang Quanjing, the former head of the CCP Organization Department and an influential patron of the neo-Maoists, wrote of the book, "This is a distortion of history, a typical expression of historical nihilism in the literature and art fields, a concrete example of the struggle between 'peaceful transformation' and anti–'peaceful transformation' [of the political system]."[71] For her part, Fang Fang was both defiant and concerned, vowing to continue writing despite the attacks, but also worried about the growing power of radical online voices. "The authorities are somehow afraid of [Utopia]," she told me. "Every time the [neo-Maoists] cause trouble, the government always does their best to satisfy them."[72]

In July 2018, Mao Yushi's outspoken liberal think tank, the Unirule Institute of Economics, had its doors literally welded shut by Beijing authorities, leaving the organization's future operations in peril. "We're very pessimistic because we clearly understand that there are more senior people behind this, although we don't have the evidence to prove it," the institute's executive director, Sheng Hong, told Chris Buckley of the *New York Times*.[73] Later that year, Sheng and his colleague Jiang Hao were refused permission to leave China to attend a conference at Harvard University. As Sheng told the *South China Morning Post*, "They told me I would endanger national security and was not allowed to leave the country. I was completely shocked. How can my attendance at an academic conference affect national security? This is absolutely absurd."[74]

But perhaps the biggest victory for the neo-Maoists was the effective takeover of Yang Jisheng's employer, *Yanhuang Chunqiu* magazine, which for more than two decades had served as a bastion for liberal and reformist writing.

In June 2016, Yang's colleague at the magazine, Hong Zhenkuai, was found guilty of libel for damaging the "heroic image and spiritual value" of the "Five Heroes of Langya Mountain," after he published a series of articles poking holes in the widely accepted facts surrounding the WWII-era tale of self-sacrifice and heroism by a group of Red Army soldiers. The next month, the magazine's official sponsor, the Chinese National Academy of Arts, announced it was replacing the magazine's editorial board. For a time, current employees tried to block the move and use their remaining political connections to stall until a solution could be found. "The maneuvers for us are like playing chess," said Wu Si, one of the magazine's long-time editors. "Moves like this have to be carefully thought out."[75] After it soon became clear that the storm wouldn't pass, most employees chose to resign rather than submit. "It's better to be shattered jade than an intact tile," said founding publisher Du Daozheng in an interview with the *New York Times*.[76]

The revamped magazine, whose masthead was now replete with party loyalists, called a last-minute meeting on August 15 and invited several well-known neo-Maoists and nationalist hardliners to attend, including Dai Xu, the PLA propagandist who opened this chapter. "I thought it was a joke," said an elated Sima Nan, one of Utopia's most outspoken figures. "I've never written for *Yanhuang Chunqiu*. How could they invite me? Impossible."[77]

The neo-Maoist Guo Songmin was also there. "Attending this writers' round table feels a little extraordinary," he wrote on his Weibo account, "and I suddenly thought of a line from Chairman Mao, 'Today the autumn wind still sighs, but the world has changed!'"[78]

7

Red Nation

Our red nation will never change color.

—Xi Jinping, 2013

IN A DINGY WALK-UP apartment in the far west of Beijing, retired PLA colonel Li Kaicheng ran a small consultancy firm. It was an incongruous setting for a man of his rank and standing. He'd joined the military in 1969 and served as an instructor at a military academy in Wuhan, in southern China, following in the family tradition of service to the country and to the party. His father had been an important official in China's early intelligence efforts and a member of the party's prestigious Central Committee. During the 1980s, Li began reading some of the multitude of texts on Western management theory being translated into Chinese to satisfy the country's rapidly expanding private sector. He thought that in studying them, he might learn how to be a better leader, but the more he read, the more frustrated he grew with how callously employees were being described. They were being treated as if they were mere business inputs to be added and subtracted in the same way one treats inventory or machinery. Li had seen enough. He put aside these texts and began reading Mao Zedong, he told me.

He retired in 2007 and decided to take what he'd learned from the military and from Mao Zedong Thought and apply it to China's private sector. He called it "red management theory," and his company, the Oriental Junheng Red Management Learning Institute, set out to "build a bridge between Mao Zedong management and Western management." According to Li, the value of continued learning from the West had long since plateaued, and what entrepreneurs around the globe needed was an appreciation for the techniques and values set forth in Mao Zedong Thought and the Communist Party's approach to talent management and overall strategy. "We've basically studied all we need to study from Western management techniques," he said.

At the time I first interviewed Li in 2015, he was just about covering his business expenses, but he remained optimistic about the future. "I suspect that in the next few years, red management will become a growth industry," he assured me.

When I went to see him two years later, Li's company had just moved into a brand-new 180-square-meter office, complete with glass-walled conference rooms and a receptionist. Business in the preceding two years had clearly boomed. "The difference is huge," Li said.

It was a difference he directly attributed to Xi Jinping. Under his direction, Li explained, the Communist Party was pushing for greater awareness of China's history and unique culture, and this was driving more business to his firm. He was now doing more training for SOEs and had started teaching an executive MBA course at Peking University. Li said the majority of his students believed that Mao was a *weiren*, a "great individual." Their logic was simple: "Mao Zedong led a country of this size to a victory this large." He also saw more of China's private entrepreneurs embracing red management theory. "Most big entrepreneurs in China are fans of Mao," he said, and most of the bosses who came to Li's classes were already wealthy. "They come to study Mao's thoughts, to get back to basics, and to think about why they started a company in the first place."

Looking to the future, he saw new growth areas, specifically in Communist Party management theory, which he believed would help multinational companies become better at identifying and promoting talent. He also wanted to take his message global, even asking me if I could help organize seminars in the United States.

Under Xi, China now has "cultural confidence" and a sense of purpose it hadn't had since the Mao era, Li said. Armed with this confidence, there were no limits to what could be achieved and no challenge China couldn't confront, he added.

Li was not alone in feeling that sense of renewed confidence. Liu Yang, one of the co-authors of *Unhappy China*, also saw Xi's unabashed pride in the Chinese system as a crucial change from the country's other recent leaders. After 1989 and 1991, China lost all sense of self-worth, Liu told me. "China's collapse of confidence stemmed from the collapse of the Soviet Union," he said. "If *their* system could end, what about ours? And with intellectuals and politicians from the West predicting the collapse of China's system, this only aggravated the problem," he added. A host of problems China was experiencing, including official corruption and the rush by China's financial elites for foreign passports, were the product of this lack of confidence in the political system.

Liu read *China Can Say No* after its publication in 1996, and he was one of the millions for whom the book gave voice. During the 1990s, it was popular for the young, talented, and ambitious to go abroad, but Liu Yang wasn't interested. He had already learned enough about the United States to know that it wasn't for him. "There was this idea out there that if you were smart and had skills, and you had to go abroad, and if you didn't, there was something wrong with you," he said. That angered him. Besides, he'd already started to sour on the United States, having heard reports of rampant drug use, open prostitution, and reckless gambling. He vividly remembers one of his relatives, unable to afford health insurance in the United States, returning to China to see a doctor. He'd also been watching the hit TV show *A Beijinger in New York*, which had "shattered the idea that it was paradise abroad." The show was based on a 1991 novel of the same name, and it told the story of two Beijing residents who traveled to the United States to seek fame and fortune, only to find the reality of life in America filled with stress, chaos, and disappointment. The book was later adapted for TV in 1993 and became a smash hit. The moral was clear, as summarized by one viewer: "There has never been a savior. In New York, Beijingers must completely rely on themselves."[1] One critic wrote that the show could also be titled "Screw You, America."[2]

While Liu was never as radical as some of the writers who hung around Utopia, he was sympathetic to many of the concerns the neo-Maoists had in the years before Xi took office. He saw the open attacks on Mao Zedong by liberal intellectuals and historians as potentially destabilizing to the country, and he believed the United States had long ago decided it couldn't tolerate a strong and independent China. He'd also previously been generally unhappy with China's political leadership, which he felt was hesitant, corrupt, and unprincipled.

In the wake of the 2008 Global Financial Crisis, America's failed wars in the Middle East, and the recent upheaval in Europe (Brexit) and the United States (Trump), Liu believed China should no longer be looking to Western nations for advice. "We can see that the problems facing the West are increasing. We can see what they've done wrong and what we need to do right," he says. With Xi Jinping, "this is a key step for China." Indeed, Liu argued that China was finally on the cusp of reclaiming its national greatness, but he cautioned, "the final steps are the hardest."

In 2015, Liu published *Confident China: Great Thinking on the National Rejuvenation*, a celebration of Xi Jinping's idea of the "China Dream" and of the return of confidence to China and the Chinese people. If *Unhappy China* set out to puncture the idea that the West was superior, *Confident China* celebrated the country's indigenous institutions and culture.

Liu told me that he was hopeful about the future and optimistic about the leadership of Xi Jinping. There was still work to be done, particularly in guarding against historical nihilism, but with Xi in charge, China's prospects were bright.

For a time after Xi took power, observers in China and around the world were unsure of what to make of him. Early signs indicated he might be a reformer in the mold of Deng Xiaoping. Certainly, that was the kind of leader China needed, many believed. By the time of his ascension in 2012, conventional wisdom held that China was on the verge of an economic crisis. It had built up a precipitous and mounting pile of debt as a result of its response to the Global Financial Crisis, its SOEs needed painful reforms to boost their productivity and profitability, and it needed to open up its financial sector to increased foreign investment. A 473-page report jointly produced by the State Council's Development Research Center and the World Bank was published in February 2012 in anticipation of Xi's tenure, and it laid out the needed reform blueprint in laborious detail. All Xi needed to do was put these policy prescriptions in effect.

The initial indications were positive.

In early December 2012, less than a month after taking power, Xi visited the southern city of Shenzhen, the same city Deng had visited on his Southern Tour twenty years earlier. "Reform and Opening Up is a guiding policy that the Communist Party must stick to," he said. "We must keep to this correct path. We must stay unwavering on the road to a prosperous country and people, and there must be new pioneering." On December 8, Xi laid a wreath beneath a statue of Deng Xiaoping and declared that China must "dare to tackle tough issues and tread dangerous waters, dare to smash all inhibiting ideas and concepts, and dare to break free from the barriers of vested interests." Edward Wong of the *New York Times* saw Xi's visit as a "strong signal of support for greater market-oriented economic policies."[3] Xi's trip stood in contrast to Hu Jintao's inaugural trip to Xibaipo back in 2002, which anticipated the "left tilt" of the 2000s. "If [Xi] indeed went to Shenzhen that means he intends to make reform a subject of priority," political commentator Li Weidong said.[4] Wong's colleague at the *Times*, Nicholas Kristof, went further. On the same day Xi Jinping delivered his speech fusing the eras of Mao and Deng, Kristof predicted, "The new paramount leader, Xi Jinping, will spearhead a resurgence of economic reform, and probably some political easing as well. Mao's body will be hauled out of Tiananmen Square on his watch, and Liu Xiaobo, the Nobel Peace Prize–winning writer, will be released from prison."[5]

In the fall of 2013, another positive sign emerged from the Third Plenary meeting of the Eighteenth Party Congress, at which the party leadership declared that henceforth markets would play a "decisive role" in China's economy. *The Economist* described the decision as the party's "most wide-ranging and reform-tinged proposals for economic and social change in many years."[6]

Optimists held out hope for as long as they could, acknowledging that, sure, Xi was consolidating and personalizing power, but only, they insisted, so that he could carry out these badly needed reforms. While a few continued to believe this line in spite of the mounting evidence to the contrary, for most, the reformist sheen was wearing off. Or more accurately, the realization was sinking in that when Xi used the word "reform"—and he used it a lot—he wasn't talking about increased liberalization and privatization. Rather, reform meant the optimization of China's political system and the strengthening of the Communist

Party Xi led. Reform was about consolidating the party's grasp over the economy, not relinquishing it. It was about improving the party's hold over technology, not being subsumed by it. It was about dominating the public square, not being held hostage by it.

In retrospect, Xi agreed that China was approaching a crisis when he took office. But this was not the crisis others thought it was. The crisis Xi saw was not the urgency of economic reforms and a reckoning with state-owned enterprises, but rather a *political* crisis within the Communist Party. This was both a matter of national consequence and intensely personal. His father, Xi Zhongxun, was one of the party's revolutionary heroes, and had served the Communist Party his entire life. And Xi Jinping, in turn, had devoted his own life to what he believed was the single most important guarantor of China's survival. If Xi Jinping seemed easygoing, even aloof, in the decades he'd spent rising through the party ranks, those days were over. Immediately after taking office, he began taking control. Xi was setting out to make China great again.[7]

His drive to *re-form* the Chinese political system spared few, least of all the Communist Party itself. The wide-reaching "anti-graft" campaign led by Politburo Standing Committee member Wang Qishan was the most visible manifestation of Xi's intra-party rectification, but there were other significant reconstitutions of the CCP's organization and operations. Traditional bastions of elite-level patronage, such as the CCP Party School system and the Communist Youth League, came under sustained political pressure to increase their allegiance to Xi. Intra-party ideological and disciplinary campaigns began increasing in frequency and severity, while a raft of new organizational regulations and guidelines reshaped incentive structures for cadres up and down the party hierarchy.

The goal of these reforms was to arrest and reverse the CCP's internal decay by restoring rigid political and organizational discipline so that the party could lead the Chinese people to a "national rejuvenation," which Xi first outlined in November 2012. Far from being a relic of the twentieth century, in Xi's mind the party was bold, capable, disciplined, and absolutely vital to the country's continuing rise. As he declared in January 2016, "The Party leads all affairs—Party, political, military, civil, and academic—east, west, south, north, and center." On

July 1, 2016, the CCP celebrated its ninety-fifth anniversary—sixty-five of those years as the sole governing authority of the PRC. To mark the occasion, Xi delivered an eighty-minute speech in Beijing's Great Hall of the People in which he repeated one phrase ten times: "Don't forget your original intentions." His message to the eighty-nine million party members was clear: don't forget where the party came from or why you joined it in the first place.

If it took foreign observers at least a year to get a sense of Xi, neo-Maoists saw promise almost immediately.

For Zhang Hongliang, there were early signs that Xi's tenure would set China on a new political and economic trajectory. In a series of speeches, Zhang declared that Xi would bring "order out of chaos" to China and deliver a "victory for [China's] left wing."

"Xi Jinping basically agrees with me," he told me, "and if he can turn the neo-Maoists into his own political force, then he will certainly realize his goals."

Zhang had split with Utopia in the wake of the Bo Xilai affair. "They have departed from reality," he said, "and they are too extreme for me now." This was an odd statement coming from the individual who was largely responsible for the organization's radical turn after 2006, but Zhang believed that the main function of the neo-Maoists moving forward should be to rally around Xi and help him realize the China Dream. He wasn't sure if Utopia was willing to continue with this struggle, so he set out on this own.

One outstanding issue for Zhang was Xi's unwillingness to reassess the Cultural Revolution. So long as Xi declined to embrace the legacy from the Cultural Revolution, Zhang argued, China would never realize its full political potential. Harkening back to Ma Bin's call for a second Cultural Revolution in 2007, Zhang likewise saw revolution as an imperative to purify and revitalize the country's political system. "Intellectuals look at the Cultural Revolution but miss the process for its meaning," he told me. "It's like only seeing the blood of childbirth without taking note of the newly born baby. The mess is unavoidable."

There was also the issue of historical nihilism. So long as the Cultural Revolution remained enshrined in the 1981 History Resolution as a "catastrophe," it could be used as a cudgel against the party by its enemies. "In recent years, we have repeatedly stressed that the comprehensive denial of the Cultural Revolution has become a political knife for extreme right-wing forces at home and abroad to slaughter the party and the Chinese nation," Zhang wrote in early 2013. "The reason is very simple: so long as the Cultural Revolution is a catastrophe in human history, the system that produced this catastrophe is an evil system and the party that caused the catastrophe is a sinful party; the nation that caused the catastrophe is an evil nation."[8]

But he wasn't arguing that there should be a revolution against Xi Jinping. Rather, he was calling for Xi to lead one himself. "My hope is on the shoulders of Xi Jinping," he said. "It's only through him that China can rejuvenate."

After years of disappointment with the leadership in Beijing, Hu Muying was also finally satisfied with the party leadership now that Xi was in charge. "The breeze is blowing away the evil air," she declared to members of the Children of Yan'an Fellowship, an organization comprising descendants of the first generation of CCP revolutionaries. Hu, the daughter of Hu Qiaomu, was also an important backer of Utopia, having appeared at several of their events, including their first public event after their shuttering in response to the purge of Bo Xilai. In early 2014, Hu made a public display of support for Xi Jinping at a gathering of a thousand members of China's red aristocracy at the PLA propaganda film studio in Beijing to celebrate the Chinese New Year. She declared she was impressed with Xi's campaign to eradicate corruption from the CCP, although she warned that the struggle against graft would not be easy. "It's not like fighting landlords, Japanese devils, or the Kuomintang army, where the enemies are clear."[9]

For the neo-Maoist writer Sima Pingbang, the realization that Xi was a different type of party leader came in one sudden moment. It was December 26, 2013, the 120th anniversary of Mao Zedong's birth, and he was attending a calligraphy exhibition in a shabby Beijing hotel when someone pointed to a TV in the corner of the room that showed Xi Jinping and the entire Politburo Standing Committee visiting Mao's body in Tiananmen Square. He noticed people around the room starting to weep.

Sima Pingbang once considered himself a liberal, but beginning in the mid-2000s, he felt his political views were increasingly at odds with his sense of patriotism. He'd read *Unhappy China*, which had a profound impact on him, and he started to visit the Utopia website. Now, he said, he considered himself a nationalist. "My bottom line is that you can't attack or destroy the foundation of our political stability," he said.

"We won," the nationalist writer Wang Xiaodong told me. "Maybe I didn't win personally, but our ideas won." Looking at the policies Xi adopted in his first five years in power, Wang saw much to commend. China had moved away from relying on the market to allocate resources, it had reversed what he saw as a decade-long trend of restricting the growth of China's state sector, and the party was now embracing the idea of "national champion" firms serving China Inc. "The state of SOEs today is strong, roughly what I called for in the 1990s," Wang said. "My position has basically been realized."

"Xi Jinping is China's hope," said "Red Wing," the nom de plume of a young neo-Maoist writer who, after the purge of Bo Xilai, founded the *China Mao Zedong Paper*, an underground newspaper printed in Hong Kong and mailed to readers in the mainland. I first met Red Wing at the Utopia offices in the summer of 2015, and we stayed in contact. I saw him again in 2017, and although he'd shut down the newspaper ("We didn't have enough money . . . and the political situation was changing."), he remained active in neo-Maoist circles.

He said he'd started to do some research on Xi before he took office in 2012, and he saw promising signs, including Xi's clear desire for China to be a strong nation. After Xi's speech calling for the fusing of the pre- and post-Reform periods (i.e., the Mao and Deng years), Red Wing began to believe that Xi was "combining the best of Mao and the best of the Reform era so that China could travel in a new direction." When asked about neo-Maoist support for Xi, he told me that the movement today was "much calmer" than in its more restive years, culminating in the downfall of Bo Xilai. "For us, the most important thing is that the road is relatively correct," he said.

But did this mean Xi had tamed neo-Maoism?

Before his death in 2014, dissident and democracy advocate Chen Zeming wrote a detailed analysis of the neo-Maoist movement, which he saw as being composed of two basic groups: royalists and rebels.[10] This taxonomy, unsurprisingly, dates to the Cultural Revolution and the two primary categories of Red Guards. The royalists were the children of high-ranking cadres who had an interest in maintaining the status quo of the party power structure. The rebels, on the other hand, sought to tear down the existing order on behalf of Mao Zedong, who had instructed them, "To rebel is justified."

Chen saw neo-Maoists such as Zhang Hongliang as fundamentally *conservative*—as royalists—interested in defending the current regime from outside attacks and ensuring that its red color never changes.

The rebel faction, on the other hand, believed the party so corrupt and debased that it could not be saved from within. It was the rebel faction the party leadership needed to worry about, for they would never come to heel, Chen concluded.

That warning was prescient. In February 2015, rumors began circulating online that activists from across China had recently converged in Luoyang, a city in Henan Province, for the inaugural meeting of the China Maoist Alliance. Luoyang was an old Mao-era industrial base and was one of the region's most severely impacted by layoffs during the SOE reforms of the 1990s. Nostalgia for the Mao era runs deep in the city, and there were dozens of small organizations dedicated to Mao-era songs and dances, some dating back nearly twenty years.

A written summary of the two-day conference entitled "China's Maoist Communists Have United!" claimed that individuals traveled to Luoyang from thirteen provinces, cities, and autonomous regions to attend the event, with declarations of support being sent from "proletarian revolutionaries" in Shanghai and Beijing.[11]

"Over the past forty years, the Maoist communists have undertaken an arduous struggle to oppose the revisionist regime," the alliance declared. The "revisionist regime" here was the Communist Party of China under the leadership of Xi Jinping. "As the battle has deepened," the statement continued, "we have all wished for the [Maoists] to join forces, to unite, and to organize. With the Luoyang conference, the support and effort of the Maoist communists has finally allowed us to take this first step." The unknown author or authors of the statement concluded, "Chairman Mao has not died, Chairman Mao is forever with us, guiding the way forward. We firmly believe in these two phrases: the future is bright, and the road is winding. We will be victorious; we will inevitably be victorious."

News of the meeting spread rapidly on left-leaning blogs and on Weibo, and was posted on several neo-Maoist websites, including Redchina.net. "Raise both hands in resolute support!" one online supporter declared. "Maoists must welcome the great development of a wave of revolution!" wrote another.[12] Utopia was silent on the meeting at first, as were other established neo-Maoist websites such as Red Song Society. At Zhang Hongliang's website, National Rejuvenation, they believed the Luoyang meeting to be the work of "black hands" seeking to split the neo-Maoists from the Communist Party and to attack the leadership of Xi Jinping.[13]

In a show of support for Xi, or perhaps to publicly signal that they were not involved with the Luoyang meeting, establishment neo-Maoists held an event on March 21. Li Dingkai, the co-founder of Maoflag, was there, as were Gong Xiantian, Guo Songmin, Zhang Qinde, and Utopia's general manager Fan Jinggang. In total there were forty participants, and the neo-Maoists wanted the current party leadership to know they were on their side.

In his remarks, Fan Jinggang made it clear there was much for the neo-Maoists to be happy about. After twenty-three years of attacking the party and spreading historical nihilism, *Yanhuang Chunqiu* was finally being tamed. Recently planned lectures by He Weifang and Mao Yushi had been canceled after vocal online opposition. Cheng Enfu, a Marxist scholar and an early participant at Utopia events, had recently met with Politburo Standing Committee member Liu Yunshan. This was a sign, Fan believed, that Utopia's ideas were being taken seriously at the very top. Xi's anti-corruption campaign was finally attacking the rot within the party. After years on the sidelines, official publications such as *Red Flag* and the *PLA Daily* were finally willing to "flash their swords" and join the struggle in the ideological realm.

Overall, Fan remarked, "our domestic political situation is gradually improving."[14]

Fan's optimism aside, there remained a core tension between the neo-Maoists (Utopia included) and the party's top leadership. For all of the moves Xi had made to clamp down on liberal voices, to glorify the Communist Party, and to rehabilitate Mao Zedong, his party was still pursuing a broadly state capitalist agenda, even if the "state" had become more pronounced since 2012. Multinational firms were still setting up factories, employing Chinese nationals, and making products to serve the global marketplace. *Hanjian* intellectuals still held prominent positions in academia and in the government. Leftist websites were still occasionally censored. And Xi's vision of a tightly disciplined political order was about as far away from Mao's millenarian radicalism as could be. All in all, if you were a thoroughgoing neo-Maoist in Xi Jinping's China, there should be a great deal to be dissatisfied with.

Just ask the workers at Shenzhen Jasic Technology, a private manufacturer of welding equipment listed on the Shenzhen Stock Exchange. In May 2018, employees attempted to unionize after frequent complaints over their poor working conditions, abusive treatment by management, and chronic low pay. One former employee told journalists from *Reuters*, "Sometimes we would work for one month straight without any time off. . . . They wouldn't let us freely quit and they even watched us go to the toilet."[15] Workers at the factory contacted the local branch of China's sole recognized labor union organizer, the All-China Federation of Trade Unions, and after being rebuffed, they took matters into their own hands.

The party's reaction to the attempted unionization included a mixture of force and innuendo.

On July 27, twenty-nine workers from the Jasic factory were detained for "picking quarrels and stirring up trouble," a vague charge frequently used by the authorities to quash speech or action that isn't covered by more specific legal statutes. One month later, heavily armed police arrested fifty students and workers who had begun a campaign to push for the release of the detained workers. Back in Beijing, the government raided the offices of the sympathetic *Red Reference* magazine, detaining one employee. "They searched every corner of our offices, and even smashed a cupboard, and took our computers, our books away in a bunch of boxes," said magazine editor-in-chief Cheng Hongtao.[16]

State media made similarly opaque accusations of "foreign-funded advocacy groups" seeking to "instigate illegal labor action." An anonymous "Beijing-based analyst" told the *Global Times*, "Those who advocate 'independent workers' unions' want to impact the Chinese society at its very core because a trade union without government involvement is not in accordance with Chinese characteristics."[17]

On August 4, Utopia organized a protest with forty of its supporters outside the police station holding the Jasic workers. Photos from the event show protestors holding photos of Mao Zedong and holding banners reading, "WORKERS ARE INNOCENT." Zhang Qinde gave an impromptu speech, in which he said, "We hold that party members and veteran cadres must walk at the front of this struggle. We must stand with the working classes and advance and retreat with the Jasic workers. We must see this struggle through till the end!"[18] He later released a public statement calling for the immediate release of the workers and for a full investigation into the complaints made about Jasic's management.[19]

One of the detained was a regular reader of Utopia named Tang Xiangwei. He later drafted a statement explaining how he'd come to join the struggle to unionize:

> When I was at the steel factory, I slowly started to become familiar with Utopia, Maoflag, Red Song Union, Red Flag, etc. I gradually began to understand Mao Zedong and Maoism as well as the history leading up to the Reform and Opening Up and the events that followed. It became increasingly clear to me why my grandfather recalls so fondly the era of state-owned enterprises.[20]

Yue Xin, a twenty-two-year-old graduate of Peking University, also took seriously Mao's exhortation to "serve the people." She posted a video online admonishing her fellow classmates for not taking a greater interest in the unfolding labor dispute in Shenzhen. "Lots of fellow students say: this incident is about workers, what does this have to do with students? I'll tell them one thing: today's students are tomorrow's workers."[21] On August 19, she took the extraordinary step of writing an open letter to Xi Jinping and the Party's Central Committee in which she declared that her commitment to socialism demanded solidarity with the detained workers. "As a young person who grew up in socialist New China, a youth who lives in the New Era [a reference to China under Xi Jinping], I have no excuse to stand by and do nothing, to look on helplessly as the workers of Shenzhen struggle alone."[22]

Shen Mengyu also took the party's claims of socialism seriously. She studied mathematics at Sun Yat-sen University, located in the heartland of China's manufacturing industry. In an open letter, Shen wrote,

During my time studying at Sun Yat-sen, a variety of seminars and talks gave me a window into understanding workers. I saw victims of occupational injuries, crippled under the turning wheel of economic development; and Foxconn workers free-falling from factory rooftops, their lives worth but a trifle; I learned about a type of occupational illness called silicosis, which put its victims through living hell, and also benzene poisoning, leukemia, noise-induced deafness.[23]

She was detained by local authorities in August for aiding the Jasic workers. Two student activists who were present told a reporter that she was "bundled into a car by three unidentified men" after eating dinner with her parents.[24]

Another activist said of Shen, "She believes in Mao Zedong and she believes in communism. That's what makes this unfortunate."[25]

As of early 2019, the campaign to crush these Marxist students and labor activists continues. For all its many platitudes about upholding socialism, the CCP still has little tolerance for actual socialists. As it was for Deng Xiaoping in 1992, so it is for Xi Jinping in 2019: "China should maintain vigilance against the Right but primarily against the 'Left.'"

EPILOGUE

———◆———

DO THE NEO-MAOISTS STILL MATTER?

AS I NEARED COMPLETION of the final draft of this book in late 2018, I had already concluded that if I had a time machine, I would have warned my 2011 self to pick a different subject to focus on. The phenomenon that originally animated this book—leftist dissident forces that appeared to be flanking the Chinese Communist Party—was, six years into the reign of Xi Jinping, already showing signs of distress, even irrelevance. While a few pockets of hard leftist protest occasionally burst forth, such as demonstrations of worker-student solidarity described in the final chapter, for all intents and purposes, leftism *as an organized movement* had succumbed to the same forces of repression that had quieted the rest of China's once-vibrant public square.

In this, the many intense political debates and policy controversies that animated intellectual discussion in the decade following China's accession to the WTO in 2001 now seem a distant memory. I remember helping organize a conference in 2010 or 2011 at a university in the northeast of Beijing where the keynote speaker was an American expert on Tocqueville's *Democracy in America*. Dozens of curious and engaged students filled the small classroom to hear a subdued American scholar explain the significance of Tocqueville's magnum opus for the United

States and for China. There were once scores of intellectual salons in Beijing with speakers from across the ideological spectrum gathered to discuss and debate serious issues about socialism, democracy, capitalism, and imperialism. The Unirule Institute, Mao Yushi's creation, famously hosted a biweekly symposium at its offices in Haidian district for more than a decade. Looking back on my notes, the topics under discussion ranged from "the Thought of F. A. Hayek" to "Hukou and Gender Discrimination." And it wasn't just Beijing. In 2015, I took an overnight train to Changsha, the provincial capital of Hunan, to meet with leftist activists who had started a fortnightly salon dedicated to "visions of democracy." To be sure, most of these visions were illiberal visions, but still, the passion to explore alternative trajectories for the country's future was widespread.

Unfortunately, the Communist Party's pursuit of political stability has come at a steep price. Now, less than a decade later, such activities are unimaginable.

As of this writing, in early winter of 2021, the intellectual climate in China is a sorry shadow of its once-thriving self. Over the past decade, Xi Jinping has erected a fearsome system of technologically enabled repression and surveillance. At its extremes, it has enveloped the entirety of the Xinjiang Uyghur Autonomous Region, transforming it into a virtual prison. But even in the thriving "first tier" cities of Beijing and Shenzhen, signs of Xi's all-encompassing national security vision are evident. Where political discussion was once robust, it is now muted, taking place under the din of noisy restaurants or in the relative safety of once's apartment.

The space for contestation has been severely constricted for both the left and the right.

On the right, the once visible cast of economists, legal scholars, political scientists, and historians who not long ago pushed a bold agenda of constitutionalism, market reforms, and a blunt reconciliation with the Maoist past have all but vanished from public debate. Journals like *Yanhuang Chunqiu*, the legendary bastion of liberal-leaning soft authoritarianism, now churns out paeans to the Eighth Route Army or superficial oral histories of retired CCP cadres. Members of the once active legal reform community have been harassed or imprisoned. Intellectuals who challenged the Party's historical line quickly came under intense criticism for the supposed crime of "historical nihilism," a catch-all term for anything that deviates from established orthodoxy. Most tragically, the movement to realize Hong Kong's democracy (as promised by the CCP) has been utterly crushed, with more than one hundred individuals now awaiting trial on charges of violating "national security."

Yet the left too has come under attack, albeit to a much lesser extent than the voices pushing China in a more liberal direction. In some ways, the neo-Maoists never recovered after the Bo Xilai affair, which fully and finally signaled to the CCP that the group wasn't just a nuisance, but also a political force. Never again would they organize street marches, hold raucous salon events, physically disrupt speaking events, or solicit tens of thousands of signatures for public petitions. Instead, many of them filled the only space allowed for them—acting as ideological cyber guardians for the Xi regime. Here they could act as online police, bullying and hectoring writers, bloggers, intellectuals, and regular citizens who published content that violated their nationalist sentiments.

Unsurprisingly, the outbreak of the Covid-19 virus has resurfaced many of the nationalist left's most conspiratorial instincts, which have found a welcome home on Utopia and other nationalist left and neo-Maoist websites. Inevitably, commentary on these websites assigns blame for the origins of the virus to the United States (in this way, parroting the official line from Beijing), but also goes further in seeing Covid-19 as a deliberate bioweapon designed by the "Western elite" to wipe out large swaths of the global population.[1] The writer Fang Fang, who was briefly discussed in chapter 5, was recently (and yet again) pilloried as a "race traitor" after her firsthand account of the Covid-19 lockdown in Wuhan was published in English. She had become, one author on the Utopia website wrote, a "pawn of the global anti-China and anti-Chinese national forces."[2] Yet another Utopia writer speculated, without offering any evidence, "After Fang Fang's diary was finished, it was translated at the speed of light and quickly published in Europe, America, and in other countries. Is there no shadow of the CIA behind this?"[3]

This is not to say that the neo-Maoists, or the nationalist left, are completely subservient to Xi. Clear themes of dissent run through their analysis. One continues to see warnings that "Western capital" plays a dominant, even controlling, role in China's political and economic system. Ironically, at precisely the same time that Western capitals and corporations are decrying their lack of fair market access in China, neo-Maoists are proclaiming "Western capital has actually kidnapped Chinese politics."[4] This mentality of "Western infiltration" of China's political and economic institutions isn't necessarily at odds with the Party's own outlook, but it does come with an intensity and a thoroughness that Beijing, undoubtedly, would prefer to see muted.

The neo-Maoist vision for socialism also stands in tension with Xi's actual existing economic policies. Despite his frequent invocations of "socialism," Xi has not fundamentally broken with the trajectory of Leninist capitalism that his predecessors created beginning in the early 1990s. State-led, bureaucratic capitalism is still the order of the day, even if it comes wrapped in encomiums to equity and social justice. As of this writing, Xi has rolled out the phrase "common prosperity," which would seem to mark a shift to the left, but as the rush of neo-Maoist commentary makes clear, few see this as anything but signboard socialism. Neoliberal logic, albeit of an increasingly totalitarian variety, continues to govern the Party's economic behavior, even as Xi promotes campaigns around poverty alleviation and environmental protection.

Returning to the title affixed to this epilogue: do the neo-Maoists matter? As an emergent, independent political force that can fundamentally reshape Chinese politics, no. Xi Jinping isn't worried about neo-Maoists and he doesn't need to worry about being outflanked to the left, as, perhaps, his predecessors once did. The Party holds a firm grip on both the digital and physical realm, which means neo-Maoists have few avenues for dissent. And, broadly speaking, they aren't inclined to press the challenge so long as Xi proclaims the glory of the CCP, shows sympathy for Mao Zedong, and asserts China's interests on the global stage. He may not be as radical as some neo-Maoists would like, but when compared to the "compradors" they believed ran Party for much of the Reform and Opening period, he's a big improvement.

Had I known the story would end here, in the cul-de-sac of Xi Jinping's autocratic rule, I likely wouldn't have started this book. But perhaps this isn't the right way to assess their relevance. Rather than seen as a *sui generis* phenomenon, neo-Maoists and neo-Maoism represent but one strain of conservative nationalism that has evolved and persisted since the death of Mao Zedong and the beginning of the reform period. While neo-Maoists might be losing influence, many of their underlying ideas—about the glory of the Party, the need for an aggressively nationalist foreign policy—are, if anything, gaining credence.

And as we've seen here in America, the forces of crude nationalism and illiberalism, even when pushed to the margins of society, can still exert a profoundly corrosive effect on the health of a polity. In the same way that the toxicity of Twitter stems almost entirely from the actions of an outspoken minority, so too can such actors poison a nation's civil discourse. The xenophobic paranoia of the neo-Maoists, combined with their antipathy to pluralistic discourse, mean they will continue to degrade China's intellectual climate so long as the Party blocks counterbalancing voices from the public square.

This, then, is the critical question. How much longer will *this* iteration of the CCP leadership be in power? It is tempting to end on a note of optimism. Xi Jinping will relinquish power in the near future, won't he? Or perhaps his overly aggressive and statist approach to governance will elicit a backlash that will force a course correction. Perhaps, as some have predicted, his colleagues at the senior echelons of the party-state apparatus will "request" that Xi step aside. Indeed, in his wonderful 1991 essay, "Now Out of Never: The Element of Surprise in the East European Revolution of 1989," the economist Timur Kuran observed, "Time and again entrenched authority has vanished suddenly, leaving the victors astonished at their triumph and the vanquished, at their defeat."

All of these scenarios are possible. Yet for the time being, improbable. Xi is in his late sixties—young for a dictator—and there are no signs that he intends to yield power, nor that anyone has the ability to do anything about it even if they object. The Chinese Communist Party of 2021 is not the Communist Party of the Soviet Union of 1989. It is far better resourced and organized. The Chinese economy of today, its many problems notwithstanding, shares little with the Soviet economy of the 1980s. It is far more dynamic and institutionalized.

Perhaps, then, instead of ending with a grand prognostication about Xi Jinping's or the Party's future—and thus, China's future—I will instead issue a call to action. It is easy to be indignant about Xi's increasingly totalitarian rule. We should be indignant. Yet the task ahead is not to ramp up our moral revulsion, but to expand our cognitive empathy so that we better understand how the political system thinks and works, refine our tools of objective analysis, and drop the (often condescending) illusions about where we think the country is headed (or more often, where we think it *should* head). This is a deeply unsatisfying conclusion, especially for us Americans, long accustomed to comforting visions of convergence with our way of life. China, now, is clearly headed in a new direction, one that does not accord with our mental maps of either market capitalism or Soviet drudgery. To understand where it's going, we need to listen and observe.

NOTES

Introduction

1. Deng Xiaoping, "Excerpts From Talks Given in Wuchang, Shenzhen, Zhuhai, and Shanghai, January 18–February 21, 1991," *Collected Works*, Vol. 3. http://www.china.org.cn/english/features/dengxiaoping/103331.htm

2. "Kim Jong-un's "Bitter Sorrow" as Bus Crash Kills Chinese Tourists," BBC, April 24, 2018. https://www.bbc.com/news/world-asia-43875526

3. "韓媒：涉中國公民在朝交通事故 4朝鮮官員被槍決3要員被降職" https://www.hk01.com/外媒視點/196248/ 韓媒-涉中國公民在朝交通事故-4朝鮮官員被槍決3要員被降職

4. "2017红色旅游热度报告：客群年轻化 '红绿配'受关注," travel. people.com.cn/n1/2017/0706/c41570-29386127.html

5. "Prominent Maoist Editor Among Chinese Who Died in North Korean Bus Crash," Radio Free Asia, April 25, 2018. https://www.rfa.org/english/ news/china/crash-04252018115303.html

6. 郭松民：刁伟铭同志不朽！斯人已去，事业永存!, www.szhgh.com/ Article/opinion/xuezhe/2018-04-28/168641.html

7. Andrew Higgins, "Confucius Descendant Incites Controversy with Insults to Hong Kongers," *Washington Post*, January 22, 2012; 孔庆东：建议授予刁伟铭 "中朝友好勋章"和 "中朝人民友谊使者"光荣称号, www.szhgh.com/Article/opinion/xuezhe/2018-05-08/169658.html

8. 王立华：悼念红色旅游事业的开拓者刁伟铭, www.szhgh.com/ Article/opinion/xuezhe/2018-05-02/168993.html

9. For a fascinating history of the Cultural Revolution, see Wu Yiching, *The Cultural Revolution at the Margins: Chinese Socialism in Crisis* (Cambridge, MA: Harvard University Press, 2014).

10. William Hurst, *The Chinese Worker after Socialism*
(Cambridge: Cambridge University Press, 2009), 1.

11. Quoted in Victor Shih, " 'Nauseating' Displays of Loyalty: Monitoring
the Factional Bargain Through Ideological Campaigns," *Journal of Politics*
70, no. 4 (2008): 1177–92.

12. 韩德强, 我为什么反对中国加入世贸组织, November 19, 2001,
https://www.china-week.com/html/1261.htm

13. Author interview with Zhang Hongliang, June 2015.

14. Chris Buckley, "China's Leftists Dig In for Fight Over Bo Xilai," Reuters,
August 20, 2012.

15. For the only extent study of the neo-Maoists, see 催金珂, 当代 "毛泽东
左派"思潮分析—以"乌有之乡"网站为例.

16. 韩德强, "我崇拜毛泽东," December 28, 2008. www.aisixiang.com/data/
24275.html

17. Ching Kwan Lee, *Against the Law: Labor Protests in China's Rustbelt and
Sunbelt* (Berkeley: University of California Press, 2007), 145.

18. Author interview, July 23, 2014.

19. "中国工人网为什么被扼杀了," www.wyzxwk.com/Article/zatan/2009/
09/31403.html

20. 范景刚, "悼念刁伟铭同志," www.wyzxwk.com/Article/shidai/2018/05/
389226.html

21. 赵思乐, "揭秘乌有之乡," http://minzhuzhongguo.org/MainArtShow.
aspx?AID=32326

22. Alan Taylor, "The Last Maoist Village in China," The Atlantic.com,
October 1, 2012. http://www.theatlantic.com/photo/2012/10/the-last-
maoist-village-in-china/100378/

23. "纪念抗美援朝战争胜利61周年暨张宏良北京讲座活动公告," www.
wyzxwk.com/Article/gonggao/2014/06/321733.html

24. 南方人物周刊, "'乌有之乡'在朝鲜," https://bit.ly/2SJujOI

25. "郑州爱国群众颂议中朝友谊使者刁伟铭," www.wyzxwk.com/
Article/shidai/2018/05/389049.html

26. 热烈祝贺朝鲜第三次核试验成功，redchinacn.net/portal.
php?mod=view&aid=7516

27. 特别报道：乌有之乡成功举办朝鲜文化艺术之夜活动 艾跃进主,
www.szhgh.com/Article/thirdworld/korea/201404/49599.html

28. 当局禁 "乌有之乡"只为避免 "卖国"指控？, https://www.rfa.org/
mandarin/yataibaodao/jingmao/gf1-05212018100922.html

29. It's important to point out here that I'm referring primarily to the non-
specialist literature on modern China, and excluding James Mann's
prophetic book, *The China Fantasy: Why Capitalism Will Not Bring
Democracy to China.*

30. Chris Miller, *The Struggle to Save the Soviet Economy: Mikhail Gorbachev
and the Collapse of the USSR* (Chapel Hill: University of North Carolina
Press, 2016), 42.

31. Nicholas D. Kristof, "China: The End of the Golden Road," *New York Times,* December 1, 1991.

32. Max Frankel, "A Great, Irrelevant Wall," *New York Times*, October 25, 1998.

33. "In Bush's Words: 'Join Together in Making China a Normal Trading Partner'", *New York Times*, May 18, 2000.

34. Nicholas D. Kristof, "The Tiananmen Victor," *New York Times*, June 2, 2004.

35. Andy Kennedy, "For China, the Tighter the Grip, the Weaker the Hand," *Washington Post*, January 17, 1999.

36. Roger Cohen, "Peaceful Evolution Angst," *New York Times*, May 24, 2009.

37. https://asiancorrespondent.com/2008/10/mr-lee-kuan-yew-an-interview/

38. Author interview, July 9, 2017.

39. William A. Joseph, *The Critique of Ultra-Leftism in China, 1958–1981* (Stanford, CA: Stanford University Press, 1984).

40. Feng Chen, "An Unfinished Battle in China: The Leftist Criticism of the Reform and the Third Thought Emancipation," *China Quarterly*, no. 158 (June 1999): 447–67.

41. Mark Mazower, *Dark Continent: Europe's Twentieth Century* (London: Penguin Books, 1999), 375–76.

42. For a compelling version of this argument, see John Garnaut's speech "Engineers of the Soul: What Australia Needs to Know About Ideology in Xi Jinping's China," available online at https://nb.sinocism.com/p/engineers-of-the-soul-ideology-in. For a persuasive rebuttal, see Christian Sorace, "From the Outside Looking In: A Response to John Garnaut's Primer on Ideology," https://madeinchinajournal.com/2019/02/07/from-the-outside-looking-in-a-response-to-john-garnauts-primer-on-ideology/.

43. Tu Wei-ming, "The Modern Chinese Intellectual Quest," in *Way, Learning, and Politics: Essays on the Confucian Intellectual* (Albany: State University of New York Press, 1993), 173.

44. "右派分析：为何有人害怕张宏良教授?", www.szhgh.com/Article/opinion/zatan/20695.html.

45. I'd like to thank Andrew Chubb for pointing me in this direction.

46. See Andrew Chubb, "Democracy Wall, Foreign Correspondents, and Deng Xiaoping," *Pacific Affairs* 89, no. 3 (September 2016). For one of the original formulations of the "radical flank" idea, see Herbert Haines, *Black Radicals and the Civil Rights Mainstream, 1954–1970* (Knoxville: University of Tennessee Press, 1988).

47. I again need to thank Andrew Chubb for this suggestion. It's both helpful and frustrating to have smart friends who can immediately see a much cleaner explanation to a problem I've been wrestling with for years.

48. Eli Friedman, "China in Revolt," *Jacobin* 7/8, 2012.

49. 中国工人网为什么被扼杀了, www.wyzxwk.com/Article/zatan/2009/09/31403.html

50. Margaret MacMillan, *Dangerous Games: The Uses and Abuses of History* (New York: Modern Library, 2010).

51. Eric Foner, *Who Owns History? Rethinking the Past in a Changing World* (New York: Farrar, Straus and Giroux, 2002), 77.

52. Sabrina Tavernise, "When History's Losers Write the Story," *New York Times*, September 15, 2017.

53. James S. Robbins, *Erasing America: Losing Our Future by Destroying Our Past* (Washington, DC: Regnery Publishing, 2018).

54. See "The Stalin Puzzle: Deciphering Post-Soviet Public Opinion," http://carnegieendowment.org/2013/03/01/stalin-puzzle-deciphering-post-soviet-public-opinion/fmz8

55. Amy Qin, "A Photographer's Quest to Reverse China's Historical Amnesia," *New York Times*, January 1, 2019.

56. Fang Lizhi, "The Chinese Amnesia," *The New York Review of Books*, September 27, 1990.

57. 习近平在中国共产党第十九次全国代表大会上的报告, cpc.people.com.cn/n1/2017/1028/c64094-29613660- 5.html

Chapter 1

1. Qian Liqun, "Refusing to Forget," in Wang Chaohua, *One China, Many Paths* (London: Verso, 2003), 305.

2. "Text of the Announcement Issued by Peking Reporting Death of Chairman Mao," Xinhua News Agency, September 10, 1976.

3. "China Cancels National Holiday Because of the Death of Mao," *New York Times*, September 25, 1976.

4. 李振盛, 1976年9月9日毛泽东逝世, blog.sina.com.cn/s/blog_62aefc6a0100x44g.html. Accessed on April 16, 2017.

5. 辛子陵: 红太阳的陨落 : 千秋功罪毛泽东, 书作坊出版社 , 2008, 446.

6. Pankaj Mishra, "The Bonfire of China's Vanities," *New York Times*, January 23, 2009.

7. 沈应维 "9月9日忆中国伟人," http://www.szhgh.com/Article/opinion/zatan/201509/95426.html. Accessed September 26, 2015.

8. Ibid.

9. "Chinese in Peking Sob Loudly at Hearing About Mao's Death," Agence France-Presse, September 9, 1976.

10. Quoted in Lowell Dittmer, *China's Continuous Revolution: The Post-Liberation Epoch, 1949–1981* (Berkeley: University of California Press, 1989), 118.

11. Bill Bishop, "Badges of Chairman Mao Zedong," *China News Digest International*, http://www.cnd.org/CR/old/Foreign_public_opinion/maobadge/index.html. Accessed February 14, 2016.

12. Joanna Wardęga, "Mao Zedong in Present-Day China: Forms of Deification," *Politics and Religion* 6, no. 2 (2017), 181–97.

13. Ji Chaozhu, *The Man on Mao's Right: From Harvard Yard to Tiananmen Square, My Life Inside China's Foreign Ministry* (New York: Random House, 2008), 291.

14. 人民网, "1976年9月悼念毛泽东纪实" http://www.mod.gov.cn/hist/2014-02/26/content_4492803.htm. Accessed January 12, 2016.

15. Li Zhisui, *The Private Life of Chairman Mao* (New York: Random House, 2011), 15.

16. Sidney Rittenberg, *The Man Who Stayed Behind* (Durham, NC: Duke University Press, 2001), 427.

17. Fox Butterfield, "Chinese Conflicts Are Persisting After Mao's Death," *New York Times*, October 1, 1976.

18. Quoted in Andrew G. Walder, *China Under Mao: A Revolution Derailed* (Cambridge, MA: Harvard University Press, 2015), 217.

19. Harrison Salisbury, *The New Emperors* (New York: Avon Books, 1992), 367.

20. Richard Baum, *Burying Mao: Chinese Politics in the Age of Deng Xiaoping* (Princeton, NJ: Princeton University Pres, 1996), 404.

21. Fox Butterfield, "So Far, Hua Maintaining a Calm Hold on the Helm," *New York Times*, December 19, 1976.

22. William A. Joseph, *The Critique of Ultra-Leftism in China, 1958–1981* (Stanford, CA: Stanford University Press, 1984), 157.

23. Joseph, *The Critique of Ultra-Leftism in China*, 154.

24. Oriana Fallaci, "Deng: Cleaning Up Mao's Mistakes," *Washington Post*, August 31, 1980.

25. Fox Butterfield, "Chinese Emphasize More Study of Mao," *New York Times*, October 2, 1976.

26. Quoted in James Palmer, *Heaven Cracks, Earth Shakes: The Tangshan Earthquake and the Death of Mao's China* (New York: Basic Books, 2012), 179.

27. Fox Butterfield, "Chinese Conflicts Are Persisting After Mao's Death," *New York Times*, October 1, 1976.

28. Ross Munro, "In China, Writing on Wall Can Be Fatal," *Chicago Tribune*, October 11, 1977.

29. See especially the pioneering work of Frederick C. Teiwes and Warren Sun in "China's New Economic Policy Under Hua Guofeng: Party Consensus and Party Myth," *China Journal*, no. 66 (2011), and their book *Paradoxes of Post-Mao Rural Reform: Initial Steps Toward a New Chinese Countryside, 1976–1981* (New York: Routledge, 2016).

30. Strobe Talbot, ed., *Khrushchev Remembers: The Last Testament* (Boston: Little, Brown, 1974), 253.

31. Quoted in Michael Schoenhals, "The 1978 Truth Criterion Controversy," *China Quarterly*, no. 126 (June 1991): 243–68.

32. Frederick C. Teiwes and Warren Sun in "China's New Economic Policy Under Hua Guofeng: Party Consensus and Party Myth," *China Journal*, no. 66 (2011).

33. Alexander V. Pantsov and Steven I. Levine, *Deng Xiaoping: A Revolutionary Life* (New York: Oxford University Press, 2015), 336.

34. Ezra Vogel, *Deng Xiaoping and the Transformation of China* (Cambridge, MA: Harvard University Press, 2011), 218.

35. 于光远, 1978: 我亲历的那次历史大转折: 一十一届三中全会的台前幕后, 中央编译出版社, 2008.

36. 黄一兵, "理论工作务虚会与《关于建国以来党的若干历史问题的决议》的起草," 中共党史研究. 2013 (04).

37. 廖盖隆, "怎样回答社会主义制度的优越性问题?," 1979年1月25日, 理论工作务虚会简报, 总第63期. .

38. 中共中央党史研究室, "中国共产党的九十年: 改革开放和社会主义现代化建设新时期," 2016, 659.

39. Quoted in 吴江, "1979年理论工作务虚会追忆," 炎黄春秋杂志, 2001年第11期.

40. Quoted in 吴江, "1979年理论工作务虚会追忆," 炎黄春秋杂志, 2001年第11期.

41. 薛庆超, 革故与鼎新:红墙决策, 中共中央党校出版社, 2006年, 7–8.

42. 于浩成, "参加理论务虚会的经过," 炎黄春秋, 2016年第1期..

43. Quoted in 吴江, "1979年理论工作务虚会追忆," 炎黄春秋杂志, 2001年第11期. In Chinese, this is the difference between 毛泽东同志的思想 and 毛泽东思想.

44. 于浩成, "参加理论务虚会的经过," 炎黄春秋, 2016年第1期.

45. Merle Goldman, "Hu Yaobang's Intellectual Network and the Theory Conference of 1979," *China Quarterly*, no. 126 (June 1991): 219–42.

46. "吴德口述: 十年风雨纪事—我在北京工作的一些经历," 当代中国出版社, 2004年, 第251页. .

47. Ruan Ming, *Deng Xiaoping: Chronicle of an Empire* (Boulder, CO: Westview Press, 1994), 53.

48. Ming, *Deng Xiaoping: Chronicle of an Empire*, 53.

49. Quoted in Vogel, *Deng Xiaoping and the Transformation of China*, 707.

50. Ming, *Deng Xiaoping: Chronicle of an Empire*, 46.

51. Andrew Chubb, "Democracy Wall, Foreign Correspondents, and Deng Xiaoping," *Pacific Affairs* 89, no. 3 (September 2016).

52. Fox Butterfield, "New Peking Posters Ask for Democracy and Praise the US," *New York Times*, November 26, 1978.

53. Jay Mathews, "Wall Posters Deepen Puzzle About Mao's Eventual Status," *Washington Post*, January 7, 1979.

54. This anecdote comes from Oriana Fallaci's 1980 interview with Deng Xiaoping. See "Deng: Cleaning Up Mao's 'Feudal Mistakes,'" *Washington Post*, August 31, 1980.

55. Quoted in Pantsov and Levine, *Deng Xiaoping: A Revolutionary Life*, 327.

56. Merle Goldman, "Hu Yaobang's Intellectual Network and the Theory Conference of 1979," *China Quarterly* 126 (June 1991): 219–42.

57. Jay Mathews, "Peking Officials Planning Action Against Democracy Wall," *Washington Post*, December 2, 1979.

58. Michael Dutton, *Policing Chinese Politics* (Durham, NC: Duke University Press, 2005), 270.

59. Quoted in Simon Leys, *The Burning Forest: Essays on Chinese Culture and Politics* (London: Paladin Grafton Books, 1988), 157.

60. 邓力群自述：十二个春秋, http://6ond.org/Article_Print. asp?ArticleID=562, Accessed on April 16, 2017.

61. 邓力群自述：十二个春秋, http://6ond.org/Article_Print. asp?ArticleID=562, Accessed on April 16, 2017.

62. Deng Xiaoping, "Uphold the Four Cardinal Principles," *Selected Works of Deng Xiaoping*, Vol. 3, *1982–1992*.

63. 叶永烈, 胡乔木：中共中央一支笔, 广西人民出版社 , 2007, 228.

64. Oriana Fallaci, "Deng: Cleaning Up Mao's 'Feudal Mistakes,'" *Washington Post*, August 31, 1980.

65. Deng Xiaoping, "Remarks on Successive Drafts of the 'Resolution on Certain Questions in the History of Our Party Since the Founding of the People's Republic of China,'" *Selected Works of Deng Xiaoping*, Vol. 2, *1975–1982*.

66. The final document was unanimously approved at the Sixth Plenary Session of the Eleventh Central Committee of the Communist Party of China on June 27, 1981.

67. 逄先知, 金冲及"1976年毛泽东自评文革：基本正确 成绩占七分," August 23, 2012. news.ifeng.com/history/zhongguoxiandaishi/detail_ 2012_08/23/17039415_0.shtml

68. Mao Zedong, "Be Activists in Promoting the Revolution," *Selected Works of Mao Tse-Tung*, Vol. 5, https://www.marxists.org/reference/archive/mao/ selected-works/volume-5/index.htm

69. Oriana Fallaci, "Deng: Cleaning Up Mao's 'Feudal Mistakes,'" *Washington Post*, August 31, 1980.

70. Deng Xiaoping, "The 'Two Whatevers' Do Not Accord With Marxism," *Selected Works of Deng Xiaoping*, Vol. 2, *1975–1982*.

71. Ming, *Deng Xiaoping: Chronicle of an Empire*, 89.

Chapter 2

1. Quoted in Christopher Wren, "Peking Reshaping Ideology to Fit New Economic Policy," *New York Times*, December 17, 1984.

2. 吴松营, "1992 年邓小平南巡'最高机密'刊发记," 广闻博览, 2012年09期. Ezra Vogel contends Deng set off from Beijing with one journalist and one photographer. See Ezra F. Vogel, *Deng Xiaoping and the Transformation of China* (Cambridge, MA: Harvard University Press, 2011), 672.

3. Vogel, *Deng Xiaoping and the Transformation of China* (Cambridge, MA: Harvard University Press, 2011), 669.

4. 吴松营, "1992 年邓小平南巡'最高机密'刊发记," 广闻博览, 2012年09期.

5. Z., "To the Stalin Mausoleum," *Daedalus* 119, no. 1 (Winter 1990): 295–344.

6. Deng Xiaoping, "With Stable Policies of Reform and Opening to the Outside World, China Can Have Great Hopes for the Future," *Selected Works of Deng Xiaoping*, Vol. 3, *1982–1992*.

7. It's important to add a caveat to this statement: although there was no wholesale political reform program, there were important innovations at the local level that sought to increase political participation. The fate of these 1990s' reforms is the subject of Joseph Fewsmith's *The Logic and Limits of Political Reform in China* (Cambridge: Cambridge University Press, 2013).

8. Deng Xiaoping, "The International Situation and Economic Problems," *Selected Works of Deng Xiaoping*, Vol. 3, *1982–1992*.

9. Deng Xiaoping, "With Stable Policies of Reform and Opening to the Outside World," *Selected Works of Deng Xiaoping*, Vol. 3, *1982–1992*.

10. Quoted in Michael E. Marti, *China and the Legacy of Deng Xiaoping: From Communist Revolution to Capitalist Evolution* (Lincoln, NE: Potomac Books, 2002).

11. Lena H. Sun, "Chinese Battening Hatches," *Washington Post*, September 11, 1991.

12. 龚学增, 民族危机与苏联解体——苏联民族问题的反思, 理论前沿1992年第18期.

13. Quoted in Barry Naughton, *Growing Out of the Plan* (Cambridge: Cambridge University Press, 1995), 275.

14. Zhao Suisheng, "Deng Xiaoping's Southern Tour: Elite Politics in Post-Tiananmen China," *Asian Survey* 23, no. 8 (August 1993): 739–56.

15. Joseph Fewsmith, *China Since Tiananmen: From Deng Xiaoping to Hu Jintao* (Cambridge: Cambridge University Press, 2008), 33.

16. Li Tieying, "Strengthen Party Building in Institutions of Higher Education, Train Successors to the Socialist Cause," *Seeking Truth*, no. 22 (November 1990): 2–9. Translation available at http://www.dtic.mil/dtic/tr/fulltext/u2/a336135.pdf

17. "Ideological Battles Between Hardliners, Liberals Viewed," *Hong Kong PAI HSING*, no. 231 (January 1991): 3. Translation available at https://apps.dtic.mil/dtic/tr/fulltext/u2/a336298.pdf

18. Deng Xiaoping, "We Have to Clear Away Obstacles and Continue to Advance," *Selected Works of Deng Xiaoping*, Vol. 3, 1982-1992.

19. This taxonomy is far from universally accepted, and a number of prominent scholars, Joseph Torigian being one of the most compelling, argue persuasively that figures widely considered to be "conservative," such as Chen Yun, Deng Liqun, and Hu Qiaomu, defy such neat categorizations. Nonetheless, I find the labels useful in simplifying the vast and complex network of ideas, organs, and individuals who shaped the politics of the late 1970s and 1980s. For an interesting early attempt to wrestle with the limitations of such categories, see the 1987 CIA report, "Hu's a Reformist, Hu's a Conservative," available at https://www.cia.gov/library/readingroom/docs/DOC_0000620553.pdf

20. Lawrence R. Sullivan, "Assault on the Reforms: Conservative Criticism of Political and Economic Liberalization in China, 1985–86," *China Quarterly*, no. 114 (June 1988): 198–222.

21. For a short biography of Chen Yun, see David M. Bachman, *Chen Yun and the Chinese Political System* (Berkeley, CA: Institute of East Asian Studies, 1985).

22. Ezra Vogel, "Chen Yun: His Life," *Journal of Contemporary China* 14, no. 45 (November 2005): 741–59.

23. Ezra Vogel, "Chen Yun: His Life," *Journal of Contemporary China* 14, no. 45 (November 2005): 741–59.

24. Mao Zedong, "On the Co-Operative Transformation of Agriculture," July 31, 1955. https://www.marxists.org/reference/archive/mao/selected-works/volume-5/mswv5_44.htm

25. Ezra Vogel, "Chen Yun: His Life," *Journal of Contemporary China* 14, no. 45 (November 2005): 741–59.

26. 陈东林, "陈云为何力排众议反对杀江青?" 人民网中国共产党新闻网, March 12, 2013. http://dangshi.people.com.cn/n/2013/0312/c85037-20756531.html

27. Frederick C. Teiwes and Warren Sun, "China's Economic Reorientation After the Third Plenum: Conflict Surrounding 'Chen Yun's' Readjustment Program, 1979–80," *China Journal*, no. 70 (July 2013): 163–87.

28. Zhu Minzhi and Zou Aiguo, "Chen Yun on Planned Economy," *Beijing Review* 12, no. 12 (March 22, 1982): 16–18.

29. For more on Deng's early life, see his autobiography, 邓力群自述(1915–1974), 人民出版社,2015.

30. 黎虹, "我所知道的胡乔木与邓力群的交往," 百年潮, 2015年第12期.

31. Chris Buckley, "Deng Liqun, Who Battled China's Liberals, Dies at 99," *New York Times*, February 12, 2015.

32. 邓力群, 我为少奇同志说些话 (当代中国出版社, 2016), 177.

33. Chris Buckley, "Deng Liqun, Who Battled China's Liberals, Dies at 99," *New York Times*, February 12, 2015.

34. Zhao Ziyang, *Prisoner of the State* (New York: Simon and Schuster, 2012).

35. Deng Xiaoping, "The Organizational Line Guarantees the
     Implementation of the Ideological and Political Lines," *Selected Works of
     Deng Xiaoping*, Vol. 3, *1982–1992*.

36. Ding Xuelieng, *The Decline of Communism in China: Legitimacy Crisis,
     1977–1989* (Cambridge: Cambridge University Press, 2006), 96.

37. Orville Schell, *Discos and Democracy: China in the Throes of Reform*
     (New York: Doubleday, 1988).

38. Yan Yunxiang, "The Impact of Rural Reform on Economic and Social
     Stratification in a Chinese Village," *Australian Journal of Chinese Affairs*,
     no. 27 (January 1992): 1–23.

39. https://www.cia.gov/library/readingroom/docs/
     CIA-RDP85T00287R001000240001-6.pdf

40. David Zweig, "Opposition to Change in Rural China: The System of
     Responsibility and People's Communes," *Asian Survey* 23, no. 7 (July
     1983): 879–900.

41. Randall Stross, "The Return of Advertising in China: A Survey of
     the Ideological Reversal," *China Quarterly* 123, no. 123 (September
     1990): 485–502.

42. Christopher Wren, "Peking Reshaping Ideology to Fit New Economic
     Policy," *New York Times*, December 17, 1984.

43. Hu Yaobang, "The Best Way to Remember Mao Zedong," *Beijing Review*
     27, no. 1 (January 2, 1984), 16–18.

44. Wren, "Peking Reshaping Ideology to Fit New Economic Policy."

45. Stanley Rosen, "The Effect of Post-4 June Re-Education Campaigns on
     Chinese Students," *China Quarterly*, no. 134 (June 1993): 310–34.

46. Stanley Rosen, "The Effect of Post-4 June Re-Education Campaigns on
     Chinese Students," *China Quarterly*, no. 134 (June 1993): 310–34.

47. 李荣希,马强, 田铁林 "对高校反对和平演变的调查与思考,"
     辽宁高等教育研究, 1991年06期.

48. See, for example, 和育东, "当代大学生爱国思想之研究," 青年研究,
     1995年第11期.

49. Sullivan, "Assault on the Reforms."

50. Hu Yaobang, "Create a New Situation in All Fields of Socialist
     Modernization," Report to the Twelfth National Congress of the CPC,
     September 1, 1982. *Beijing Review* 37 (September 13, 1982): 21.

51. Sullivan, "Assault on the Reforms."

52. Keith Forster, "The 1982 Campaign Against Economic Crime in China,"
     Australian Journal of Chinese Affairs, no. 14 (July 1985): 1–19.

53. Richard Baum, *Burying Mao: Chinese Politics in the Age of Deng Xiaoping*
     (Princeton, NJ: Princeton University Press, 1996), 229.

54. Benedict Stavis, "Contradictions in Communist Reform: China Before 4
     June 1989," *Political Science Quarterly* 105, no. 1 (1990), 31–52.

55. Bruce Dickson, "Conflict and Non-Compliance in Chinese Politics: Party
     Rectification, 1983–1987," *Pacific Affairs* 63, no. 2 (Summer 1990): 170–90.

56. Bruce Dickson, "Conflict and Non-Compliance in Chinese Politics: Party Rectification, 1983–1987," *Pacific Affairs* 63, no. 2 (Summer 1990): 170–90.

57. Baum, *Burying Mao*, 176.

58. Fox Butterfield, "Under Deng, Running China Has Become a Family Affair," *New York Times*, July 2, 1989.

59. Edward A. Gargan, "As China's Economy Grows, So Does Official Corruption," *New York Times*, July 10, 1988.

60. Gargan, "As China's Economy Grows, So Does Official Corruption."

61. Nathan Gardels, "The Price China Has Paid: An Interview With Liu Binyan," *New York Review of Books*, January 19, 1989.

62. Quoted in Frederick C. Teiwes and Warren Sun, "China's Economic Reorientation After the Third Plenum: Conflict Surrounding 'Chen Yun's' Readjustment Program, 1979–80," *China Journal*, no. 70 (July 2013): 163–87.

63. "Clearing Cultural Contamination," *Beijing Review*, November 7, 1983.

64. Christopher Wren, "China Is Said to End a Campaign to Stop 'Spiritual Pollution,'" *New York Times*, January 24, 1984.

65. Harry Harding, *China's Second Revolution: Reform After Mao* (Washington, DC: Brookings Institution, 1987), 70.

66. Harding, *China's Second Revolution*, 70.

67. Harding, *China's Second Revolution*, 71.

68. For a book-length treatment of these pendulum swings, see Baum, *Burying Mao*.

69. Deng Xiaoping, "Remarks Made During an Inspection Tour of Shanghai," *Selected Works of Deng Xiaoping*, Vol. 3, 1982–1992.

70. Vogel, *Deng Xiaoping and the Transformation of China*, 670.

71. Deng Xiaoping, "Excerpts from Talks Given in Wuchang, Shenzhen, Zhuhai, and Shanghai, January 18–February 21, 1991," *Selected Works of Deng Xiaoping*, Vol. 3, 1982–1992.

72. 田炳信, "最困难的时候小平来了!— 邓小平1992年南巡见证者梁广大的回忆," 中共珠海市委党校珠海市行政学院学报, 2004年第4期.

73. Bruce Gilley, *Tiger on the Brink: Jiang Zemin and China's New Elite* (Berkeley: University of California Press, 1998), 184.

74. Nicholas D. Kristof, "China Is Softening Its Economic Line," *New York Times,* February 24, 1992.

75. Sheryl Wu Dunn, "Bootleg Tape of Aide's Jab Is Hit in China," *New York Times*, May 31, 1992.

76. Quoted in Barry Naughton, "Deng Xiaoping: The Economist," *China Quarterly*, no. 135 (September 1993): 491–514.

77. This dilemma is brilliantly explored in Feng Chen, "An Unfinished Battle in China: The Leftist Criticism of the Reform and the Third Thought Emancipation," *China Quarterly*, no. 158 (June 1999): 447–67.

78.   Robert Lawrence Kuhn, *How China's Leaders Think: The Inside Story of China's Reform and What This Means for the Future* (Hoboken, NJ: John Wiley, 2010), 81.

79.   Feng Chen, "Order and Stability in Social Transition: Neoconservative Political Thought in Post-1989 China," *China Quarterly*, no. 151 (September 1997): 593–613.

80.   Author interview, July 9, 2017, Beijing.

81.   Joseph Fewsmith, "Neoconservatism and the End of the Dengist Era," *Asian Survey* 35, no. 7 (July 1995): 635–51.

82.   王沪宁, 社会主义市场经济的政治要求:新权力结构," 《社会科学》 1993年 第2期.

83.   https://www.thechinastory.org/key-intellectual/ wu-jiaxiang-%E5%90%B4%E7%A8%BC%E7%A5%A5-2/

84.   王沪宁, "顾问手记: 93新加坡辩论感想," www.aisixiang.com/data/ 39868.html#

85.   Barry Sautman, "Sirens of the Strongman: Neo-Authoritarianism in Recent Chinese Political Theory," *China Quarterly*, no. 129 (March 1992): 72–102.

86.   萧功秦, "民族主义与中国转型时期的意识形态," 战略与管理, 1994年04期.

87.   For a recent overviews of the New Left, see Shi Anshu, Francois Lachapelle, and Matthew Galway, "The Recasting of Chinese Socialism: The Chinese New Left Since 2000," *China Information* 32, no. 1 (2018): 139–59, and Ban Wang and Jie Lu, *China and New Left Visions: Political and Cultural Interventions* (Lanham, MD: Lexington Books, 2012).

88.   Ariana Eunjung Cha, "For China's New Left, Old Values," *Washington Post*, April 19, 2009.

89.   Quoted in Bruce Gilley, *Tiger on the Brink: Jiang Zemin and China's New Elite* (Berkeley: University of California Press, 1998), 265.

90.   Quoted in Steven Mufson, "Can China's Party Survive Prosperity? Competing Articles by Propagandist, Reformer Bring Debate Into Open," *Washington Post*, October 17, 1996.

91.   Steven Mufson, "Can China's Party Survive Prosperity? Competing Articles by Propagandist, Reformer Bring Debate Into Open," *Washington Post*, October 17, 1996.

92.   Feng Chen, "An Unfinished Battle in China: The Leftist Criticism of the Reform and the Third Thought Emancipation," *China Quarterly* no. 158 (June 1999): 447–67.

93.   Michael Schoenhals, "Political Movements, Change, and Stability: The Chinese Communist Party in Power," *China Quarterly* no. 159 (September 1999): 595–605.

94. Quoted in Roderick MacFarquhar, ed., *The Politics of China: Sixty Years of the People's Republic of China* (Cambridge: Cambridge University Press, 2011), 539.

95. For a critical take on the *wanyanshu*, see 马立诚, "最近四十年中国社会思潮," 东方出版社, 2015.

96. Jiang Zemin, "Jiang Zemin's Speech at the Meeting Celebrating the Eightieth Anniversary of the Founding of the Communist Party of China," July 1, 2001.

97. Bruce Dickson, *Wealth Into Power* (Cambridge: Cambridge University Press, 2008), 34.

98. 孙瑞林, "生命不息战斗不止——忆恩师魏巍同志," www.wyzxwk.com/Article/lishi/2009/09/57894.html

99. 中共浙江省委书记张德江撰文说:"要明确私营企业主不能入党" 真理的追求2001-05-11.

100. 喻权域, "开国际玩笑—资本家加入共产党," 真理的追, 2001年05期.

101. A translation of the letter can be found at https://monthlyreview.org/commentary/letter-of-the-fourteen/

102. Joseph Fewsmith, "Is Political Reform Ahead?—Beijing Confronts Problems Facing Society—and the CCP," *China Leadership Monitor*, no. 1 (January 2002). https://www.hoover.org/research/political-reform-ahead-beijing-confronts-problems-facing-society-and-ccp

103. Quoted in Zhao Yuezhi, *Communication in China: Political Economy, Power, and Conflict* (Lanham, MD: Rowman & Littlefield, 2008), 55.

104. Erik Eckholm, "Chinese Censors Shut Down Marxist Journal Critical of Jiang," *New York Times*, August 16, 2001.

105. Schoenhals, "Political Movements, Change, and Stability," 595–605.

Chapter 3

1. 刘国光谈西化严重者不宜在高校及研究机构任领导, m.wyzxwk.com/content.php?classid=13&id=3144

2. Philip Pan, "A Study Group is Crushed in China's Grip," *Washington Post*, April 23, 2004.

3. Author interview with Yang Zili, March 20, 2015.

4. https://www.marxists.org/reference/archive/mao/selected-works/volume-1/mswv1_6.htm

5. Andy Kennedy, "For China, the Tighter the Grip, the Weaker the Hand," *Washington Post*, January 17, 1999.

6. For a book-length treatment of the case, see 徐连胜, 世纪冤狱：新青年学会桉揭秘, 劳改基金会, 2014.

7. 关军和张蕾, "获得邓小平南巡消息后"非常失望甚至绝望" 南方人物周刊, October 10, 2012.

8. 关军和张蕾, "获得邓小平南巡消息后"非常失望甚至绝望" 南方人物周刊, October 10, 2012.

9. 关军和张蕾，"获得邓小平南巡消息后"非常失望甚至绝望"
南方人物周刊, October 10, 2012.

10. Han Deqiang, "The Advantages and Disadvantages of China's Accession to the WTO," www.spectrezine.org/global/wtochina.html

11. 韩德强, 碰撞:全球化陷阱与中国现实选择, 经济管理出版社, 2000.

12. 韩德强, 碰撞, 35.

13. Nicholas R. Lardy, *Integrating China Into the Global Economy* (Washington, DC: Brookings Institution Press, 2004), 21.

14. 房宁, 王小东, 宋强, 全球化阴影下的中国之路,
中国社会科学出版社, 1999.

15. 杨斌, 威胁中国隐蔽战争:美国隐蔽经济战与改革陷阱,
经济管理出版社, 2000.

16. "Internet Users in China Reach 45.8 Million: CNNIC Report," July 23, 2002, en.people.cn/200207/22/eng20020722_100150.shtml

17. Author interview, June 22, 2014.

18. Adi Ignatius, "Beijing, Faced With Economic Crisis, Draws Back From Liberalization Drive," *Wall Street Journal*, September 26, 1988.

19. Author interview, July 16, 2015.

20. Author interview, July 16, 2015.

21. http://www.washingtonpost.com/wp-srv/world/foreignpolicy/bushchina.html

22. "Clinton's Words on China: Trade Is the Smart Thing," *New York Times*, March 9, 2000.

23. Liu Junning, "Open Society Spells Liberal Regime: The Political Consequences of WTO, PNTR, and the Internet in China." https://web.stanford.edu/dept/iis/democracy/Seminar/LiuJunning.htm

24. This nice phrase comes from Kaiser Kuo. See https://asiasociety.org/blog/asia/kaiser-kuo-baidu-foreign-reportage-and-paradoxes-china

25. "400中国学者联名反战 反对美国攻打伊拉克," February 17, 2003. news.sina.com.cn/c/2003-02-17/1425911306.shtml

26. 中国学者反战声明发起人韩德强王小东聊天实录, February 18, 2003. news.sina.com.cn/c/2003-02-18/1833913132.shtml

27. "400中国学者联名反战 反对美国攻打伊拉克," February 17, 2003. news.sina.com.cn/c/2003-02-17/1425911306.shtml

28. 徐景安 杨帆 : 左派与右派的分歧在哪里?, 2008-12-27, http://www.aisixiang.com/data/23706.html

29. Ho Pin and Gao Xin, *Princes and Princesses of Red China* (Toronto: Canada Mirror Books, 1993), 117–19.

30. Author interview with Yang Fan, July 6, 2017.

31. Author interview with Yang Fan, July 9, 2015.

32. 关军和张蕾，"获得邓小平南巡消息后"非常失望甚至绝望"
南方人物周刊, October 10, 2012.

33. Andy Hu, Andy Hu, "Swimming Against the Tide" (master's thesis, School of Communication, Simon Fraser University, 2006), 161.

34. 杨帆讲座简迅：痛斥张维迎，提醒中国暴富阶层莫上当, www.wyzxwk.com/Article/jiangtang/2011/03/111.html

35. Author interview with Guo Songmin, July 9, 2017.

36. Author interview with Guo Songmin, July 9, 2017.

37. Quoted in Barry Naughton, "China's Left Tilt: Pendulum Swing or Midcourse Correction," in *China's Changing Political Landscape*, ed. Cheng Li (Washington, DC: Brookings Institution Press, 2008), 144.

38. Mao Zedong, "Report to the Second Plenary Session of the Seventh Central Committee of the Communist Party of China," *Selected Works of Mao Tse-tung*, Vol. 4.

39. Quoted in Naughton, "China's Left Tilt," 143.

40. Chun Lin, "The Socialist Market Economy: Step Forward or Backward for China?" *Science & Society* 73, no. 2 (April 2009): 228–35.

41. Ching Kwan Lee, "From the Specter of Mao to the Spirit of the Law: Labor Insurgency in China," *Theory and Society* 31, no. 2 (April 2002): 189–228.

42. Alexander F. Day, *The Peasant in Postsocialist China: History, Politics, and Capitalism* (Cambridge: Cambridge University Press, 2013), 6.

43. Joseph Kahn, "Painting the Peasants Into the Portrait of China's Economic Boom," *New York Times*, August 7, 2006.

44. Quoted in Zhao Yuezhi, *Communication in China: Political Economy, Power, and Conflict* (Lanham, MD: Rowman & Littlefield, 2008), 289.

45. 乌有之乡部分顾问学者出席《新自由主义评析》出版座谈会, www.wyzxwk.com/Article/lixiang/2010/12/356.html

46. 乌有之乡部分顾问学者出席《新自由主义评析》出版座谈会, www.wyzxwk.com/Article/lixiang/2010/12/356.html

47. https://www.forbes.com/global/2001/1112/032tab.html#20db71c2213e

48. 郎咸平质疑顾雏军"七板斧"伎俩席卷国家财富, August 11, 2004. finance.sina.com.cn/g/20040811/0923940584.shtml

49. Bill Schiller, "Economic Bust Is Big Boom for Mao," *Toronto Star*, March 25, 2009.

50. 郎咸平是谁? September 9, 2004. www.aisixiang.com/data/4122.html

51. "告死郎咸平," January 3, 2018. news.ifeng.com/a/20180103/54783342_0.shtml

52. 中山大学博士生炮轰郎咸平 自称证据100 percent真实, 每日经济新闻, 2006年06月07日 finance.people.com.cn/GB/42774/4446064.html

53. 被郎咸平坑了的顾雏军, 竟然告赢了中国证监会https://new.qq.com/omn/20171226/20171226A100W3.html

54. http://finance.ifeng.com/news/history/rwpz/20090407/515459.shtml

55. 张程, "好与人斗的张维迎, www.wyzxwk.com/Article/shidai/2009/09/72648.html

56. 左大培、杨帆、韩德强就阻止国有资产流失、搞好国有企业致党和国家领导人的公开信，www.wyzxwk.com/Article/sichao/2009/09/618.html

57. 郎咸平，"我反对'国退民进,'" news.sina.com.cn/c/2004-08-31/10524186042.shtml

58. 学者左大培书面声明：我坚决站在郎咸平一边，finance.people.com.cn/GB/43429/125491/125503/125550/7472592.html

59. 2004–2006中国第三次改革论争始末，news.sina.com.cn/c/2006-03-16/10379365018.shtml

60. 关于郎咸平教授质疑流行产权理论和侵吞国有资产问题的学术声明，www.aisixiang.com/data/4183.html

61. Quoted in Zhao, *Communication in China*, 311.

62. Geoff Dyer and Richard McGregor, "China's Answer to Larry King," *Financial Times*, January 31, 2005.

63. Wieland Wagner, "Challenging the Communists With 'Larry Lang Live,'" *Der Spiegel*, August 12, 2005.

64. 刘国光，"社会主义市场经济也需要计划," March 20, 2006. politics.people.com.cn/GB/30178/4215790.html

65. 刘国光：社会主义与市场经济不容割裂，March 24, 2006. business.sohu.com/20050324/n224835489.shtml

66. 刘国光:谈经济学教学和研究中的一些问题www.xinfajia.net/579.html

67. 刘国光11·23研讨会重要发言，www.wyzxwk.com/Article/lixiang/2010/12/3559.html

68. 一部违背宪法和背离社会主义基本原则的《物权法（草案）》(全文), https://news.qq.com/a/20061221/002288.htm

69. 巩献田这个人，finance.sina.com.cn/g/20070318/06243416735.shtml

70. 巩献田这个人，finance.sina.com.cn/g/20070318/06243416735.shtml

71. 巩献田这个人，finance.sina.com.cn/g/20070318/06243416735.shtml

72. 大教授公开信称物权法违宪 姓社姓资再起争议，news.sina.com.cn/c/2006-02-23/15019183436.shtml

73. 北大教授公开信称物权法违宪 姓社姓资再起争议，news.sina.com.cn/c/2006-02-23/15019183436.shtml

74. Joseph Kahn, "A Sharp Debate Erupts in China Over Ideologies," *New York Times*, March 12, 2006.

Chapter 4

1. www.cser.org.cn

2. Andy Hu, *Swimming Against the Tide*, 116.

3. Joseph Kahn, "At a Secret Meeting, Chinese Analysts Clashed Over Reforms," *New York Times*, April 7, 2006.

4. 新望：警惕民间和高层的反改革潮流，September 3, 2005, finance.sina.com.cn/review/20050903/15181940076.shtml

5. Kahn, "At a Secret Meeting, Chinese Analysts Clashed Over Reforms."

6. His remarks can be found in English translation in He Weifang, *In the Name of Justice: Striving for the Rule of Law in China* (Washington, DC: Brookings Institution Press, 2012).

7. Richard Hofstadter, "The Paranoid Style in American Politics," *Harper's*, November 1964.

8. Dulles's statement is available at http://teachingamericanhistory.org/library/document/statement-on-liberation-policy/

9. For a fascinating study of Khrushchev's speech, see Kathleen E. Smith, *Moscow 1956: The Silenced Spring* (Cambridge, MA: Harvard University Press, 2017).

10. Qiang Zhai, "1959: Preventing Peaceful Evolution," *China Heritage Quarterly*, no. 18 (June 2009), http://www.chinaheritagequarterly.org/features.php?searchterm=018_1959preventingpeace.inc&issue=018

11. Michael Dutton, *Policing the Revolution* (Durham, NC: Duke University Press, 2005), 3.

12. Mao Zedong, "Basic Tactics," *Selected Works of Mao Tse-tung*, Vol. 2, https://www.marxists.org/reference/archive/mao/selected-works/volume-6/mswv6_28.htm

13. Mao Zedong, "The Role of the Chinese Communist Party in the National War," *Selected Works of Mao Tse-tung*, Vol. 2, https://www.marxists.org/reference/archive/mao/selected-works/volume-2/mswv2_10.htm

14. 钱钢, "'敌对势力'一词的使用频率," 炎黄春秋, 2015年第3期.

15. Quoted in Allen S. Whiting, "Chinese Nationalism and Foreign Policy After Deng," *China Quarterly*, no. 142 (June 1995): 295–316.

16. Alastair Iain Johnston, "Anti-Foreigner Propaganda Is Not Spiking in China," *Washington Post*, Monkey Cage blog, December 2, 2014. https://www.washingtonpost.com/news/monkey-cage/wp/2014/12/02/anti-foreigner-propaganda-is-not-spiking-in-china/?utm_term=.f5fb7a02d2ce

17. For a full account of the campaign, see Zheng Wang, *Never Forget National Humiliation: Historical Memory in Chinese Politics and Foreign Relations* (New York: Columbia University Press, 2012).

18. 李荣希, 马强, 田铁林 "对高校反对和平演变的调查与思考," 辽宁高等教育研究, 1991年06期.

19. 陈琪, "抵御'和平演变', 是高校教育面临的严峻课题," http://www.pkulaw.cn/fulltext_form.aspx?Db=qikan&Gid=1509960223&EncodingName=

20. Author interview, July 28, 2017.

21. David Schweisberg, "China Denounces U.S. for Okaying F-16 Sale to Taiwan," UPI, September 3, 1992.

22. Jim Mann, "China's Feelings of Betrayal on Taiwan Fed Anger at US," *Los Angeles Times*, September 9, 1996.

23. Mann, "China's Feelings of Betrayal on Taiwan Fed Anger at US."

24. Charles Krauthammer, "Universal Dominion: Toward a Unipolar World," *National Interest* 18 (Winter 1989–1990): 46–49.

25. Jack Goldstone, "The Coming Chinese Collapse," *Foreign Policy*, no. 99 (Summer 1995): 35–53.

26. Gerald Segal, "Does China Matter?" *Foreign Affairs* 78, no. 5 (September–October 1999): 24–36.

27. Quoted in Joseph Fewsmith, "Neoconservatism and the End of the Dengist Era," *Asian Survey* 35, no. 7 (July 1995): 635–51.

28. 石中, 未来的冲突, 战略与管理, 1993年第1期.

29. "从'逆向种族主义' 到 '中国的民族主义'", 明报月刊, 9月1996.

30. 王小东, 思维方法更新改革才有希望, 北京青年报, 1992年1月12日.

31. Quoted in Zhao Suisheng, *A Nation-State by Construction* (Ithaca, NY: Cornell University Press, 2004), 232.

32. Quoted in Suisheng, *A Nation-State by Construction*, 139.

33. Patrick E. Tyler, "Rebels' New Cause: A Book for Yankee Bashing," *New York Times*, September 4, 1996.

34. Quoted in Peter Hays Gries, *China's New Nationalism: Pride, Politics, and Diplomacy* (Berkeley: University of California Press, 2004), 125.

35. Maurice Brosseau, Hsin-chi Kuan, and Y. Y. Kueh, *China Review 1997* (Hong Kong: Chinese University Press, 1997), 21.

36. *China Can Say No*, by Song Qiang, Zhang Zangzang, Qiao Ben, Gu Qingsheng, and Tang Zhengyu; *Studying in the USA*, by Qian Ning; *China Can Still Say No*, by Song Qiang, Zhang Zangzang, Qiao Ben, Gu Qingsheng, and Tang Zhengyu, reviewed by Peter Gries, *China Journal*, no. 37 (January 1997): 180–85.

37. http://www.cnn.com/ASIANOW/asiaweek/96/0927/feat10.html

38. Maurice Brosseau, Hsin-chi Kuan, and Y. Y. Kueh, *China Review 1997* (Hong Kong: Chinese University Press, 1997), 21.

39. 讲座：防人之心不可无——
童增王小东谈SARS是否是美国针对中国人的武器, www.wyzxwk.com/Article/jiangtang/2011/03/142.html

40. Stephen Philion, "The Social Cost of Neoliberalism in China," *Dollars & Sense* (July–August 2007): 22–24.

41. 张勤德, "注意防止改革的性质发生'演变'," 理论探索, 1992年02期.

42. The book is discussed in Stephen E. Philion, *Workers' Democracy in China's Transition From State Socialism* (New York: Routledge, 2009), 10.

43. 张勤德, "西山事件"的三点警示, www.wyzxwk.com/Article/qingnian/2009/09/5530.html

44. 郑胜利, "'张勤德现象' 值得警惕, www.wyzxwk.com/Article/sichao/2009/09/7126.html

45. For more on the "angry youth," see Yang Lijun and Zheng Yongniang, "*Fen Qings* [Angry Youth] in Contemporary China," *Journal of Contemporary China* 21, issue 76 (2012): 637–53.

46. Jason Ng, *Blocked on Weibo: What Gets Suppressed on China s Version of Twitter (and Why)* (New York: New Press, 2013), 31.

47. 张宏良：从"郑胜利现象"看精英集团历史本质, http://www.wyzxwk.com/Article/sichao/2009/09/7719.html

48. 郑胜利教授的声明, www.wyzxwk.com/Article/sichao/2009/09/8079.html

49. 张宏良：当前中国左派和右派的斗争, www.mzfxw.com/e/action/ShowInfo.php?classid=12&id=14619

50. 马宾新著《纪念毛泽东》读书交流会, www.wyzxwk.com/Article/lixiang/2014/04/318776.html

51. 马宾新著《纪念毛泽东》读书交流会, www.wyzxwk.com/Article/lixiang/2014/04/318776.html

52. C. K. Lee, *Against the Law: Labor Protests in China's Rustbelt and Sunbelt* (Berkeley: University of California Press, 2007), 141.

53. Dominik Bartmanski, "Successful Icons of Failed Time: Rethinking Post-Communist Nostalgia," *Acta Sociologica* 54, no. 3 (2011): 213–31.

54. Fritz Stern, *Five Germanys I Have Known* (Basingstoke, UK: Macmillan, 2007), 479.

55. Edward Wong and Chris Buckley, "At Bo Xilai Trial, a Goal to Blast Acts, Not Ideas," *New York Times*, August 20, 2013.

56. http://www.chinadaily.com.cn/china/2008-04/14/content_6614357.htm

57. "China's Coming-Out Party," *The Economist*, November 16, 2006.

58. Author interview with Wang Xiaodong, Beijing, July 9, 2017.

59. Author interview with Song Qiang, July 28, 2017.

60. 《中国不高兴》：你高兴还是不高兴, https://www.xzbu.com/6/view-2372740.htm

61. 冰点：评《中国不高兴》所推销的病态民族主义, news.sina.com.cn/c/sd/2009-04-08/060717565626.shtml

62. http://chinamediaproject.org/2009/04/02/unhappy-china-and-why-it-is-cause-for-unhappiness/

63. 曾梦龙, "1996 年，《中国可以说不》和更大的民族主义浪潮 | 畅销书让我们看到了什么样的中国," http://www.qdaily.com/articles/40262.html

64. Li Li, "Happy or Unhappy Is the Question," *Beijing Review*, April 13, 2009.

65. Damian Grammaticas, "China's Rising Nationalism Troubles West," news.bbc.co.uk/2/hi/asia-pacific/8363260.stm

66. Zhao Suisheng, "Nationalism's Double Edge," *Wilson Quarterly*, Autumn 2005.

67. Jessica Chen Weiss, *Powerful Patriots: Nationalist Protest in China Foreign Relations* (Oxford: Oxford University Press, 2014), 19–20.

68. Author interviews.

69. Fu Qi and Li Huizi, "Book 'Unhappy China' Stirs a Controversy," *Xinhua*, March 27, 2009.

70. Chris Buckley, "China Bestseller Sees Plots and Profit in Financial Crisis," *Reuters*, September 21, 2009.

71. 摩罗, "中国站起来: 我们的前途, 命运与精神解放," 长江文艺出版社, 2010.

72. 沙龙简讯：中国不高兴：道出了谁的心声？踩了谁的尾巴？www. wyzxwk.com/Article/lixiang/2010/12/73227.html

73. Stephen Philion, "An Interview with Yan Yuanzhang," *Monthly Review* online, March 13, 2006. https://mronline.org/2006/03/13/an-interview-with-yan-yuanzhang/

74. http://wikileaks.ikiru.ch/cable/09BEIJING1970/

75. The original declaration exists on several overseas websites, including http://www.wengewang.org/read.php?tid=26426

Chapter 5

1. "Premier Wen Jiabao Attends Press Conference of the 5th Session of the 11th NPC," March 15, 2012. Available at http://www.chinese-embassy.no/eng/zjsg_2/sgxw/t914991.htm

2. "乌有之乡恩怨:创始人杨帆与张宏良 公开决裂" 时代周报, 03-31-2012.

3. Andrew Higgins, "Fans of Bo Xilai Rally to Ousted Chief in China," *Washington Post*, April 14, 2012.

4. 萃岚, 文革中薄一波：虽然已无自由 我依然崇拜毛主席, news. ifeng.com/history/zhongguoxiandaishi/special/maozedongdanchen/detail_2011_12/14/11323389_0.shtml

5. John Garnaut, "The Revenge of Wen Jiabao," *Foreign Policy*, March 29, 2012.

6. Chris Buckley, "Children of Mao's Wrath Vie for Power in China," *Reuters*, June 21, 2012.

7. Carrie Gracie, "Murder in the Lucky Holiday Hotel," BBC, March 17, 2017. https://www.bbc.co.uk/news/resources/idt-sh/Murder_lucky_hotel

8. Victor Chung-Hon Shih, "'Nauseating' Displays of Loyalty: Monitoring the Factional Bargain Through Ideological Campaigns in China," *Journal of Politics* 70, no. 4 (October 2008): 1177–92.

9. In June 2007, Ma Bin joined thirty former high-ranking CCP officials in condemning the party's handling of the brick kiln scandal. The opening line read, "For us communists, it is neither right nor possible to treat or even speak of such incidents as the inevitable result of the primary state of socialism. This was obviously a capitalist event, incorporating certain scenes of cruel exploitation, and the tragic, dog-eat-dog world of primitive accumulation under feudalism and slavery."

10. "重庆，我们支持你," 2011-05-06, www.wyzxwk.com/Article/zatan/2011/05/223636.html

11. Romain Lafarguette, "Chongqing: Model for a New Economic and Social Policy?," *China Perspectives* 4 (2012): 62–64.

12. 亚洲周刊：重庆模式创中国经济反攻新路径, February 6, 2009. www.chinanews.com/hb/news/2009/02-06/1552353.shtml

13. Quoted in Cui Zhiyuan, "Making Sense of the Chinese 'Socialist Market Economy': A Note," *Modern China*, 38, no. 6, "State Capitalism" or "Socialist Market Economy"?—Dialogues Among Western and Chinese Scholars 5 (November 2012): 665–76.

14. 崔之元：从危旧房改造看"重庆模式," February 20, 2011. www.aisixiang.com/data/38922.html

15. 王绍光：探索中国式社会主义3.0：重庆经验, www.aisixiang.com/data/38896-2.html

16. 李希光, "重庆梦与中国模式," 社会观察, November 11, 2010, www.guancha.cn/indexnews/2010_11_11_50705.shtml

17. 郎咸平："重庆模式"可以拯救中国房地产, 南京日报, August 3, 2010.

18. http://travel.cnn.com/explorations/none/who-mattered-most-2009-regional-978863/

19. 基辛格：重庆神奇巨变让人兴奋, 2011-09-07, news.163.com/11/0907/12/7DBL3CMC00011124J.html

20. "Henry Kissinger Talks to Simon Schama," *Financial Times*, May 20, 2011.

21. https://www.bbc.co.uk/news/resources/idt-sh/Murder_lucky_hotel

22. Geoff Dyer, "China: A Populist Rising," *Financial Times*, March 9, 2010.

23. Tania Branigan, "'Godmother of the Underworld' Jailed in China," *The Guardian*, November 3, 2009.

24. 崔之元：公平可以促进效率, May 4, 2011. www.aisixiang.com/data/40440.html

25. A translation of He's letter can be found on the indispensable China Media Project website, at http://chinamediaproject.org/2011/04/12/letter-to-my-chongqing-colleagues.

26. Xiao Mei, *Chongqing's Red Culture Campaign: Simulation and Its Social Implications* (New York: Routledge, 2017), 40.

27. 薄熙来："唱红就是回归文革为无稽之谈," http://dailynews.sina.com/gb/chn/chnnews/ausdaily/20110619/18412537116.html

28. 薄熙来：搞乌七八糟的东西无人管 唱红歌何罪之有？china.huanqiu.com/roll/2011-07/1796085_3.html

29. 张宏良推荐：薄熙来在重庆纪念中国共产党建党九十周年大会上的讲话, www.szhgh.com/Article/red-china/ideal/2803.html

30. Chris Buckley, "China's Leftists Dig In for Fight Over Bo Xilai," Reuters, August 21, 2012.

31. Author interview, Utopia, June 23, 2015

32. 乌有之乡第二次"重庆模式"研讨会纪要, January 8, 2011. www.wyzxwk.com/Article/lixiang/2011/01/199909.html

33. 世界危机下的重庆模式与中国未来——
    乌有之乡第三次重庆模式研讨会纪要, September 8, 2011. www.szhgh.
    com/Article/opinion/xuezhe/4260.html?from=groupmessage\

34. "韩德强：析贺卫方的公开信," http://www.aisixiang.com/data/41109.
    html

35. "文化红卫兵, 十赞重庆模式," March 15, 2011. www.wyzxwk.com/
    Article/zatan/2011/03/212528.html

36. Sun Wenhao, "The Chongqing Model Revisited," Utopia, February 9,
    2012. Translation available at https://policycn.com/wp-content/uploads/
    2016/05/The-Chongqing-model-is-dead-long-live-the-Chongqing-model.
    pdf.

37. 苏伟, 杨帆, 刘士文, 重庆模式, 中国经济出版社 , 2011, 258.

38. 茅于轼, 无悔的历程, 浙江出版集团数字传媒有限公司, 2010.

39. Stephen John Hartnett, "To 'Dance With Lost Souls': Liu Xiaobo,
    Charter 08, and the Contested Rhetorics of Democracy and Human
    Rights in China," *Rhetoric and Public Affairs* 16, no. 2 (Summer
    2013): 223–74.

40. The Progress Society website has been taken offline, but a cached version
    is still available. http://web.archive.org/web/20120802144258if_/http://
    xinu.jinbushe.org/index.php?doc-view-176.html

41. 红太阳的陨落——千秋功罪毛泽东, 香港书作坊 2008 年增订本.

42. An excerpt of the full piece was translated by the present author and
    published in the *Wall Street Journal*. See Mao Yushi, "Judging Mao as a
    Man," *Wall Street Journal*, July 6, 2011.

43. Text of the petition can be found at http://www.szhgh.com/Article/
    opinion/zatan/927.html

44. "陈奉孝：为什么当政者不敢清算毛泽东的罪错," http://cn.rfi.fr/
    中国/20110611-陈奉孝：为什么当政者不敢清算毛泽东的罪错

45. Translation by Jeremiah Jenne can be found on his blog *Jottings from the
    Granite Studio*, http://granitestudio.org/2011/05/30/mao-more-than-ever-
    on-the-legacy-of-mao-and-the-moonbat-denunciations-of-mao-yushi-no-
    relation. Accessed on January 18, 2015.

46. "'六一九'首都大学生揭露茅于轼汉奸言行大会内容纪要," June 20,
    2011, www.wyzxwk.com/Article/zatan/2011/09/234491.html

47. Darren Wee, "Smog Is China's Top Defence Against US Laser Weapons,
    says PLA Navy Admiral," *South China Morning Post*, February 24, 2014.

48. 张召忠将军：希望建立专门机构研究中国汉奸问题, www.wyzxwk.
    com/Article/zatan/2011/06/231597.html

49. See "Proposal to Restore Punishment for Traitors to Constitution," at
    http://www.thechinastory.org/archive/china-texts. Accessed on January
    19, 2015.

50. Zhao Yuezhi, *Communication in China: Political Economy, Power, and
    Conflict* (Lanham, MD: Rowman & Littlefield, 2008), 57–58.

51. 中国拟制定《惩治汉奸言论法》遭团体抗议, https://www.rfa.org/mandarin/yataibaodao/kangyi-20070308.html

52. 喻权域：制定惩治汉奸言论法不是以言定罪, www.wyzxwk.com/Article/zatan/2009/09/14117.html

53. Quoted in profile of Yuan Weishi available at www.thechinastory.org/key-intellectual/yuan-weishi

54. "中国左派票选当代十大汉奸," http://www.iask.ca/news/china/2012/0102/110459.html. Accessed on January 19, 2015.

55. Although the original announcement has been deleted from Utopia's website, it has been archived at http://www.thechinastory.org/wp-content/uploads/2012/08/Arc_UtopiaTraitors.pdf

56. John Garnaut, "'Dark Forces' Attack Chinese Leftist Website in Resurgent Culture War," *Sydney Morning Herald*, June 1, 2011.

57. 杨帆，乌有之乡如何走向极左的?
杨帆答《时代周报》记者徐伟问, March 28, 2012.

58. See 乌有之乡恩怨：创始人杨帆与张宏良公开决裂，https://m.sohu.com/n/339479770/

59. Author interview, July 2017.

60. 杨帆：乌有之乡是如何走向极左的？杨帆答《时代周报》记者徐伟问, March 28, 2012.

61. John Garnaut, "Bo Can Do! One Man Does His Bit to Be the Great Will of China," *Sydney Morning Herald*, August 7, 2011.

62. Author interview, Beijing, July 6. 2017.

63. Jonathan Ansfield and Ian Johnson, "China's Hierarchy Strives to Regain Unity After Chongqing Leader's Ouster," *New York Times*, March 29, 2012.

64. 孙立平：有关重庆模式的两点看法, March 15, 2012. Available at http://2newcenturynet.blogspot.com/2012/03/blog-post_8081.html

65. 焦点对话：茅于轼谈他与中国左派之争, May 13, 2013.

66. 范景刚答《时代周报》记者，blog.sina.cn/dpool/blog/s/blog_4e2f86430100ycnr.html?md=gd&wm=1833

67. Wang Hui, "The Rumour Machine," *London Review of Books*, May 10, 2012.

68. 时代周报："乌有之乡"分崩, www.aisixiang.com/data/51663.html

69. See, for example, Barbara Demick, "China Puts a Stop to Maoist Revival," *Los Angeles Times*, March 20, 2012.

Chapter 6

1. Deng Xiaoping, "Remarks on Successive Drafts of the 'Resolution on Certain Questions in the History of Our Party Since the Founding of the People's Republic of China,'" *Selected Works of Deng Xiaoping*, Volume 2, 1975–1982.

2. 戴旭齐齐哈尔大学演讲视频：锻造中华民族的精神品格(完整版), www.szhgh.com/Article/opinion/xuezhe/2017-11-22/153592.html

3. 戴旭齐齐哈尔大学演讲视频：锻造中华民族的精神品格(完整版),
   www.szhgh.com/Article/opinion/xuezhe/2017-11-22/153592.html

4. 戴旭齐齐哈尔大学演讲视频：锻造中华民族的精神品格(完整版),
   www.szhgh.com/Article/opinion/xuezhe/2017-11-22/153592.html

5. Dai Xu, "U.S. Building 'Asian NATO' to Encircle China," August 11,
   2010. www.china.org.cn/opinion/2010-08/11/content_20687335.htm

6. David Lague, "China's Military Hawks Take the Offensive,"
   Reuters, January 16, 2013. https://www.reuters.com/article/us-china-
   hawks/special-report-chinas-military-hawks-take-the-offensive-
   idUSBRE90G00C20130117

7. 空军大校戴旭：对禽流感不要高调 死不了几个人, finance.people.
   com.cn/n/2013/0408/c1004-21048399.html

8. 戴旭：美对华攻心战思想总纲曝光, youth.chinamil.com.cn/view/
   2014-06/23/content_5991456.htm

9. 戴旭：新战争形态——信息思想战隐然成形, www.wyzxwk.com/
   Article/guofang/2014/01/312217.html

10. 戴旭, 警惕西方敌对势力抹黑毛泽东的险恶图谋, www.81.cn/jkhc/
    2014-01/07/content_5724427.htm

11. 戴旭, 警惕西方敌对势力抹黑毛泽东的险恶图谋, www.81.cn/jkhc/
    2014-01/07/content_5724427.htm

12. 余斌：历史虚无主义批判，www.wyzxwk.com/Article/sichao/2018/
    05/389495.html

13. Chris Buckley, "Scholars Fight a Milder Version of Mao's Calamities,"
    New York Times, October 17, 2013.

14. 文章内容乌有之乡被敌人反对是好事, m.wyzxwk.com/content.php?c
    lassid=12&id=68639&actid=4

15. Author interview, July 6, 2017.

16. Patrick Tayler, "Deng Xiaoping: A Political Wizard Who Put China on
    the Capitalist Road," *New York Times*, February 20, 1997.

17. Qian Yingyi and Wu Jinglian, "China's Transition to a Market
    Economy: How Far Across the River?" globalpoverty.stanford.edu/sites/
    default/files/publications/69wp.pdf

18. See Feng Chen, "The Dilemma of Eudaemonic Legitimacy in Post-Mao
    China," *Polity* 29, no. 3 (Spring 1997): 421–39.

19. Quoted in Mikhail Heller, *Cogs in the Wheel: The Formation of Soviet Man*
    (New York: Knopf, 1988), viii.

20. Deng Xiaoping, "To Uphold Socialism We Must Eliminate Poverty,"
    April 26, 1987. http://www.china.org.cn/english/features/dengxiaoping/
    103350.htm

21. "Address to Officers at the Rank of General and Above in Command
    of the Troops Enforcing Martial Law in Beijing," June 9, 1989. https://
    dengxiaopingworks.wordpress.com/2013/03/18/address-to-officers-at-the-
    rank-of-general-and-above-in-command-of-the-troops-enforcing-martial-
    law-in-beijing/

22. Ian Johnson, "China's Memory Manipulators," *The Guardian*, June 8, 2016.

23. Perry, "Is the Chinese Communist Regime Legitimate?" https://scholar.harvard.edu/files/elizabethperry/files/perry_is_the_chinese_communist_regime_legitimate_v2_jr_edits.pdf

24. 还历史以真相: 关于我国 20 世纪 60 年代人口变动问题的研究报告, available for download at blog.sciencenet.cn/home.php?mod=attachment&id=29685

25. Author interview, June 19, 2015.

26. 杨松林：我为什么要写 "关于饿死三千万"真相一书?, www.wyzxwk.com/Article/lishi/2013/08/304777.html

27. 杨松林：我为什么要写 "关于饿死三千万"真相一书?, www.wyzxwk.com/Article/lishi/2013/08/304777.html

28. 杨松林:《总要有人说出真相》, history.sina.com.cn/his/hs/2013-11-25/155674926.shtml

29. 老田沙龙：在新一轮 "否定文革"运动的高潮中回顾文革的认识论价值, www.wyzxwk.com/Article/lixiang/2010/12/445.html

30. First published in Hong Kong as 墓碑:中国六十年代大饥荒记实. The book was translated into English and published in abridged form as *Tombstone: The Great Chinese Famine, 1958–1962* (New York: Farrar, Straus and Giroux, 2012).

31. Ian Johnson, "Finding the Facts About Mao's Victims," *New York Review of Books* Daily, December 20, 2010, www.nybooks.com/daily/2010/12/20/finding-facts-about-maos-victims.

32. For a concise history of the Great Leap Forward, see Andrew Walder, *China Under Mao: A Revolution Derailed* (Cambridge, MA: Harvard University Press, 2015), 153–79.

33. This quote comes from the English transition. See Yang Jisheng, *Tombstone: The Great Chinese Famine, 1958–1962* (New York: Farrar, Straus and Giroux, 2012).

34. Author interview, July 17, 2017.

35. Ian Johnson, "Finding the Facts About Mao's Victims," *New York Review of Books* Daily, December 20, 2010, www.nybooks.com/daily/2010/12/20/finding-facts-about-maos-victims.

36. 孙经先, "饿死3600万"的重大谬误是怎样产生的?, theory.people.com.cn/n/2014/0124/c143844-24217270.html

37. E-mail correspondence.

38. E-mail correspondence.

39. 孙经先, "'中国饿死三千万'的谣言是怎样形成的?" 中国社会科学报, September 9, 2013. www.cssn.cn/zt/zt_xkzt/zt_lsxzt/23858/lishixuwuzhuyibx/lsxwzybx2/201508/t20150826_2136470.shtml

40. Sun Jingxian, "Population Change During China's 'Three Years of Hardship' (1959–1961)," *Contemporary Chinese Political Economy and Strategic Relations: An International Journal* 2, no. 1 (April 2016): 453–500.

41. 孙经先：关于"非正常死亡1700万人"与蒋正华先生商榷, www. wyzxwk.com/Article/lishi/2011/07/243248.html

42. 孙景泽, 破解国家统计局户籍统计数据矛盾之谜— 关于我国六十年代人口变动问题, economy.guoxue.com/?p=1034

43. Quoted in Liu Mingfu and Wang Zhongyuan, *The Thoughts of Xi Jinping* (Salt Lake City, UT: American Academic Press, 2017), 348.

44. 习近平：历史不可虚无, www.qstheory.cn/2018-01/08/c_1122225580. htm

45. http://www.chinadaily.com.cn/china/2013massline/2013-07/19/content_16800244.htm

46. A translation of the document can be found at http://www.chinafile.com/document-9-chinafile-translation

47. It should be noted that the communiqué contains a slight dig at the neo-Maoists, noting that one of the manifestations of historical nihilism includes "[cleaving] apart the period that preceded Reform and Opening from the period that followed, or even to set these two periods in opposition to one another." This applies to the neo-Maoists as much as it does liberals and reformers.

48. 唐 莉, 当代中国历史虚无主义的政治诉求与双重应对, theory. people.com.cn/n/2013/0704/c168825-22081026.html

49. David L Shambaugh, *China's Communist Party: Atrophy and Adaptation* (Berkeley: University of California Press, 2008).

50. Zhao Suisheng, "The Ideological Campaign in Xi's China," *Asian Survey* 56, no. 6 (November–December 2016): 1168–93.

51. For a thought-provoking meditation on Xi's speech, see Paul Gewirtz, "Xi, Mao, and China's Search for a Usable Past," January 14, 2014. http://www.chinafile.com/reporting-opinion/viewpoint/xi-mao-and-chinas-search-usable-past

52. Susanne Weigelin-Schwiedrzik, "Party Historiography in the People's Republic of China," *Australian Journal of Chinese Affairs* 17 (January 1987): 77–94.

53. Weigelin-Schwiedrzik, "Party Historiography in the People's Republic of China," 77–94.

54. For Deng's crucial roles in the anti-rightist campaign and the Great Leap Forward, see Chung Yen-lin, "The Witch-Hunting Vanguard: The Central Secretariat's Roles and Activities in the Anti-Rightist Campaign," *China Quarterly*, no. 206 (June 2011): 391–411, and "The CEO of the Utopian Project: Deng Xiaoping's Roles and Activities in the Great Leap Forward," *China Journal*, no. 69 (January 2013): 154–73.

55. Xiaoping, "Remarks on Successive Drafts of the 'Resolution on Certain Questions in the History of Our Party Since the Founding of the People's

Republic of China,'" *Collected Works*, Vol. 2, https://dengxiaopingworks. wordpress.com/2013/02/25/remarks-on-successive-drafts-of-the-resolution-on-certain-questions-in-the-history-of-our-party-since-the-founding-of-the-peoples-republic-of-china/

56. "杨尚昆, 薄一波, 胡乔木希望党史工作者担负历史重任加强党史研究尽快写出一部完整的中共党史," 福建党史月刊, 1990年04期.

57. Ann Scott Tyson, "China Stifles Army History," *Christian Science Monitor*, November 9, 1990.

58. A translation of Zhang's open letter can be found at http://www.zonaeuropa.com/20070120_1.htm

59. Anthony Garnaut, "The Mass Line on a Massive Famine," https://www.thechinastory.org/2014/10/the-mass-line-on-a-massive-famine/

60. 杨继绳：关于武汉会议的声明, hx.cnd.org/2014/07/22/杨继绳：关于武汉会议的声明/

61. 杨继绳, "关于大饥荒年代人口损失的讨论," 炎黄春秋杂志 2014年第9期.

62. 杨继绳关于武汉会议的声明, https://www.chinainperspective.com/ArtShow.aspx?AID=26499

63. 孙经先与杨继绳直接对话: "饿死三千万"弥天大谎被当场戳穿, http://mzd.szhgh.com/maoshidai/2014-07-11/56759.html

64. Garnaut, "The Mass Line on a Massive Famine," https://www.thechinastory.org/2014/10/the-mass-line-on-a-massive-famine/

65. Ben Blanchard, "Chinese Official Fired After Calling Mao 'a Devil,'" Reuters, January 16, 2017.

66. Te-Ping Chen, "History Lesson: Mao Remarks Get Chinese Professor Fired," *Wall Street Journal*, China Real Time Report, January 10, 2017. https://blogs.wsj.com/chinarealtime/2017/01/10/history-lesson-chinese-professors-mao-remarks-get-him-fired/

67. Jun Mai, "Criticising Mao Still Not a Good Career Move," *South China Morning Post*, January 10, 2017.

68. Chris Buckley, "Chinese Legal Maverick, Facing Political Gales, Bides His Time," *New York Times*, May 18, 2018.

69. "History Teacher's Anti-Mao Weibo Account Removed," *Global Times*, September 11, 2017.

70. Kathrin Hille, "Mocking Mao Good for Business but Not Career," *Financial Times*, June 11, 2010.

71. https://globalvoices.org/2017/06/08/china-bans-soft-burial-an-award-winning-novel-about-the-deadly-consequences-of-land-reform. Chinese version can be found at http://www.globalview.cn/m/show.php?classid=4&id=18075

72. Email correspondence with Fang Fang.

73. Chris Buckley, "In Beijing, Doors Shut on a Bastion of Independent Ideas," July 11, 2018.

74. Nectar Gan, "Think Tank Chief Barred From Leaving Country," *South China Morning Post*, November 5, 2018.
75. Author interview, July 17, 2017.
76. Chris Buckley, "Liberal Magazine, 'Forced Into a Corner' by China, Girds for Battle," *New York Times*, July 27, 2016.
77. Chris Buckley, "Revamped Chinese History Journal Welcomes Hard-Line Writers," *New York Times*, August 17, 2016.
78. https://www.weibo.com/1065618283/E3FJ9yFkd?from=page_ 1005051065618283_profile&wvr=6&mod=weibotime&type=comment#_ rnd1540649383563

Chapter 7

1. 高丽民, "从来就没有什么救世主—看《北京人在纽约》, 中国电视, 1994年01期.
2. Quoted in Geremie R. Barme, "To Screw Foreigners Is Patriotic: China's Avant-Garde Nationalists," in J. Unger (ed.), *Chinese Nationalism* (Armonk, NY: M. E. Sharpe, 1996), 183–208.
3. Edward Wong, "Signals of a More Open Economy in China," *New York Times*, December 9, 2012.
4. Wong, "Signals of a More Open Economy in China."
5. Nicholas Kristof, "Looking for a Jump-Start in China," *New York Times*, January 5, 2013.
6. "The Party's New Blueprint," *The Economist*, November 16, 2013.
7. Evan Osnos, "Making China Great Again," *The New Yorker*, January 8, 2018.
8. 张宏良：左翼的理论胜利和右翼的政治反击, March 10, 2013, www. wyzxwk.com/Article/shiping/2013/03/10/300415.html
9. Philip Wen, "Red Aristocracy Urge Party to Rally Behind Xi Jinping's Anti-Corruption Crusade," *Fairfax Media*, February 16, 2014.
10. 陈子明, "简析两种毛派: 保皇派与造反派," www.aisixiang.com/data/ 63649.html
11. http://www.chinaelections.org/article/915/236409.html
12. 围绕洛阳会议的争论, redchinacn.net/portal. php?mod=view&aid=28014
13. 李波：在毛泽东继续革命理论指导下，团结起来，奋勇前进, www.mzfxw.com/e/DoPrint/index.php?classid=11&id=35260
14. 乌有之乡负责人范景刚在左翼形势分析会上的发言, www.szhgh. com/Article/opinion/xuezhe/201503/79539.html
15. Sue-Lin Wong and Christian Shepherd, "China's Student Activists Cast Rare Light on Brewing Labor Unrest," Reuters, August 14, 2018.
16. "China Raids Maoist Websites, Detains Editors Who Supported Jasic Labor Movement," August 28, 2018. https://www.rfa.org/english/news/ china/labor-shenzhen-08282018132845.html

17.   Zhao Yusha, "Chinese Workers Warned Against Foreign-Funded Advocacy Groups," *Global Times*, August 26, 2018.

18.   中共原老干部声援深圳佳士工人组建工会, https://www.voachinese.com/a/More-Support-For-Shenzhen-Workers-20180807/4516870.html

19.   关于尽快解决佳士公司有关问题的紧急呼吁, redchinacn.net/portal.php?mod=view&aid=36250

20.   http://www.chinalaborwatch.org/newscast/667

21.   Wong and Shepherd, "China's Student Activists."

22.   A translation of Yue's letter can be found at https://chinadigitaltimes.net/2018/08/no-one-can-resist-the-tides-of-history-detained-activist-yue-xin-on-the-jasic-workers/

23.   http://redballoonsolidarity.org/3104.html

24.   Wong and Shepherd, "China's Student Activists."

25.   毛派发起工运 深圳佳士科技工潮30人被拘, https://www.rfa.org/cantonese/news/labor-07302018080830.html

Epilogue

1.   See 黄卫东, "危险！美国资本绑架中国政治，推行消灭人口的群体免疫," https://www.kunlunce.com/ssjj/guojipinglun/2021-08-22/154547.html

2.   "方方卖国日记的脏钱捐了就能脱罪吗？" www.wyzxwk.com/Article/yulun/2021/03/432760.html

3.   中情局收买记者当间谍，方方算不算间谍？www.wyzxwk.com/Article/yulun/2021/04/433181.html

4.   黄卫东, "危险！美国资本绑架中国政治，推行消灭人口的群体免疫," https://www.kunlunce.com/ssjj/guojipinglun/2021-08-22/154547.html

INDEX